SPEECH PRACTICES

A Resource Book for the Student of Public Speaking

WALDO W. BRADEN

Professor of Speech
Louisiana State University

AND

MARY LOUISE GEHRING

Professor of Speech
Stetson University

HARPER & ROW, PUBLISHERS

New York, Evanston, and London

**SPEECH PRACTICES: A RESOURCE BOOK FOR THE
STUDENT OF PUBLIC SPEAKING**

Library of Congress catalog card number: 58-8362

E-Q

Contents

Illustrations

Preface

Speech Practices is based upon the belief that the student gains significantly by studying how other speakers have actually handled the problems of public speaking. The purpose of this book, therefore, is to provide through examples and testimony a collection of practical speech materials which will lead the student to a better understanding of the elements of speech composition and speech criticism.

In our teaching we have found that famous speeches are not always helpful to the beginner, who may fail to see the parallel between a speech model and his own faltering efforts. The eloquence of Webster, the terse logic of Calhoun, and the simple diction of Lincoln often seem to the student beyond his attainment. He frequently asks, "But where can I find examples that will help me see my problems?" *Speech Practices* seeks to answer this question.

In making our selections, we considered hundreds of speeches—classical and contemporary, professional and amateur. From these we have chosen mainly recent utterances and student speeches; consequently, we have omitted many of the old favorites. These speeches and speech excerpts are not necessarily models to be imitated; they should be regarded as materials for case studies of principles. In some instances they show what not to do as well as what to do. Most chapters of the book use an inductive approach; that is, first the speech is given, then follows a series of questions to stimulate the discovery of the principle.

Speech Practices may be used in three ways.

First, it may be used to supplement any of the standard textbooks. We have attempted to coördinate the development with that of eleven of these works. (See the list at the close of each chapter.)

Second, it may serve as a basic textbook in a course employing a multiple-book approach. The list of references at the close of each chapter should help the teacher make an appropriate selection of readings. We have also prepared a variety of exercises including many speaking assignments.

Third, it may be used as a guide for undergraduates in speech criticism or speech composition. Many of the exercises have as their objective to develop the student's critical appreciation and to provide him with opportunities to analyze selected aspects of speaking.

W. W. B.
M. L. G.

December, 1957

The Notes of Russell Conwell, Used the Last Time He Delivered the Lecture "Acres of Diamonds."

Chapter I

THE STUDY OF SPEECHES AND SPEAKERS

Augustine, churchman and student of rhetoric, once said that he knew of no eloquent man who had not "read and listened to the speeches and debates of eloquent men." In explaining how to make the Christian message more impelling, the great preacher further said: "But if a man desire to speak not only with wisdom, but with eloquence also (and assuredly he will prove of greater service if he can do both), I would rather send him to read, and listen to, and exercise himself in imitating eloquent men, than advise him to spend time with the teachers of rhetoric. . . ."[1]

What the great churchman recommended has certainly proved true in practice; the great speakers have steeped themselves in the eloquence of the past. Students of public speaking have learned much from the speakers who have come before. Cicero studied the oratory of Demosthenes and the great Roman orators. Edmund Burke, parliamentary debater and speaker of the eighteenth century, found profit in the speeches of Cicero and Demosthenes. Lord Mansfield, distinguished Lord Chief Justice of England, went so far as to translate Cicero's orations into English and back again into Latin. Young William Pitt, later England's Prime Minister for over 20 years, listened to the parliamentary debating of Burke, Fox, and Sheridan.

These same habits and influences are observable in American speakers. Daniel Webster was well acquainted with the utterances and careers of Chatham, Burke, Fox, Pitt, and Sheridan. The pleading of an able opponent, Jeremiah Mason, caused Webster to change completely his speaking style. Ralph Waldo Emerson, popular lecturer and philosopher, whenever possible heard Webster, Everett, Channing, and other prominent speakers. Albert J. Beveridge became an authority on the Lincoln-Douglas debates. William Jennings Bryan, while a student at Illinois College, listened intently to Wendell Phillips and Russell H. Conwell. Woodrow Wilson was so impressed with the

---

[1] Aureleus Augustine, "On Christian Doctrine," bk. I, chaps. 3, 5, in Philip Scharff (ed.), *A Selected Library on Nicene and Post Nicene Fathers of the Christian Church*, The Christian Literature Company, 1887, vol. II, p. 576.

speeches of Burke that he sprinkled through his writings and speeches numerous quotations of the Englishman. He also studied the eloquence of Patrick Henry and Daniel Webster. William E. Borah, largely a self-taught orator, could quote from memory Pitt, Fox, Burke, and Bright. If there is any lesson to be learned from the education of the great speakers, it is that the study of speeches and speaking is an important part of speech training.

The student of today is unusually fortunate to have close at hand many of the great models of the past as well as to have almost daily opportunities to see and to hear prominent living speakers in action. Seldom a day passes that any American cannot hear some outstanding speaker. Radio and television bring to the living room the political convention, the legislative session, the congressional committee investigation, and the great commemorative events. Since the days of Franklin D. Roosevelt's Fireside Chats, citizens have come to expect frequent direct reports from the President of the United States as well as from other important governmental officials. Because of rapid transportation, political speakers now make hundreds of personal appearances during a typical campaign; a campaigner may travel thousands of miles visiting villages as well as metropolitan areas. Representatives of business, labor, education, and social reform take to the air and to the stump to present their views and programs. The diligent student will find challenge and profit in studying speeches and speaking careers and in listening to live speakers.

Why Study Speech Practices?

First, of course, the study of speech practices provides greater insight and a deeper understanding of speech theory. The textbook writer necessarily must abstract and simplify his exposition in order to stay within the limitation of space. Often he condenses a discussion of an important principle into a page, a paragraph, or sometimes even a sentence or two. As a result the student, who is unfamiliar with the material, may fail to realize the real significance or to see the practical application of what is said. These gaps in understanding disappear when illustrations are found. Comprehension and appreciation come when a principle is associated with how other speakers have mastered the particular problem.

Second, the study of speech practices encourages the adoption of more challenging goals. The beginning speaker may measure his own efforts by what he hears at the neighborhood church, in the county courtroom, or from the village bandstand. His acceptance of these speakers as models is likely to limit his development, for in many cases the student has no difficulty in equaling or even excelling these performances. Study of more eloquent speakers leads the student to view his own abilities and achievements in perspective and to be more objective about his accomplishments. Consequently, he becomes more difficult to satisfy and demands of himself a more rigorous program in self-discipline and self-improvement.

Perhaps some great speaker will stir the student's imagination and fire his enthusiasm the way Lord Chatham is reported to have affected Henry Grattan, Irish orator and statesman. The Englishman's debating in Parliament so fascinated the young Irishman that he forgot everything "in the one great object of cultivating his powers as a public speaker. To emulate and express, though in the peculiar forms of his own genius, the lofty conceptions of the great English orator, was from this time the object of his continual study and most fervent aspirations."[2]

Third, the study of speech practices provides a fruitful source of ideas, speech materials, and inspiration. A powerful speech may prod the student to think great thoughts and to pursue his own speaking with greater enthusiasm. In the words of Lionel Crocker, he is "catapulted on to the public platform where heated issues of the day are threshed out."[3]

Walter Reuther or John L. Lewis by their vigorous communications give the cause of labor a dramatic quality. Eric Johnston makes the aspirations of business live in his speeches. Dr. Ralph Sockman, Dr. Louis Evans, or Father Vincent Sheen bring new and deeper meaning to the concepts of Christianity. The beginner who feels that he has nothing to talk about should look to the speeches of others for ideas and stimulation.

Fourth, the study of speech practices sharpens the ability to make critical judgments concerning speeches. The uncritical person often accepts what is said with no attempt to examine the soundness and validity of the ideas. This type of listener often may become the dupe and tool of the persuader who makes use of emotions and directive language. Obviously, in a world saturated by persuasive media, the intelligent listener must be able to judge what he attends, remembers, and accepts. The thoughtful study of speeches makes the listener more discerning of techniques and strategies of the speaker. Instead of being influenced by smooth talk, suave manner, and impressive language, he commences to question *why* the speaker uses particular devices. No longer is he satisfied so easily, for he develops a basis for comparing the performance of the speaker with what other speakers have done on similar occasions.

Fifth, the study of speeches leads to a greater appreciation of the place of public address in a free society. The spoken word has always played a significant role in the upward struggle of free people against tyranny and oppression. William Norwood Brigance has said:

[2] Chauncey A. Goodrich, *Select British Eloquence,* Harper & Brothers, 1852, p. 382.
[3] Lionel Crocker, *Vital Speeches of the Day,* September 1, 1956, p. 693.

Not only is history written with words. It is made with words. Most of the mighty movements . . . have gathered strength in obscure places from the talk of nameless men, and gained final momentum from leaders who could state in common words the needs and hopes of common people. Great movements, in fact, are usually led by men of action who are also men of words, who use words as instruments of power, who voice their aims in words of historic simplicity. . . .[4]

No finer expression of democratic principles can be found than in speeches and debates of Englishmen of the eighteenth century. The aspirations of the Founding Fathers are found in their utterances. Much of the basic philosophy of the nation is enunciated in the debates of Webster and Calhoun, Lincoln and Douglas. In the modern period, Woodrow Wilson, Franklin D. Roosevelt, Adlai Stevenson, and Dwight Eisenhower have put the ideals of the nation into powerful and compelling language. The war oratory of Winston Churchill still stirs pride and reverence for democratic institutions. Great speeches and vigorous debaters give the reader and listener a sense of the dynamic quality of our institutions.

What to Study

To study a speech the critic must consider the four interacting elements of the speech situation: the speaker, the occasion, the audience, and the speech. That is, he must concern himself with (1) how the speaker adapted (2) his speech materials (3) to the occasion (time and place) and (4) to the listeners.

THE SPEAKER

A person may enjoy a painting, a poem, or a selection of music without knowing about the artist who produced it. But a speech represents the effort of an individual to inform, to stimulate, or to persuade listeners. It definitely expresses the speaker's personality and reveals his attitudes, sentiments, aspirations, and desires. The critic can therefore profit from an understanding of the events of the speaker's life. Significant are questions like the following ones: (1) What was the speaker's training in speech making? (2) What are the speaker's general study habits and his specific methods of speech preparation? (3) What is the speaker's general background with reference to subject? (4) How did the speaker prepare the speech under consideration? (5) What factors motivated the speaker to speak?

[4] William Norwood Brigance (ed.), *A History and Criticism of American Public Address*, McGraw-Hill Book Company, Inc., 1943, vol. I, p. vii.

THE OCCASION

A speech can never be divorced from its social and political contexts, from its historical setting. The critic must be keenly aware of the forces which influence the speaker and his listeners. Edmund Burke's speech on "Conciliation with America" is only meaningful against a setting of the events of late eighteenth-century England. The Webster-Hayne debate and the Webster-Calhoun debate grew out of the great struggle between the North and the South. Churchill's wartime oratory might be considered overdramatic at any other time than when the Germans were menacing Britain's very life by land, air, and sea. The Fireside Chats of Roosevelt developed from a need to inform the people about depression and war.

The critic is concerned with the answers to the following questions: (1) Of what large historical trends was the speech a part? (2) What were the specific events that gave rise to the speech? (3) Was the speaker's decision to speak a part of some campaign or some grand strategy? (4) Did the speaker select the time and place or was he invited to speak? (5) What were the peculiar requirements of the time and place?

THE LISTENERS

Beginning physics students sometimes ponder whether sound exists when a tree falls in the forest with no ear nearby to record and interpret the waves. But there can be no similar debate about a speech. An oral discourse without listeners is not a speech; it must be *heard* to qualify as a *speech*. Of course, the listeners may be confined to those within the sound of the speaker's voice or they may be spread over a vast radio or television network. The critic's task is to weigh the problems which the listeners present the speaker and to judge how the speaker adapts his materials to ever changing reactions of his listeners.

The study of a speaker's audience should involve an investigation of questions like the following: (1) What was the extent of the speaker's listeners? (2) Were listening conditions conducive to comprehension and retention? (3) What did the listeners demand and expect of the speaker? (4) Was the controlling segment of the listeners hostile, neutral, or favorable toward the speaker, his cause, and his subject?

THE SPEECH

The Speech Purpose or Goal. The successful speech is purposive; it is planned to gain a definite response from the listeners. The skillful speaker does not "hitch his wagon to a star." Instead he keeps his feet very much on the ground and selects an immediate goal which he has a reasonable expectation of achieving. He includes or discards materials on the basis of whether they keep the speech moving toward his desired goal.

The speaker may announce a goal within his speech, but he may sometimes conceal his real and ultimate purpose, knowing that the concealment is a surer way to success. A speaker may appear to be speaking for a worthy charity when in reality he is speaking in order to present himself in a favorable light. His announced goal may be money for the needy; his real and ultimate goal may be to win the respect of his listeners and hence election to public office. Often in determining real and ultimate goals the critic must rely upon a tentative hypothesis which he is willing to change when new facts become available. These guesses may be based upon previous utterances, past conduct, platform behavior, speech development, choice of materials, and sometimes even upon subsequent actions and utterances.

In judging a speech, the critic will find the determination of the speaker's purpose an excellent starting point, for it becomes the measuring-stick by which to judge the speaker's ultimate success. In the final evaluation the critic must answer two important questions: (1) What response did the speaker seek? (2) How did the actual response aroused by the speech compare with the speaker's desired response?

In addition, the critic must make a judgment concerning the wisdom of the speaker in selecting his objective in light of listener attitudes and the requirements of the occasion. He must also give serious consideration to whether the selected goals were socially commendable and whether the speaker was thoroughly aware of his social responsibilities.

Choice of Subject.   According to his goal the speaker selects and limits his subject.

The critic must decide whether the subject is one which the speaker is capable of developing. At this point the critic must again turn to a study of the speaker's background. The average presidential campaign provides many examples of what happens when a candidate attempts to speak on all the subjects his advisers give him. For example, many political writers suggested that Adlai Stevenson in 1956 was less effective when he attempted to present the "canned" arguments of his advisers than when he discussed those subjects on which he had personal convictions.

The critic must likewise consider whether the subject is appropriate to the interests and aspirations of the listeners. Many classroom speeches, for example, are "speaker centered"; they are about favorite topics of the speakers, but they are of little interest to the listeners. Certainly the subject must grow out of the interests of the speaker, but it must be expressed in terms of the wants and interests of the listeners.

The critic must consider a third aspect of the subject: Does it fit the time and place of the speech? The subject which is appropriate for an after-dinner occasion may be highly inappropriate for a Sunday worship service. A successful classroom lecture may fall flat before a women's club meeting. A speech on politics or religion may be considered taboo at a businessmen's luncheon club. The time and the place impose limitations upon the speaker which he cannot afford to ignore.

The Speaker's Ideas. Significant speaking attempts to communicate significant ideas. The critic must, of course, thoroughly understand these ideas in order to evaluate the speech.

As a starting point he should look for the speaker's basic beliefs. Often those underlying premises from which the speaker argues are not specifically stated within the speech proper; nevertheless, they undergird every argument of the speech. To understand unstated premises the critic must look to the speaker's other utterances, writings, and past actions. He must seek information about the speaker's philosophical, political, social, and economic points of view.

After ascertaining the basic beliefs of the speaker, the critic is better able to analyze and evaluate the speaker's main lines of argument and to weigh carefully their reliability or credibility. For tests he should consult a more exhaustive source than the present discussion.[5]

One final word of warning. Not all speakers are interested in communicating ideas to their listeners. Many high-power persuaders strive to gain action by weaving together a series of vague words and intense emotional appeals. They hope through directive language to hit enough sensitive spots to produce action without reflective thinking. Too often political speaking falls within this category. The critic, of course, must not make the mistake of attempting to read into these persuasive attempts thought content where none exists.

The Structure of the Speech. After understanding a speaker's ideas the critic should next look at how the speech is organized or how the parts fit together. Is the speech clear, orderly, and logical?

On testing the structure, the critic should weigh the following questions: (1) Is the organization consistent with the speech purpose and the nature of the subject? (2) Does the time allotted to the introduction, the discussion, and the conclusion seem consistent with the demands of the listeners and occasion? (3) Do the structure and the ordering of the points contribute to achieving the desired goal?

The Forms of Support. The ideas or arguments are the bones; the structure is the skeleton; the forms of the support constitute the substance of the speech. The supporting material may, of course, be either visual or oral.

[5] Giles Wilkeson Gray and Waldo W. Braden, *Public Speaking, Principles and Practice,* Harper & Brothers, 1951, chap. 11. Lester Thonssen and A. Craig Baird, *Speech Criticism,* The Ronald Press, 1948. Max Black (ed.), *Critical Thinking,* Prentice-Hall, Inc., 2nd ed., 1952.

At the outset in studying a speech the critic needs to determine whether the speaker is using exposition or argument. How does the speaker substantiate his premises? (1) Is he using authority? If so, is the authority identified by the speaker? Is the authority recognized by other competent observers? (2) Is he using examples (specific instances) or statistics? If so, are the cases cited typical or nontypical? (3) Is he using assertions without any support—either authority or examples? If so, what right does he have to make assertions? Is he considered a competent observer?

Language. The critic must weigh carefully the speaker's language. Often the principal difference between the mediocre and the superior speaker is found in the choice of words, in the sentence structure, and in the other elements of style. At the outset, the critic must remember that he is judging oral style which to be effective generally must be instantly intelligible. In other words, the critic must judge the oral quality of the language even when it is recorded on the printed page. This demand for immediacy of understanding requires simple words and sentence structure, sign posts, obvious transitions, and many summaries.

Textbooks in public speaking list as important four qualities of style: (1) clarity, (2) appropriateness, (3) vividness, and (4) impressiveness. Let us put these four qualities into four questions: (1) Does the language convey meaning? (2) Does the language meet the requirements of the listeners, the occasion, and the time limit? (3) Does the language arouse or stir imagery with the listener: visual, auditory, gustatory, olfactory, kinaesthetic, tactual, and thermal? (4) Does the language arouse a surge of powerful feelings? Or, is the language rich in its connotative qualities?

Delivery. A speech on a printed page is an essay; the words are transformed into a speech when the speaker delivers them orally. The critic must determine how these elements of delivery—voice, pronunciation, and bodily behavior—contribute to the process of the communication of thoughts. The techniques of speaking—use of voice, correctness of pronunciation, attractiveness of posture and movement—have no virtue in themselves; they become significant when they convey to listeners significant ideas.

Total Impact of the Speech. The final question which the critic must consider is: Did the speaker achieve his goal? To put the question another way, what was the immediate and the long-range effect of the speech?

The speaker must now see the speech as a whole. As Thonssen and Baird have put it,

Finally the criticism of a speech implies a philosophic judgment. . . . His [the critic's] is the added responsibility for ultimate synthesis. . . . His generalizations concerning the speaker, speech, audience, occasion must in turn be completed by a comprehensive view of the speaking event. Unlike the subjectivist he rests his interpretation squarely on the discipline of history, logic, rhetoric. His catholicity is tempered by insight into his own individual attitudes and handicaps. His philosophical methods then apply both to his materials and to his own methods of evaluating those materials.[6]

In considering the ultimate effect of the speech, the critic is faced with an analysis and evaluation of the speaker's broader influences. In this sense he must consider whether the speaker contributed to man's betterment and whether the speaker promoted the larger goals of his society.

EXERCISES

1. Deliver a short speech in which you introduce yourself to your classmates. Relate some interesting personal experience which will help your classmates to know you.
2. Present to your class an eight- to ten-minute evaluation of some living speaker whom you personally have heard. Include in your report the following:
   a. A brief description of the speaker and his speaking manner.
   b. What impressed you most about the speaker?
   c. What did you observe about the speaker that you could apply to your own speaking?
3. Write a brief evaluation of a recent speech which you have read. You may wish to consult the *New York Times*, *Representative American Speeches*, *Vital Speeches of the Day*, or the *Congressional Record*. Divide your report into four parts: (1) the speaker, (2) the occasion, (3) the audience and (4) the speech.
4. Evaluate for your classmates one of your own speaking experiences. You may wish to consider a topic like one of the following:
   a. How a lack of confidence in myself caused me to fail.
   b. How I succeeded because of my speaking ability.
   c. The day I wished for eloquence.
   d. How I prepared for a speaking contest.
   e. How I won (or lost) a speech contest.
   f. Why I am taking this course.
   g. The problem I hope to solve in this course.
   h. My ideal speaker.
   i. The speech I shall never forget.
   j. How I talked my way out of a tight spot.
5. Make a careful study of a television news commentator. Study carefully how he attempts to present the news in his own individual style. Does he attempt to achieve individuality by his interpretations, his language, his manner, or by sound effects or some other technique?

[6] A. Craig Baird and Lester Thonssen, "Methodology in Criticism of Public Address," *Quarterly Journal of Speech*, April, 1947, p. 138.

REFERENCES

Readings to Be Assigned with Chapter I

NOTE TO THE TEACHER: The following references are included in order to assist in coördinating the chapters on *Speech Practices* with materials found in standard text books. In some cases the teacher may wish to use *Speech Practices* with only one text, such as Gray and Braden, *Public Speaking: Principles and Practice.* In other cases the teacher may choose to supplement *Speech Practices* with readings from several books.

Baird, A. Craig, and Knower, Franklin H., *General Speech: An Introduction,* McGraw-Hill Book Company, 2nd ed., 1957, chap. 1, "Essentials of Effective Speech."

Brigance, William Norwood, *Speech: Its Techniques and Disciplines in a Free Society.* Appleton-Century-Crofts, Inc., 1952, chap. 1, "The Rights of Listeners"; chap. 2, "Four Fundamentals for Speakers"; chap. 5, "Efficient Listening."

Bryant, Donald C., and Wallace, Karl R., *Fundamentals of Public Speaking,* Appleton-Century-Crofts, Inc., 1953, chap. 1, "Approaching the Study of Public Speaking."

Crocker, Lionel, *Public Speaking for College Students,* American Book Company, 3rd ed., 1956, chap. 1, "Public Speaking and Your Competitive Position."

Gilman, Wilbur E., Aly, Bower, and Reid, Loren, *The Fundamentals of Speaking,* The Macmillan Company, 1951, chap. 1, "Learning to Speak Effectively"; chap. 17, "The Field of Speechmaking."

Gray, Giles W., and Braden, Waldo W., *Public Speaking: Principles and Practice,* Harper & Brothers, 1951, chap. 1, "The Attitude of the Speaker."

McBurney, James H., and Wrage, Ernest J., *The Art of Good Speech,* Prentice-Hall, Inc., 1953, chap. I, "The Role of Speech"; chap. II, "Standards of Good Speech"; chap. III, "Principles of Good Speech."

Monroe, Alan H., *Principles and Types of Speech,* Scott, Foresman and Company, 4th ed., 1955, chap. 1, "Essentials of Effective Speaking."

Oliver, Robert T., and Cortright, Rupert L., *New Training for Effective Speech,* The Dryden Press, 1951, chap. 1, "Speech and You"; chap. 4, "The Role of the Listener."

Thonssen, Lester, and Baird, A. Craig, *Speech Criticism, The Development of Standards for Rhetorical Appraisal,* The Ronald Press Co., 1948, chap. 1, "The Nature of Rhetorical Criticism."

White, Eugene E., and Henderlider, Clair R., *Practical Public Speaking: A Guide to Effective Communication,* The Macmillan Company, 1954, chap. 1, "Approaching Public Speaking Positively."

Readings on Speech Criticism for Advanced Students

Aly, Bower, "The Criticism of Oratory," *The Rhetoric of Alexander Hamilton,* Columbia University Press, 1941, pp. 25-32.

Baird, A. Craig, "Why Study Speeches?" *American Public Addresses 1740-1952,* McGraw-Hill Book Company, Inc., 1956, pp. 1-14.

Baird, A. Craig, and Thonssen, Lester, "Methodology in the Criticism of Public Address," *Quarterly Journal of Speech,* April, 1947, 33:134-138.

Baskerville, Barnet, "The Critical Method in Speech," *Central States Speech Journal*, July, 1953, 4:1-5.
Brigance, William Norwood (ed.), *A History and Criticism of American Public Address*, McGraw-Hill Book Company, Inc., vols. 1 and 2, 1943; Marie Hochmuth (ed.), Longmans, Green and Co. vol. 3, 1955.
Crofts, Albert J., "The Functions of Rhetorical Criticism," *Quarterly Journal of Speech*, October, 1956, 42:283-291.
Harding, Harold F., "The College Student as a Critic," *Vital Speeches of the Day*, September 15, 1952, 18:733-736.
Henderlider, Clair R., and White, Eugene, "A New Emphasis in Teaching Public Speaking," *The Speech Teacher*, November, 1952, 1:265-270.
Nilsen, Thomas R., "Criticism and Social Consequences," *Quarterly Journal of Speech*, April, 1956, 42:173-178.
Parrish, Wayland Maxfield, "The Study of Speeches," *American Speeches*, Longmans, Green and Company, 1954, pp. 1-20.
Reid, Loren D., "The Perils of Rhetorical Criticism," *Quarterly Journal of Speech*, December, 1944, 30:416-422.
Thompson, Wayne, "Contemporary Public Address: A Problem of Criticism," *Quarterly Journal of Speech*, February, 1954, 40:24-30.
Wichelns, Herbert A., "The Literary Criticism of Oratory," *Studies in Rhetoric and Public Speaking in Honor of James Albert Winans*, Appleton-Century-Crofts, 1925, pp. 181-216.

Single-Volume Collections of Speeches

Baird, A. Craig, *American Public Addresses 1740-1952*, McGraw-Hill Book Company, 1956.
 The anthology contains 38 of the best known American speeches from 26 speakers. The introduction gives an excellent discussion of speech criticism.
Brigance, William Norwood, *Classified Speech Models*, Appleton-Century-Crofts, 1928.
 The volume contains 58 speeches classified under 18 forms of public address.
Goodrich, Chauncey, *Select British Eloquence*, Harper & Brothers, 1856.
 This anthology is the best single volume of British public address. The major part of the book is devoted to orations of late eighteenth and early nineteenth centuries. The introductions to the various speakers are extremely well done and are worth careful reading for method and content. This book is now considered a collector's item.
Harding, Harold F., *The Age of Danger: Major Speeches on American Problems*, Random House, 1952.
 The book contains 68 serious modern speeches and discussions. The speeches are grouped around the principal issues of the day.
Hicks, Frederic, *Famous American Jury Speeches*, West Publishing Company, 1925.
O'Neill, James M., *Models of Speech Composition*, Appleton-Century-Crofts, 1926.
 The collection is a compilation of 95 complete speeches, including the English and American masterpieces of eloquence.
O'Neill, James M., *Modern Short Speeches*, Appleton-Century-Crofts, 1923.
 The anthology includes 98 short speeches which were delivered after 1890. The book is an excellent source of models of short ceremonial speeches.

O'Neill, James M., and Riley, Floyd K., *Contemporary Speeches*, Appleton-Century-Crofts, 1930.

A collection of speeches delivered between 1925-1930.

Parrish, Wayland Maxfield, and Hochmuth, Marie, *American Speeches*, Longmans, Green and Company, 1954.

This anthology presents 29 complete speeches from 17 speakers, dating from Jonathan Edwards to Franklin D. Roosevelt. Also included is an introductory essay on "The Study of Speeches," and a criticism of Lincoln's First Inaugural Address.

Peterson, Houston, *A Treasury of The World's Great Speeches*, Simon and Schuster, 1954.

The editor attempts in one volume (pp. 856) to present a panoramic view of the speech-making of the Western world from Moses to Eisenhower. Included are 125 speakers and 160 speeches and parts of speeches. The book is organized around 20 headings which center around historical periods, issues and movements.

Sarett, Lew, and Foster, William Trufant, *Modern Speeches on Basic Issues*, Houghton Mifflin Co., 1939.

This collection includes over 50 modern speeches. They are grouped by subject and by form.

Multi-Volume Collections of Speeches

Baird, A. Craig, *Representative American Speeches*, The H. W. Wilson Company.

These volumes, a part of the Reference Shelf Series, have appeared annually since 1938. The editor, a foremost scholar in the field of speech criticism, has included speeches from politicians, educators, ministers, and business men. He has taken great care to check authenticity of the speech texts. Each volume is opened with a terse summary of speech principles.

Bryan, William Jennings, *The World's Famous Orations*, Funk and Wagnalls Co., 1906, 10 vols.

A collection of speeches dating from Achilles to T. R. Roosevelt.

Lee, Guy C., *World's Orations*, G. P. Putnam and Sons, 1900, 3 vols.

Reed, Thomas B., *Modern Eloquence*, John D. Morris and Company, 1900, 10 vols.

Three volumes are devoted to after-dinner speaking, three to classical and popular lectures, three to occasional addresses, and a final one to selected quotations. This set appeared in a second edition under the editorship of Ashley H. Thorndike. It includes many speeches of World War I period. Modern Eloquence Corporation, 1923, 15 vols.

Evaluation Sheet

NAME_____ SUBJECT_____

Poor	11
Fair	22
Below Average	33
Average	44
Above Average	55
Excellent	66
Superior	77

	Poor	Fair	Below Average	Average	Above Average	Excellent	Superior
	1	2	3	4	5	6	7
CHOICE OF SUBJECT: appropriate to speaker, listener, assignment, time limit (2,7)[a]							
ORGANIZATION: clear, simple, orderly, logical (2,8,9)[a]							
DEVELOPMENT OF INTRODUCTION: Did it gain an attentive, friendly, intelligent hearing? (13)[a]							
DEVELOPMENT OF DISCUSSION: factual and visual support (11,12,14)[a]							
DEVELOPMENT OF CONCLUSION: summary, appeal (15)[a]							
BODILY CONTROL: facial expression, eye contact, gestures, posture, movement (2,20,22)[a]							
PUTTING OVER IDEAS: rapport, communicativeness, persuasiveness (3,4)[a]							
LANGUAGE: clarity, vividness, impressiveness (16,17,18)[a]							
VOICE AND PRONUNCIATION (21)[a]							
ATTITUDES: toward listeners and speaking situation—urge to communicate (1,2)[a]							
OVERALL EFFECTIVENESS							

TOTAL SCORE_____

[a] Numbers refer to chapters in Gray and Braden, *Public Speaking*, which discuss the item. This evaluation sheet can be similarly adapted to other text books.

Chapter II

HOW SPEAKERS PREPARE THEIR SPEECHES

SPEECH preparation is serious business. A speaker may spend hours, days, or even months in extensive research, conferences with associates, careful planning, and endless revisions. In fact, a speaker may say seriously that he has prepared all his life for a speech. Such a remark is not an exaggeration, for all of his training, reading, and experience come to bear when he meets a challenging speaking assignment. Many of the speeches of Franklin D. Roosevelt went through six to ten extensive revisions. Midnight oil was burned; reams of paper consumed; and hours of typing expended in preparing a single Fireside Chat. These speeches were read and reread by specialists in the Administration. Each sentence was carefully weighed for its possible effect on the listeners. F.D.R. carefully timed the final reading copy, sometimes jotting the reading times in the margin.

Russell H. Conwell, lecturer extraordinary, delivered his famous lecture, "Acres of Diamonds," over 6100 times during a 50-year period, and yet Conwell never stopped working on the speech. He was always seeking new illustrations which would make his presentation more meaningful and more impelling for his immediate listeners.

With a single speech, "The Cross of Gold," William Jennings Bryan won the Democratic nomination for the presidency in 1896. This famous speech was no one-night production. The Nebraskan had tested various versions of the speech before middle western audiences during the past four years.

The college student or the busy executive should not, therefore, be surprised when speeches prepared in 15 or 20 minutes seem flat and uninspired to the listeners. Any speech which is worth serious attention is carefully thought out and prepared.

A study of successful speakers will reveal that their preparation usually involves the following:

1. They have a broad background upon which to draw in their preparation.
2. They are constantly seeking and collecting speech materials to be used in some later effort.

3. They spend a considerable amount of time thinking and reading about their speech subjects.
4. They revise their best speeches many times before delivering them.
5. They constantly attempt to adapt their materials to the audience and the occasion—even after they start speaking.

However, different speakers develop individual methods of approaching preparations. These variations in approach are explained by the conditions under which the speaker works and by the demands made upon the speaker's time. The following excerpts show how some well-known personalities approach the preparation of a speech.

How a Preacher Prepares His Sermons

Dr. Ralph W. Sockman, pastor of Christ Church, Madison Avenue Methodist Church of New York, is recognized as one of the foremost pulpit and radio preachers of the country. On Sundays he is heard on the National Radio Pulpit, which has two and a half million listeners. He prepares his sermons thoughtfully and carefully; consequently he is well qualified to comment on his sermon preparation.

During the summer I plan to make my reading general and enjoyable. I read rather widely in fields which appeal to me, some books of biography, some of fiction, some of Biblical exposition, and other areas which would seem to offer something useful for the pulpit.

I come back in the fall with perhaps 75 or 100 possible sermon themes. I may use very few of them in the ensuing season, but in this way I have collected several hundred themes which may strike fire with my mind. I try to plan my sermon subjects at least six weeks in advance and follow in general the church year, so that I may cover the full-orbed gospel which we are commissioned to preach.

One of the phases which I stress with my homiletic students at Union Theological Seminary is to keep variety both in the content and story of their sermons.

The minister is always in danger of having a "line" which he voices too much. The truth which we have in Christ is so vast that there is always romance in exploring its range.

In preparing my sermon for original delivery, I consult usually some eight or ten books for each sermon. When I get a new book, I do not read it at once but look over its contents and see what it has to offer. Then when I am preparing a sermon, let us say on prayer, I recall the chapter of the book which may have material on that subject. I take down one-line notes with page references. After preparation of eight or ten hours of reading, and note-taking, I begin to consider the outline. This takes me perhaps two or three hours, to get a sermon pattern. I usually have this done by late Friday night. My usual custom then is to spend all day Saturday writing the morning sermon.[1]

[1] Charles A. McGlon (ed.), "How I Prepare My Sermons: A Symposium," *Quarterly Journal of Speech,* February, 1954, pp. 54-55. Quoted by special permission.

How a Prominent Lecturer and Politician Prepares His Speeches

Norman Thomas, politician, lecturer, and writer, is well known for five unsuccessful campaigns for the presidency as Socialist candidate and for his speaking on the lecture platform and before forums. He reports that he has talked "to all sorts of audiences . . . from soap boxes on city streets to the platform in Madison Square Garden." After 50 years of speaking, Norman Thomas has some worthwhile observations about speech preparation.

I early discovered that the best way to prepare a speech is to get firmly in mind your major theme and then live with it, carry it around with you. Fortunately we are so made that we can stow an important matter in the back of our minds, attend to necessary business, and then find that the mind has been working on our theme without our conscious attention. How else explain the fact of the sudden intrusion on your conscious attention of a phrase, an illustration, a solution of some problem of order or argument which had bothered you? Repeatedly, I have been happily surprised at the way some valuable hint or illustration would leap at me from the newspaper or from some happening as I went about my business. Looking back on the years I think that I have composed more of my speeches walking around, going to bed, getting up, or sometimes by flashes in the night, than at my desk.

I hasten to add that I lay no claim to the inspiration of genius in these flashes. For a great many years, I was almost obsessed with the notion that to advance my cause I had to speak whenever possible. Doubtless I sacrificed to some extent quality for quantity. In any case, I was carrying a load of work that made my method of composing speeches a necessity. I had no time to seek perfection in an artist's seclusion.

I have heard the theory that a truly great oration has rules for its composition almost comparable to the rules for writing a sonnet or a symphony. The comparison seems to me somewhat extreme. But an oration or even an effective speech requires a logical order. It should have a certain unity; the speaker shouldn't roam over the earth as if he were killing time in a filibuster nor drag into every speech his pet creedal formulations on the road to secular or otherworldly salvation. A speech should have a beginning, a logical development, a climax or at least a dignified end. My own sins, as my wife and other friendly critics often reminded me, were to try to make too many points in one speech and to have too many climaxes or postscripts to the climax. I personally have worried more over the proper beginnings, especially since I often was in the position of one who must get his audience's attention promptly or not at all. There isn't one formula—too much depends on the audience, the occasion, the subject. As I grew more accustomed to speaking in all sorts of places, I came more and more to depend upon some event, some remark of a preceding speaker, or, for example—on a street corner—a reference to something before my listeners' eyes and ears, to get me started.[2]

[2] Norman Thomas, *Mr. Chairman, Ladies and Gentlemen,* Hermitage House, 1955, pp. 55-56. Quoted by permission of the author.

A Radio Commentator Reveals How He Speaks Impromptu

American radio listeners are familiar with the radio newscasts of H. V. Kaltenborn, who has been on the air since 1922. This successful news analyst has become famous for his ability to give clear and graphic accounts of rapidly changing events. He is able to transform news taken directly from wire services immediately into his own inimitable style. Kaltenborn can therefore speak with authority about impromptu and extemporaneous speaking.

One of my teachers at Harvard was the great William James. Often he talked about the great capacities that are latent in every human being. Everyone of us, he said, has infinitely more mental, physical, and emotional resources than we use in our daily lives. It is only when we are faced with an unusual challenge or demand that we call upon great reserves of power. These he compared with the ocean deeps which remain unaffected by the normal play of wind and weather, but which are stirred into action when the storm is at its peak.

It is when we plunge into an unprepared speech to sink or swim that we unconsciously reach for those latent powers of feeling and expression that often bring superior performance. . . .

When I am called upon really unexpectedly—this doesn't happen too often—I voice a few banalities in my opening sentences while thinking about what I am going to say. Once I have decided on my message and get it under way I forget myself. My mind is devoted to finding the words that give expression to what I feel. One successful phrase triggers another.

The real success of most ad lib talks lies in the feeling they convey, particularly when that feeling is shared by the listeners. It is when you make yourself their spokesman and say what they would have liked to say themselves that you win their most enthusiastic response.[3]

How a Presidential Speech Was Prepared

Who prepared Franklin D. Roosevelt's speeches? John T. Flynn, a Roosevelt detractor, says, "The voice, the manner, the delivery were Roosevelt's. But the words were supplied by others. The voice was the voice of Roosevelt, the words were the words of his ghost writers."[4] Samuel I. Rosenman, who helped F.D.R. with his speeches from 1928 until his death, disagrees. This man, who might be considered a ghost writer, testifies, "The speeches as finally delivered were his [Roosevelt's]—and his alone—no matter who the collabora-

---

[3] H. V. Kaltenborn, "Speaking of Speaking on the Spur of the Moment," *The Rotarian*, April, 1956, pp. 8-9. Quoted by special permission.
[4] John T. Flynn, *The Roosevelt Myth*, Garden City Books, 1948, p. 283.

tors were. He had gone over every point, every word, time and again."[5] Other "collaborators" agree with this latter point of view.

Although the discussion over who was responsible for Roosevelt's speeches is likely to continue, there can be no debate that Franklin D. Roosevelt considered the spoken word extremely important. Consequently, he gathered about him a most remarkable group of speech writers, including Samuel I. Rosenman, Raymond Moley, Louis McHenry Howe, Harry Hopkins, Robert Sherwood, Stanley High, and many others.

The work methods of this speech writing team reveal the complexity of preparing a presidential address. Rosenman gives a good summary of how they worked.

If a visitor, familiar with the appearance of the Cabinet Room on an ordinary day, were to have looked into it, say about midnight of February 21, 1942, he would have been quite startled.

All the lights were burning. But there were black curtains pulled across the windows now; we were at war, and it was blackout time. The shining surface of the large table was hardly visible, for it was covered from one end to the other with papers, books, telegrams, letters. . . .

Seated around the table were three men. They were all in their shirt sleeves and were obviously tired, for they had been working all day on a speech. They had just said good night to the President in his study in the White House, and had then walked over to the Cabinet Room to do some more work on the speech. . . .

"What's the war news like?" I [Rosenman] asked.

"It's all terrible—we're getting one hell of a licking all over the Pacific, and it certainly looks as though it's going to get worse instead of better," Harry [Hopkins] said. . . .

"If the American people ever needed a shot in the arm, this is the time," said Bob [Sherwood]. "I hope this speech can do it. If they could only look into that room across the way and see the magnificent spirit and the confidence of the President, as we did just now, it would do them a world of good."

"They can't see it," I said, "but if I know the Boss, they'll feel it in his voice next Monday. But they won't unless we get to work—he expects the next draft with his breakfast."

Grace Tully, in her own office, had been typing some inserts and corrections which the President had dictated during our recent session with him. By this time she had brought some of them in, each on a separate piece of paper labeled "Insert A, p. 2," or "Insert B, page 15." She silently gave a copy to each of us, . . . and went back to her room to type the other inserts and to wait. . . .

We huddled over the new inserts she had brought in.

We were working on a fireside chat the President was to deliver on Washington's Birthday, 1942. . . .

"Let's see now," I said, "this is draft six"—so I took a carbon copy of draft five, which the President had just gone over with us, and changed the "five" to "six." I also kept before me the original of draft five, on which he had made deletions and corrections in his own hand.

This was the first fireside chat by the President since December 9, 1941, right

[5] Samuel I. Rosenman, *Working with Roosevelt,* Harper & Brothers, 1952, p. 11.

after Pearl Harbor. Our armed forces were being beaten and forced back at every point. . . . The President had decided to make a fireside chat explaining the global strategy of the war. . . . He had dictated parts of a first draft several days ago, and had just carefully read over and revised the fifth draft. We had each written some inserts for this fifth draft which had been submitted to him. Some had found their way into the draft—and some into the wastebasket.

"Too bad, Bob, he cut out that stuff of yours on page three; it sounded pretty good to me as he read it out loud. I wonder why," I murmured. . . .

Whatever the speech, the general pattern of our collaboration was always the same. When Bob had finished, he would silently pass to me what he had written; and Harry and I would read it together. We might say "O.K." or "fine" and clip it in the right place; or we might say "try again—that's too complicated or too oratorical for the Boss"; or we might suggest a few changes here and there. The same thing would happen with what I had dictated to Grace, and with what Harry had written.

The inserts the President himself had dictated got the same close scrutiny. We changed his language and often cut out whole sentences. When there was some dissent among us, we made a note to talk to the President about it the next day.

There was no pride of authorship; there was no carping criticism of each other. We were all trying to do the same thing—give as simple and forceful expression as possible to the thoughts and purposes and objectives that the President had in mind. Whatever language and whoever's language did it best was the language we wanted.

"Here is a suggestion from Berle which is O.K. and one from Marshall which is a peach," I said that evening, passing them around. By common consent, they went into the next draft, each marked as an insert and clipped to the right sheet.

After a few pages of the carbon copy of draft five were corrected and added to in this way, I pushed a button in the table near the President's chair. It was a bell connected with the messenger room. A messenger came in and took the pages to the girls upstairs to make six copies. This draft would be number six. From then on we sent the new draft up page by page, so that almost as soon as we were finished they could send it down retyped, and we could immediately begin working all over again on the seventh draft—polishing, correcting, adding, deleting. . . .

By two o'clock we had finished sending up the sixth draft; it was down again in a few minutes, and we were ready to begin the seventh. . . .

By three o'clock, we had finished the seventh draft. . . .

The seventh-draft original we left in a sealed envelope at the usher's office to be delivered to the President with his breakfast. . . .

This was the grind—and the glamour—of what was known as "ghostwriting" for a President of the United States.

In 1942 it was chiefly Harry [Hopkins] and Bob [Sherwood] and I [Rosenman] who did it. But there had been others before Harry and Bob: Moley, Tugwell, Johnson, Corcoran, Cohen, Berle, Bullitt, Richberg, High, MacLeish. . . .

If the preparation of speeches is so important in the development of policy, why did not the President write his own speeches; why did he have people help him?

Basically, the answer is this: the speeches as finally delivered were his—and his alone—no matter who the collaborators were. He had gone over every point, every word, time and again. He had studied, reviewed, and read aloud each draft, and had changed it again and again, either in his own handwriting, by dictating inserts, or making deletions. Because of the many hours he spent in its preparation, by the time he delivered a speech he knew it almost by heart.

But if the question is: Why did not the President . . . write the whole speech himself so that all the words were his alone? the answer is this: there just is not enough time in a President's day.

The preparation of some of the speeches or messages took as many as ten days, and very few took less than three. That does not mean actual writing time. But there were long memoranda and proposed drafts to be read, and information and statistics to be gathered. Irrelevant data had to be separated from relevant data. Many people had to be interviewed, sometimes a dozen or more for a single message. Some were consulted during the preparatory period before the speech began to take shape, others during the actual writing of the speech—either to check data or to canvass views on questions of policy. The President often asked that a full draft of a speech or certain paragraphs in it be checked by several departments and agencies. Sometimes a speech went through as many as twelve or thirteen drafts before the President was finally satisfied. Obviously, for him to undertake so exhausting and time-consuming a task from beginning to end was impossible if he wanted to continue on his other duties. As it was, a major speech invariably set his schedule back a full day or two.[6]

How a State Paper Was Prepared

In discussing why Franklin D. Roosevelt used assistants to help prepare his messages, Samuel I. Rosenman says, "There just is not enough time in the President's day" for him to write his own speeches. The time and care involved in preparing a state paper is clearly reflected in the account of how President Dwight D. Eisenhower's State of the Union message of January 5, 1956, was prepared:

Of all U.S. state papers, none is more formally conceived or more intricately worked over than the State of the Union message to Congress [of January 5, 1956]. In 1955 at least 600 Government officials were consulted during the five months in which President Eisenhower's message was prepared. . . .

The chronology:

AUG. 5. Ike summoned his Cabinet to the White House to outline the message he meant to deliver. It would be brief, he said, with an outside limit of 25 minutes' reading time; it would sum up the accomplishments of his Administration to date, and hammer home the need for completing his program. Cabinet members and department heads were instructed to submit by Oct. 15 their lists of achievements and specific requests for new legislation. The man who would coordinate everything: Kevin McCann, 51, president-on-leave of Ohio's Defiance College, . . . and currently White House Assistant for Speeches and Reports.

OCT. 15. Out of the U.S. bureaucracy came a book-size pile of research. McCann read it all, occasionally marking a paragraph or a thought he considered worthy of inclusion.

OCT. 24. McCann headed west to visit the President, recuperating from his

[6] Rosenman, op. cit., pp. 1-12. If you are interested in reading the speech of February 23, 1942, see Samuel I. Rosenman (ed.) *The Public Papers and Addresses of Franklin D. Roosevelt, 1942 Volume,* Harper & Brothers, 1950, pp. 105-116.

heart attack in Denver's Fitzsimmons Army Hospital. Settling back in his plane seat, McCann began to scratch out in pen and ink the first, 400-word outline of the State of the Union message. He put down five subject headings: 1) "World Responsibility," which later grew to "The Discharge of Our World Responsibility"; 2) "National Security," which became "The Constant Improvement of our National Security"; 3) "Fiscal Integrity"; 4) "Our Production Plant," for which the President substituted "To Foster a Strong Economy"; 5) "Human Resources," which became "The Response to Human Concerns." McCann checked his outline with Presidential Assistant Sherman Adams and Economic Assistant Gabriel Hauge, and then set out . . . to write the first draft of the message. The result: a triple-spaced sheaf of typescript that ran to precisely 30 minutes' reading time.

OCT. 27. McCann read this draft to the President. . . . Ike interrupted at almost every paragraph to make changes. His secretary, Mrs. Ann Whitman, took a shorthand transcription of his ideas. Next day, with only Mrs. Whitman present, Ike spent 90 more minutes revising and rewriting the second half of the speech. McCann flew back to Washington, D. C.

OCT. 29-NOV. 1. Over the weekend, McCann studied the Whitman transcript and turned out a second draft, or "Revise No. 1," which he sent off to the President at Denver. . . .

MID-NOVEMBER. Presidential revisions and departmental suggestions flooded into McCann's office. So did the rejoinders of consultants and constitutional lawyers, and phone calls from Cabinet members agog to learn whether their fondest projects had caught the President's fancy. To all, McCann responded: "Don't worry. It isn't frozen yet." It wasn't. McCann wrote "Revise No. 2" on Nov. 17, "Revise No. 3" on Nov. 29.

DEC. 2. Under the chairmanship of Vice President Richard Nixon, a long and trying Cabinet meeting was held at the White House. Starting with Secretary of State John Foster Dulles, the members of the Cabinet commented on the draft of the message, then commented upon one another's comments. . . . the Cabinet eventually sent out to the President a file of verbatim reaction that piled 1½ inches high. . . .

DEC. 16. With the President now convalescing at Gettysburg, the pace quickened. More Cabinet suggestions. More presidential revisions. McCann wrote a longer "Revise No. 4." By now it was obvious that the President would not deliver the message in person, so the need for brevity faded. The paragraphs on the farm problem were the most troublesome. Lights burned late at the White House as a special committee —Nixon, Adams, Attorney General Brownell, Secretary of the Treasury Humphrey and Secretary of Agriculture Ezra Taft Benson—conferred. Rough drafts were handed to Jack Martin and Bryce Harlow, White House liaison men with the Senate and House, for comment and approval of Republicans on the Hill.

DEC. 20. Ike returned to the White House for Christmas, and at once got into a 90-minute discussion with McCann. He reviewed the latest draft of the message, with its countless incorporations and changes, word by word, working on through the holiday. Out of this came "the semifinal draft."

DEC. 28. Leaving the draft of the message with the typists, Ike flew down to Key West. At 1 o'clock, two mornings later, McCann followed with a new, cleanly typed version in his briefcase. With almost no sleep he plunged into another interview with the President, 9 a.m. to noon. Once more the President went over the message line by line, finally dictating two entirely new paragraphs. . . .

DEC. 31. Back in Washington, McCann huddled from morning until 5:30 p.m., with Sherman Adams and several others, smoothing out the whole message to conform to Ike's revisions, teletyping the wording down to Key West. Page by page, as the old year died, the final version was handed out to the typists. The White House executive clerk, William J. Hopkins, supervised the preparation of the two "signature copies," which would be signed by the President and delivered to the Senate and the House.

JAN. 2. . . . White House Staff Secretary Andrew Goodpaster flew to Key West with the signature copies. The President worked over them, making new changes, adding a word here and there. Ike finally signed the copies, which Goodpaster flew back to Washington.

JAN. 4. More last-minute changes. More teletyping between Key West and Washington. Late at night, Ike decided that he was satisfied. McCann was told. Stencils in the White House were cut. Mimeograph machines began to hum on 3,000 copies of the State of the Union message for Congress and the press.

JAN. 5. Shortly after 6 a.m., Assistant Press Secretary Murray Snyder arrived at the White House, took one last exacting look at the completed draft, one hour later released it to the press marked FOR RELEASE AT NOON. The signature copies, signed and enclosed in big White House envelopes, were taken up to Capitol Hill. Shortly after noon the clerks began to read the 7,500 words of the message. It took Senate Clerk Edward E. Mansur Jr. 51 minutes and House Clerk George J. Maurer one minute more.[7]

An Englishman Comments on Speech Preparation

John Bright (1811–1889), English orator and statesman, was once called "the most powerful speaker in the House of Commons," but even more notable was his speaking before large public gatherings. His speeches were reported to have been extremely persuasive because of his intense moral fervor. The secret of his power may be suggested in his method of speech preparation.

As to the modes of preparation for public speaking, it seems to me that every man would readily discover what suits him best. To write speeches and then commit them to memory is, as you term it, a double slavery, which I could not bear. To speak without preparation, especially on great and solemn topics, is rashness and cannot be recommended. When I intend to speak on anything that seems to me important, I consider what it is that I wish to impress upon my audience. I do not write my facts or my arguments, but make notes on two or three slips of note paper, giving the line of argument and the facts as they occur to my mind, and I leave the words to come at call while I am speaking. There are occasionally short passages which for accuracy I may write down, as sometimes also—almost invariably—the concluding words or sentences may be written. This is very nearly all I can say on this question. The advantage of this plan is that while it leaves a certain and sufficient freedom to the speaker, it keeps him within the main lines of the original plan upon which the speech was framed, and what he says, therefore, is more likely to be compact and not wandering and diffuse.[8]

[7] *Time Magazine,* January 16, 1956, p. 17.

[8] From *The Times,* London, October 17, 1888, p. 7, quoted by Joseph O. Baylen, "John Bright As a Speaker and Student of Speaking," *Quarterly Journal of Speech,* April, 1955, pp. 159-168.

Brief Comments on Speech Preparation

Albert J. Beveridge, senator and biographer, recommends the following: "By being the master of your subject and of yourself, be the master of your audience. But that dominance cannot be yours if you are uncertain and ill-prepared. Dignity and power come from full knowledge, deep thought, and sure faith, as well as from personality. No wonder that the common people heard Jesus gladly, 'for he taught them as one having authority.' "[9]

Wendell Phillips, one of the most eloquent Americans of the nineteenth century said: "Practice is the best of teachers. Think out your subject, and read all you can about it. Fill your mind; and then talk simply and naturally. Forget that you are to make a speech, or are making one. You are to carry a purpose, effect an object; then having forgotten yourself, you will be likelier to do your best. Talk up to an audience, not down to it. The commonest audience can relish the best thing you can say if you say it properly. Be simple; be earnest."[10]

Eric Johnston, prominent business executive, described his method of speech preparation as follows: "First you get an idea. Then you refine it. Then do research. Then outline. Then fill in the details in a full manuscript. Refine again. Revise. Study. Deliver."[11]

Lincoln Steffens, the American journalist, wrote (to A. H. Suggett) about memorizing a speech:

In your last to me you said you had made a short speech without writing it and that it went so well that you were going to repeat it. I am sure that is right. It cost me dear to learn that. When I went out some years ago, on my first lecture trip, it was as a writer, and I wrote my lecture. Then I committed it to memory. My memory is bad. The consequence was that I was trying all the time I was talking to remember. My attention was backward, upon what I had written; not forward, not on my thought. It was a passable failure, that trip and what saved it was that I so often forgot my written speech and had so often to go ahead on my own thoughts, that parts of every lecture were extemporaneous.[12]

Woodrow Wilson, one of our most eloquent presidents, describes his method of speech preparation as follows: "I begin with a list of topics I want to cover, arranging them in my mind in their natural relations—that is, I fit the bones of the thing together; then I write it out in shorthand. I have always

[9] Albert J. Beveridge, *The Art of Public Speaking*, Houghton Mifflin Co., 1924, p. 59.

[10] Lorenzo Sears, *Wendell Phillips, Orator and Agitator*, Doubleday, Page and Co., 1909, p. 367.

[11] Personal interview with James Stansell, January 5, 1951. Quoted in *A Rhetorical Study of the Public Speaking of Eric A. Johnston During His Presidency of the United States Chamber of Commerce* (unpublished Ph.D. thesis, Louisiana State University, 1951).

[12] Ella Winter and Granville Hicks, (eds.), *The Letters of Lincoln Steffens*, Harcourt, Brace and Company, 1938, vol. II, p. 574.

been accustomed to writing in shorthand, finding it a great saver of time. This done, I copy it on my own typewriter, changing phrases, correcting sentences, and adding material as I go along."[13]

George V. Denny, Jr., founder and moderator of "America's Town Meeting of the Air," has summarized how the most successful performers on his program have prepared. He says: "If you would speak well, listen to good speeches well delivered and walk out on bad ones. Gather your own material carefully, organize it, write it out—then rewrite it until it says what it ought to say. Finally, discard the written word and face your audience with a free mind.

"If you've done your advance work properly, the actual delivery of your speech will be easy."[14]

William E. Gladstone, nineteenth-century parliamentary debater and four times Prime Minister of Great Britain, said the following about preparing for a debate: "The work of the debater I take to be as follows. He has already in his mind all the elements of his speech. He has them in the best arrangement, of easiest access: but not yet combined, or so combined as to be capable of great modification in the structure of the combination. He has even the order and succession of topics generally and clearly, though not immovably, before him. . . . The ultimate construction therefore of his speech is the work of the moment."[15]

EXERCISES

1. Speaking assignment. Prepare a ten-minute report on one of the following topics or a similar one:
   a. How a famous speech was prepared. (See Exercise No. 4.)
   b. How a prominent speaker prepares his speeches.
   c. How poor speech preparation caused a speaker to fail.
   d. A sure-fire method of speech preparation.
   e. Famous speech ghost writers.
   f. Ghost writing today.
   g. Speech writing teams of recent Presidents.

2. Interview a local minister or some prominent local speaker concerning his methods of speech preparation. (Your instructor will tell you whether the results of the interview are to be submitted orally to the class or in written report.) Ask the interviewee such questions as the following:
   a. How does the speaker get ideas for speeches?
   b. Does he keep a speech materials file or scrap book?

[13] Ida M. Tarbell, "A Talk with the President of the United States," *Colliers*, October 28, 1916, p. 5.

[14] George V. Denny, Jr., "How to Make A Good Speech," *Pageant*, November, 1945, pp. 44-49.

[15] Loren Reid, "Gladstone's Theory of Parliamentary Debating," *Bulletin of Debating Association of Pennsylvania Colleges*, December 1954, pp. 4-7.

c. What sources has he found the best for supplying ideas and materials for speeches?

d. What steps does he follow in preparing a speech?

e. In his preparation, does he prepare an outline, prepare a complete manuscript, memorize it?

f. Does he rehearse it orally? Does he have anyone who acts as a critic? Does he use a speech recorder in speech preparation?

g. Does he have any advice about speech preparation which he would give to beginning speakers?

3. Investigate the speech preparation of one of the following speakers: Daniel Webster, Abraham Lincoln, William Jennings Bryan, Booker T. Washington, Russell H. Conwell, Woodrow Wilson, or Winston Churchill.

4. For additional insight into speech preparation see the following:

Baylen, Joseph O., "John Bright As a Speaker and Student of Speaking." *Quarterly Journal of Speech*, April, 1955, pp. 159-168.

Bormann, Ernest G., "Ghostwriting Agencies," *Today's Speech*, September, 1956, pp. 20-23.

Braden, Waldo W., "The Bases of William E. Borah's Speech Preparation," *Quarterly Journal of Speech*, February, 1947, pp. 28-30.

Brandenburg, Earnest, "The Preparation of Franklin D. Roosevelt's Speeches," *Quarterly Journal of Speech*, April, 1949, pp. 214-221.

Brandenburg, Earnest and Braden, Waldo W., "Franklin Delano Roosevelt," *A History and Criticism of American Public Address*, vol. III, pp. 464-498.

Brigance, W. Norwood, "Ghostwriting Before Roosevelt," *Today's Speech*, September, 1956, pp. 10-12.

Crowell, Laura, "Building the 'Four Freedoms' Speech," *Speech Monographs*, November, 1955, pp. 266-283.

Feris, Frances, "The Speech Preparation of John Bright," *Quarterly Journal of Speech*, November, 1931, pp. 492-504.

McGlon, Charles A., "How I Prepare My Sermons: A Symposium," *Quarterly Journal of Speech*, February, 1954, pp. 49-62. Six leading preachers tell how they prepare their sermons.

Ray, Robert T., "Ghostwriting in Presidential Campaigns," *Today's Speech*, September, 1956, pp. 13-15. Also found in *Central States Speech Journal*, Fall, 1956, pp. 8-11.

Reid, Loren, "Did Charles Fox Prepare His Speeches," *Quarterly Journal of Speech*, February, 1938, pp. 17-26.

Reid, Loren, "Gladstone's Essay on Public Speaking," *Quarterly Journal of Speech*, October, 1953, pp. 265-272.

Richardson, Ralph, "Adlai E. Stevenson, Hollywood Bowl, October 9, 1954, His Preparation and His Speaking Manuscript," *Western Speech*, May, 1955, pp. 137-174.

Smith, Donald K., "The Speech-Writing Team in a State Campaign," *Today's Speech*, September, 1956, pp. 16-19.

White, Eugene E., and Henderlider, Clair R., "What Harry S. Truman Told Us About His Speaking," *Quarterly Journal of Speech*, February, 1954, pp. 37-42.

White, Eugene E., and Henderlider, Clair R., "What Norman Vincent Peale Told Us About His Speaking." *Quarterly Journal of Speech*, December, 1954, pp. 407-416.

REFERENCES

Baird, A. Craig, and Knower, Franklin H., *General Speech: An Introduction,* McGraw-Hill Book Company, 2nd ed., 1957, chap. 2, "Improving Your Speech Habits: Beginners' Problems"; chap. 3, "Choosing Your Subject and Purpose"; chap. 4, "Finding Materials."

Brigance, William Norwood, *Speech: Its Techniques and Disciplines in a Free Society,* Appleton-Century-Crofts, Inc., 1952, chap. 3, "First Steps in Managing Ideas"; chap. 9, "Selecting the Subject and Purpose"; chap. 10, "Earning the Right to Speak."

Bryant, Donald C., and Wallace, Karl R., *Fundamentals of Public Speaking,* Appleton-Century-Crofts, Inc., 1953, chap. 3, "Managing Ideas in the First Speeches"; chap. 8, "Selecting the Subject"; chap. 9, "Finding Materials."

Crocker, Lionel, *Public Speaking for College Students,* American Book Company, 3rd ed., 1956, chap. 12, "Choosing the Subject"; chap. 14, "Gathering Material."

Gilman, Wilbur E., Aly, Bower, and Reid, Loren, *The Fundamentals of Speaking,* The Macmillan Company, 1951, chap. 2, "Choosing a Topic"; chap. 3, "Discovering Material."

Gray, Giles W., and Braden, Waldo W., *Public Speaking: Principles and Practice,* Harper & Brothers, 1951, chap. 2, "Some First Principles"; chap. 7, "Subjects, Sources and Materials."

McBurney, James H., and Wrage, Ernest J., *The Art of Good Speech,* Prentice-Hall, Inc., 1953, chap. 5, "Subjects for Speaking"; chap. 7, "Exploring the Subject."

Monroe, Alan H., *Principles and Types of Speech,* Scott, Foresman and Company, 4th ed., 1955, chap. 7, "The Process of Preparing a Speech."

Oliver, Robert T., and Cortright, Rupert L., *New Training for Effective Speech,* The Dryden Press, 1951, chap. 8, "Selecting and Developing Ideas."

Thonssen, Lester, and Baird, A. Craig, *Speech Criticism, The Development of Standards for Rhetorical Appraisal,* The Ronald Press Co., 1948, chap. 8, "Determining the Areas of Investigation."

White, Eugene E., and Henderlider, Clair R., *Practical Public Speaking: A Guide to Effective Communication,* The Macmillan Company, 1954, chap. 2, "Selecting a Subject"; chap. 3, "Gathering the Speech Materials."

Chapter III

HOW SPEAKERS ORGANIZE THEIR SPEECHES

At the heart of any effective oral communication is organization. Sounds must be uttered in combinations of recognizable words; words must be joined into intelligible phrases or sentences; and isolated sentences must be woven together into a pattern which develops the speaker's thought. As a sentence is not just a sequence of unrelated words, so a speech is not a series of disconnected thoughts.

In the quotations of the preceding chapter, did you notice the emphasis which several of the speakers placed upon outlining and organization? For example, Dr. Sockman said: "After preparation of eight or ten hours of reading, and note-taking. I begin *to consider the outline*. This takes me perhaps two or three hours, *to get a sermon pattern*."[1] Norman Thomas maintained that "an effective speech requires *a logical order*. It should have *a certain unity*. . . . A speech should have *a beginning, a logical development, a climax*, or at least *a dignified end*."[2]

How, then, do speakers organize their thoughts for presentation? What are their notes and outlines like? These are the questions which this chapter will consider.

To have a unified speech, a speaker must first determine the central thought or proposition which he desires to have the audience accept. The materials to be included or omitted should be selected by this criterion: Will this material influence the audience to accept my position?

Plans of Organization

The thesis having been determined, there are, broadly speaking, two possible ways of ordering the points in relation to this central idea.

[1] Charles A. McGlon (ed.) "How I Prepare My Sermons: A Symposium," *Quarterly Journal of Speech*, February, 1954, p. 55. The italics are the present author's addition.
[2] Norman Thomas, *Mr. Chairman, Ladies and Gentlemen*, Hermitage House, 1955, p. 56. The italics are the present author's addition.

There is the deductive order, wherein the speaker states his proposition before any of the main points are introduced.

The second method is inductive, calling for the presentation of the proposition as the conclusion reached after the development of all major points. A skilled speaker who has directed the sequence of his ideas to an inescapable conclusion may occasionally present his proposition by implication. That is, he lets the audience frame the proposition in its own words instead of stating it specifically for the listeners.

Three typical student speeches, which follow the standard textbook formulas of organization, are printed below to illustrate the ways of ordering points.

A SPEECH USING THE DEDUCTIVE ORDER

"The United States Forest Ranger" is largely an expanded outline. Much vivid detail and colorful illustration have been omitted in order to emphasize the framework of the speech.

THE UNITED STATES FOREST RANGER[3]
by George W. Cabaniss

Introduction

1. Some of you may have strange and romantic ideas about the activities of the United States Forest Ranger. Let me assure you immediately that this public servant is not the dashing storybook hero who battles the raging elements and leaping flames single-handedly to save the beautiful girl. Nor is he the man pictured in the pulp magazine advertisement under the bold caption: "Be a Ranger—Hunt—Fish—Trap and Patrol."

2. Let me dispel these notions by discussing the ranger's work under five headings: (1) the ranger as a custodian of public property; (2) the ranger as a personnel manager; (3) the ranger as a fire protection expert; (4) the ranger as a timber manager; and (5) the ranger as a maintenance engineer.

Discussion

3. First, let us consider the ranger as custodian of public property. The average ranger's district consists of about 200,000 acres of publicly owned timber land covered with millions of dollars worth of timber products. In addition to trees, there may be more than 100 miles of forest roads, about the same amount of telephone lines, several residential structures for housing employees, an office building, a large warehouse filled with thousands of dollars worth of tools, supplies and special equipment—as well as trucks, cars and road machinery. This property is entrusted to the ranger for care and protection.

4. Second, let us consider the ranger as a personnel manager. Of course he cannot individually practice forestry on all of the area under his supervision. He must have help. Working under the ranger are several full time specialists, including fire control

[3] Delivered in a class of Speech 51 at Louisiana State University.

aides, timber management assistants, timber markers, and a road foreman. In addition to full time employees, there are often 50 part time workers whose duties range from working on the roads to fire watching. During the fire season additional local persons are hired to fight fires. The ranger assigns duties to the men; he takes care of their payroll and personnel records. Incidental to the personnel work, he must maintain other records and answer correspondence concerning this area. He usually puts off these tasks for rainy days when he cannot work in the field.

5. The third phase of the ranger's work is fire protection. His first duty is to protect his woods from fire. In carrying out this responsibility, he breaks it down into three main phases: (1) fire prevention, (2) fire presuppression, and (3) fire suppression.

6. A successful fire prevention program requires that the ranger personally know the families living in his district and their attitudes towards forest fires. This is to help him know how to appeal to them to prevent man-caused fires. Before each fire season, he presents a series of persuasive lectures and movies before churches, schools, clubs, and informal groups to emphasize the importance of fire prevention.

7. Presuppression of fires involves having sufficient manpower and fire fighting equipment always in readiness to put the fires out speedily. Keeping lookout vigilance from the towers and maintaining telephone and radio communication systems also fall under this heading.

8. The actual suppression of the fires is a matter of dispatching the right amount of manpower and equipment to outbreaks of fires to extinguish them before they become uncontrollable. The ranger personally visits the fires of appreciable size, for he must decide when they are officially out. For a fire to reoccur after once being declared out will bring an investigation of the ranger's competence.

9. Let us consider fourth the forest ranger as a timber manager. This is his biggest job, requiring about 60 percent of his time in marking and measuring trees for sale and in training and supervising his helpers to assist with this work. He divides the district into many small logging units and makes a master plan showing which units currently need cutting. He operates the woods in such a way as to have more timber growing than is cut during the year. The trees in need of harvesting are measured, marked, and advertised for sale. The purchaser cuts and logs the marked trees in accordance with a written contract.

10. After the logging is complete and the contract is closed, the ranger hires a crew of workers to go into the sale area and deaden the remaining undesirable trees that overshadow and suppress the growth of the young desirable trees. These men work under the direction of a foreman, previously trained by the ranger. During this clean-up work, usually called timber stand improvement, the ranger considers the needs of the forest game animals. He attempts to provide sufficient game food trees and den trees to insure a good crop of game from year to year.

11. The last aspect of the forest ranger's work which I want to discuss is that of maintenance engineer. Periodically, the ranger checks all the buildings, towers, communications systems, roads and bridges in his district. Upon completing the inspection, he estimates the costs of needed repairs and replacements, and submits to his forest supervisor a request for funds. Then he starts on the long list of jobs to be completed including repainting the tower steel, re-roofing lookout cabins, cleaning water wells, redecking bridges, ordering new parts for trucks or road machinery, and even little tasks like replacing the tattered flag that constantly waves over each occupied government station. The ranger must keep his stations and equipment in good repair.

Conclusion

12. I have attempted to enumerate for you the duties of the United States Forest Ranger. I hope you will remember him as a custodian, as a personnel manager, as a fire protection expert, as a timber manager, and as a maintenance engineer. He guards and cares for your National Forests in order that they will produce wood, water, and recreation for you and for the generations to come.

QUESTIONS FOR STUDY

1. What is the purpose of Par. 1? of Par. 2? Gray and Braden consider the function of the introduction as the following:
   (1) "to direct the listeners' attention and interest toward the subject;
   (2) to develop a friendly attitude toward the speaker; and
   (3) to prepare the listeners for understanding."[4]
   Which of these objectives does Cabaniss achieve? In the light of the speech as a whole, does the omission of any objective seriously damage the speech?
2. Are the individual points of the speech developed inductively or deductively? (That is, is the central thought at the beginning or the end of the paragraph?) Support your answer by citing the speech.
3. Among the techniques frequently suggested for use in the conclusion are: restatement, summary, suggestion, challenge, emotional appeal, personal appeal, and visualization. Which of these does Cabaniss use?
4. Does Cabaniss identify the source of his information? Is there any statement in the speech which would indicate that the speaker is qualified to talk on the ranger? If you were a member of the audience, what do you think would be your reaction to the speech as far as the accuracy of the information is concerned? Cabaniss actually spent five years in the forestry service before entering college. Should he have indicated his first-hand knowledge of his subject? How?
5. A good oral paragraph must be organized so that it is instantly intelligible to the listener. Do the paragraphs of "The United States Forest Ranger" meet the criterion of instant intelligibility?
6. What is the central thought? Where is it first stated in the speech? Is there a restatement of the central thought? Is there any material in the speech which is not properly related to the central thought?

A SPEECH USING THE INDUCTIVE ORDER

In "Some People Learn the Hard Way," J. T. Nason, an insurance adjuster, shares his experience with his listeners. The talk gains impetus because the audience recognizes that he is speaking from first-hand knowledge of his subject.

[4] Giles W. Gray and Waldo W. Braden, *Public Speaking: Principles and Practice*, Harper & Brothers, 1951, p. 334.

SOME PEOPLE LEARN THE HARD WAY[5]
by J. T. Nason

1. "I'm sorry, I can't sign it. I lost my arm!" This was a pretty startling statement, but it is what a young man told me when I had finished taking a statement from him about an accident in which he had been involved. The statement I had taken revealed that this man had been driving on a gravel road and had tried to take a curve too fast. As a result, the car skidded in loose gravel and overturned.

2. Another case I investigated required that I interview a girl in the hospital. This girl was about 22, and she had about 122 sutures in her face. The car in which she had been riding was in a bad collision. The cause was bad brakes.

3. Today we have multiple lane highways with good hard surfaces and electronic traffic signals. We have grade separations which have been designed by brilliant engineers, and we have ever-increasing traffic law enforcement. Our cars have faster pickup, power steering, power brakes, wider brake shoes for more braking surface, ball-joint suspension, safety steering wheels, and safety latches. We even have a little man that wasn't there to automatically dim our lights. In spite of all these safety factors we are experiencing an ever-increasing number of automobile accidents.

4. We could refer to statistics published by the National Safety Council and learn that some of the major causes of accidents are drinking, defective automobiles, and poor judgment. Statistics are very impressive if you are mathematically inclined, but most people don't remember a long string of numbers. I believe these factors can be stressed without the help of statistics.

5. You have probably heard the story that is told about the cow hit on the highway. It is always the best cow in the farmer's herd. Just as consistently, I have run into another story. I have probably interviewed at least a thousand drivers who acknowledged having something alcoholic to drink prior to an accident. But of all these, no more than two have ever admitted that they were intoxicated. The story they all give is, "I had a couple of beers," or "I had a couple of hi-balls, but I wasn't drunk." I don't know who they think they are fooling. Certainly they can't fool themselves since they frequently have a torn-up automobile and personal injuries. They aren't fooling the insurance company because the police report spells it out—"Driving while under the influence of alcohol."

6. A defective automobile can mean poor tires, bad brakes, or a faulty steering mechanism, among other things. These are things which can easily be controlled, and if they are not, they can just as easily create tragedy. Of these, probably the worst offender is poor brakes. Have you ever seen a trailer loaded with one or two long utility poles? If you have, you remember that these poles extend back behind the trailer a distance of 10 to 20 feet. If you had ever seen one of these poles extending back through an automobile like an apple on a sword, you would never again take a chance on driving a car with poor brakes. Just as impressive and also just as tragic was the fellow who pushed his radiator into the front seat of his car. It was a little late, but he finally learned that a car with 60,000 miles on it should be checked for loose nuts, screws and bolts. His wasn't, and when a tie rod came loose, he found that so far as he was concerned a large oak tree is a pretty immovable object. Defects? These are just a few. Poor tires cause blowouts that in turn cause an unbelievable number of accidents. I have seen blowouts cause the driver to lose con-

[5] Delivered in a class of Speech 103 at Louisiana State University.

trol and strike other cars, strike other objects, and overturn. The pitiful thing about accidents caused by poor tires is that you don't have to be a mechanic to look at tires occasionally to see if they are worn.

7. The third factor causing accidents that we have mentioned is poor judgment. To me, this is the greatest cause of automobile accidents, and at the same time the one that should be our smallest problem. By poor judgment we don't mean poor judgment of drinking while driving or driving an unsafe car. Rather, we refer to the factor of human error on the part of the driver. This embraces a lot of territory, but basically there are two main types of human error. First, the error in not knowing the proper driving rules and traffic laws. Second, the error of poor behaviour in any given incident. In speaking of the first case, I wonder how many of you know that when two cars approach an uncontrolled intersection that the car to the left is supposed to yield to the car approaching from its right? Or take the case of two cars approaching each other from opposite directions which stop for a traffic signal. When the light turns green, the southbound driver gives it the gas and starts a left turn in front of the northbound car. This driver is infuriated when the northbound car strikes him before he completes his left turn. In court his anger will do him no good because a person making a left turn must yield until the way is clear to make the turn safely. The second type of human error involves such things as knowing that you don't brake a car in the middle of a curve. Or knowing that when a car starts skidding the driver should cut the wheels in the same direction that the car is skidding. In other words, reacting properly to an emergency.

8. Where does this lead us? We have discussed the preventatives as well as some of the causes of accidents. The point I want to make with you is simply—become safety conscious every time you get into a car.

9. All of us have a tendency to be very passive when we hear someone preaching safety. If, however, just one time you could see the expression on a doctor's face when he says, "This man's brain is injured so severely that he will be nothing more than a vegetable," then you would become safety conscious. Safety is primarily common sense. Learn what you can from reading safety literature. This can be easily obtained from a number of sources including the police and your insurance agent. Have your car checked periodically. Use your head as well as your foot when you get behind the wheel and leave drinking to someone who doesn't have to drive.

10. If you will heed this warning and become safety conscious now, you will have a better chance to escape becoming a safety statistic later.

QUESTIONS FOR STUDY

1. How does Nason seek to gain the initial attention of his listeners?
2. Taking into consideration that the audience knew Nason's profession, what does the speaker include in the introduction to establish his right to speak?
3. Does the introduction disclose the subject of the speech?
4. Nason considered Pars. 1, 2, and 3 the introduction. What is the purpose of Par. 4? On what grounds could it be considered a part of the introduction?
5. Par. 5 develops the first major cause of accidents, Par. 6 the second, and Par. 7 the third. Is each paragraph developed inductively or deductively?
6. What do you consider the proposition of the speech? Some persons have suggested that the last clause of the first sentence of Par. 4 states the proposition; however, Nason considered the second sentence, Par. 8, his proposition. If the former is considered the proposition, is the speech order still inductive? What

becomes the relationship of Pars. 8, 9, and 10 to the proposition?

7. What techniques does Nason use in his conclusion? (See question 3 of the first section of this chapter for possible techniques.)

8. The inductive order is more difficult than the deductive to present in good oral paragraphs. Does Nason achieve instant intelligibility?

9. Nason relies primarily on what forms of support to establish his main points?

10. Divide a sheet of paper into two columns; in the left-hand column list the emotional appeals used by the speaker; in the right-hand column, cite the actual phrases from the speech which illustrate the appeal.

A SPEECH USING THE MOTIVATED SEQUENCE

Alan H. Monroe, Chairman of the Department of Speech at Purdue University, has developed a plan of speech organization called the motivated sequence. The steps of the sequence are: attention, need, satisfaction, visualization, and action.[6] Lewis H. Eaton, Jr., a student at Louisiana State University, planned to use the motivated sequence in the following speech.

HELP TODAY FOR HEALTH TOMORROW
by Lewis H. Eaton, Jr.

1. If you should be in an accident on your way home tonight, the chances are that you would not find an available bed at either local hospital. The hospital situation in Baton Rouge is critical. Why is it critical?

2. The formula used to determine the number of beds needed for a city is 4.5 beds per thousand population. Recent estimates place the population of East Baton Rouge Parish at 183,000. Applying the ratio of only four beds per thousand people, we should have 732 beds to provide adequate hospitalization in this parish. Based on this estimate, Baton Rouge is short 207 beds to meet the minimum requirements for adequate facilities.

3. Now let's examine why there is a shortage of beds. There are three reasons. First, like many of the other community services, the hospitals have not been able to keep up with the phenomenal growth of this community. Second, people today recognize the value of hospital care; and because of better economic conditions and more widespread hospital insurance coverage, they use these facilities more often. Third, the polio and rehabilitation program is taking up 75 badly needed beds on the fourth floor of the Baton Rouge General Hospital.

4. There is no question that the community has experienced a phenomenal growth or that more people are recognizing the value of hospital care and are better able to afford it; but what are the advantages of a polio and rehabilitation center?

5. Even though the doctors are doing as much as they can through research, a polio preventative has not been proven, and it is still necessary to have the proper equipment available for the treatment of possible cases. Local doctors, hospitals, citizens, and the National Foundation for Infantile Paralysis have cooperated to reduce the suffering and disabilities caused by polio. The polio mortality rate in the nation is 5 to 8 percent compared with the local rate of only 1 percent. This fact

[6] Alan H. Monroe, *Principles and Types of Speech,* Scott, Foresman and Company, 4th ed., 1955.

alone speaks well for the job being done by the local center. Last year more than 20,000 patients were treated here.

6. The purpose of a rehabilitation ward is to help the disabled patient develop to the fullest his physical, mental, social, and vocational abilities. The hospital itself gains, for those patients who regain their health release their beds for the use of new patients. Surely, we must maintain the polio and rehabilitation center.

7. What, then, can be done to meet the city's need for additional hospital beds? The Baton Rouge General Hospital is on a large plot of ground and is built in such a way that it can be easily added to. The proposed solution is an addition to the south wing of the Baton Rouge General. The addition will be planned to house the polio and rehabilitation unit plus 24 additional beds. These 24 added to the 75 which will be released by moving the polio and rehabilitation unit will provide 99 additional beds.

8. There will be many benefits from this new structure. The new floor space is highly desirable for polio and rehabilitation wards. There will be great psychological value in removing these patients from the atmosphere of the hospital proper. Furthermore, the new structure will have a dual-purpose pool for treatment and recreation. Having all of these facilities on the ground floor instead of the fourth floor will be much more convenient for the patients using crutches and wheel chairs. The floor space of the rehabilitation unit will also be designed to separate the polio and nonpolio patients according to their needs.

9. With the use of vaccines, it is possible that polio will decrease in the coming years. The large areas now being planned for polio patients can then be put to use for nonpolio patients.

10. Another important point is that ample property will still remain for a future addition to this building which can provide vocational rehabilitation offices, counselling and testing areas, space for a crippled children's clinic, and facilities for functional occupational therapy, teaching of exceptional children, and treatment of rheumatic fever cases.

11. As you must agree, every eventuality has been carefully considered. This is the immediate solution to the critical shortage of hospital beds in Baton Rouge. A community problem carries with it a community responsibility. Since the plans have been prepared for the new addition to the Baton Rouge General and an organization set up to raise the money to finance it, very shortly you will be approached for a voluntary contribution. It has been my experience that, when given the facts and informed of the need, people who are sincerely interested in the welfare of their community respond generously. I hope that learning the facts leading up to this proposed addition will encourage you to give generously. The need is great; the plan is feasible, the benefits many. Help today for health tomorrow!

QUESTIONS FOR STUDY

1. Is the motivated sequence essentially an inductive or a deductive order of organization?
2. Point out which paragraphs of Eaton's speech correspond with each of the five points of the motivated sequence.
3. What reasons does Eaton give for additional hospital beds? How does he develop each reason? Is the supporting material adequate to substantiate the need?
4. Should Eaton tell how much money will be needed to finance the addition? Does his solution meet the need?

5. List the benefits which Eaton visualizes as the results of the proposed addition. Are they described with sufficient vividness to influence an audience? What sort of aids could Eaton have employed to help his listeners visualize the project?
6. Outline the action step. Compare it with the conclusion of Nason's "Some People Learn the Hard Way." What techniques are included by both speakers? Are there techniques peculiar to either speaker?
7. What are the chief forms of supporting material used in the speech?
8. What are the major emotional appeals?
9. Are the paragraphs in good oral style, easily comprehended by the listener?

The Speaker's Notes

All speakers—for the sake of their listeners—should carefully plan the organization of their speeches. There is, however, no single "best way" for preparing notes for the actual platform situation. Some speakers use no notes at all; others employ a key-word outline; some may have a full content outline; while still others read from manuscript. The novice should practice several techniques until he arrives at the one best suited to his individual needs.

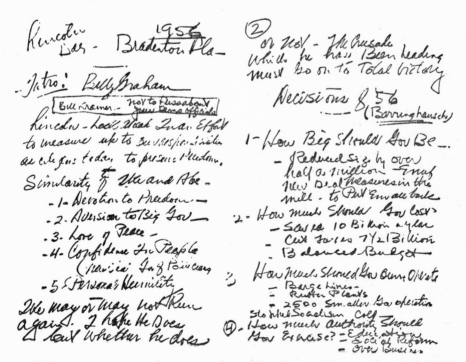

FIGURE 1. The Speaking Notes of Karl Mundt, Senator from South Dakota. These notes in the Senator's own handwriting were used in a speech delivered at Bradenton, Florida, February, 1956.

Facing p. 1 is a photograph of the note which Russell H. Conwell used when he delivered "Acres of Diamonds" for the last time. Compare this outline with the excerpt from the speech given on pp. 70-73.

Karl Mundt, Senator from South Dakota, describes himself as "one who believes in encouraging speakers to exercise their arts extemporaneously rather than try to pound through an inch or two of manuscript."[7] On p. 35

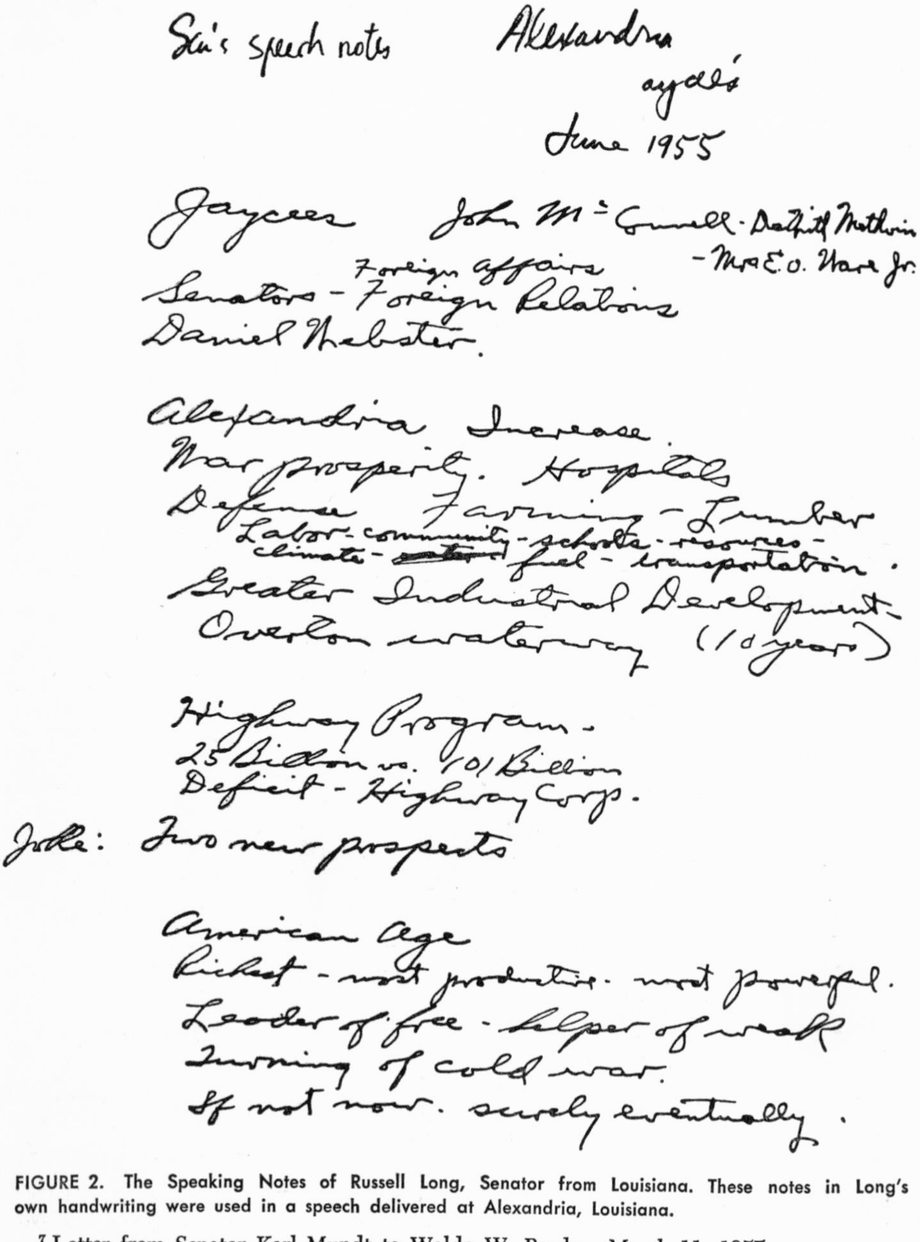
Sen's speech notes
Alexandria
June 1955
Jaycees John McConnell
Mrs E. O. Ware Jr.
Foreign affairs
Senators - Foreign Relations
Daniel Webster.
Alexandria Increase.
War prosperity. Hospitals
Defense Farming - Lumber
Labor - community - schools - resources -
climate - fuel - transportation.
Greater Industrial Development -
Overton waterway (10 years)
Highway Program -
25 Billion vs. 101 Billion
Deficit - Highway Corp.
Joke: Two new prospects
American Age
Richest - most productive - most powerful.
Leader of free - helper of weak
Turning of cold war.
If not now - surely eventually.

FIGURE 2. The Speaking Notes of Russell Long, Senator from Louisiana. These notes in Long's own handwriting were used in a speech delivered at Alexandria, Louisiana.

[7] Letter from Senator Karl Mundt to Waldo W. Braden, March 11, 1957.

are reproductions of notes which he used for a Lincoln Day address at Bradenton, Florida, in 1956. Senator Mundt says these notes are "somewhat typical" of the notes he prepares "for any political speech." Two representative pages of the five pages he actually used in delivering the speech are reproduced here. The speech ran from 45 minutes to an hour.

A set of notes used by Senator Russell Long of Louisiana appears on p. 36. The occasion was a talk for the Jaycees of Alexandria, Louisiana. Senator Long wrote his notes on an ordinary sheet of ruled notebook paper. Notice the way in which he skipped lines in order to indicate thought groupings in the speech.

A third Senator who uses notes for his talks is Hubert Humphrey of Minnesota. Below are two of the sheets he used in speaking on foreign affairs to a Career Conference sponsored by George Washington University. The audience was primarily composed of college students. Senator Humphrey states: "These are rather typical of the notes I use when I make a major speech and have prepared no formal text."[8] The pages reproduced here are not consecutive pages, but are pages two and four of the five which he used.

Thomas E. Dewey, another prominent political speaker, used the notes on

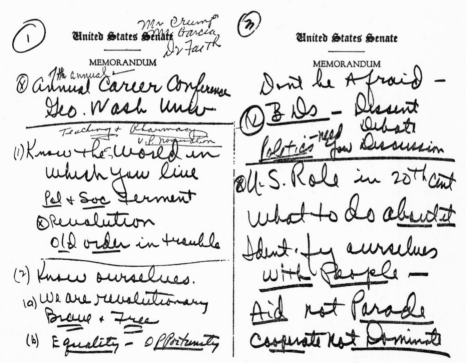

FIGURE 3. The Speaking Notes of Hubert Humphrey, Senator from Minnesota. These notes in Humphrey's own handwriting were prepared for a speech he delivered at the Career Conference at George Washington University, Washington, D.C.

[8] Letter from Senator Hubert Humphrey to Waldo W. Braden, April 10, 1957.

New Phase of World Struggle — All our lines

Common — World 1/3 Slave — 2/3 free — No
  In 1/3 Slave 1/5th free — rest in flux.

Asia | Recent Colonial peoples freed 600,000 — Not enf.
  Not beer + skittles — Beginning

Agrarian Mostly — India - Pakistan - Lines - Dead.
  All — No
  (1) Capital (Here $15,000 per job)
  (2) Raw Materials — wrong places — No technique
  (3) Food.
  (4) Not even governments or politicians
      — Civil Service (Mails) — Buildings
  5) Engineers, lawyers, accountants, Managers.

Illiteracy yes — but literacy not whole answer
Socialist — Communist - Capitalist — All capitalist
                        — State - private of people?
One Voice — Not Astonishing — 1000 mile border

Low living standard - $55 India

Know of good things — Intend to have them.
Right

So — No War — New phase - Korea - Imitation.

Asia 1/2 + 1/2 — all Africa — S. America — Europe
  "Road to Paris" — Lenin.

FIGURE 4. Speaking Notes of Thomas E. Dewey, Former Governor of New York and Prominent Republican. These notes in Dewey's own handwriting were used in a speech delivered at Harvard Law School, March 16, 1957.

p. 38 when he spoke on Asia at the Harvard Law School March 16, 1957. Mr. Dewey made these notes on a sheet of ruled yellow legal-sized paper.

Addressing a Chicago Library Luncheon, former President Truman spoke from two and a half pages of typed, double-spaced notes. His sixth and final point reads:

6. The President is the Social Head of the State. He receives and entertains high ranking visitors as well as Ambassadors of foreign nations. He gives five or six State dinners at the White House and holds long line receptions for Ambassadors, The Congress, the Supreme Court. He also has a luncheon or a dinner for high ranking visitors too. These social functions are incidental to the tremendous job he has to do and to work at constantly. His work follows him wherever he goes, at home or abroad.

The records of his transactions are in his papers which are considered his private property. Washington set the precedent. The Adamses established it and it has been the custom ever since for the President to take his papers with him when he leaves the White House.

What has happened to them, etc.

What I'm trying to do.[9]

A transcript of what Mr. Truman actually said at the luncheon reveals that this section from the notes was expanded into four full pages in delivery. Four paragraphs (approximately one page of the transcript) are printed below. Compare these paragraphs with the appropriate part of the notes above.

The President is also the social head of the state, and this is what a great many of the stuffed-shirt people like very much. They think it's just the finest thing in the world to be able to meet Princes and Queens and Kings and personages of that kind. The President, when they come to the United States, is their host, and he always is a courteous host too. . . . He receives and entertains high-ranking visitors, as well as ambassadors of foreign nations, and that is a very important job in itself. He gives five or six state dinners in the White House and holds long-line receptions, and if you don't think it's a lot of fun to stand in line and shake hands with 2700 people whose names you can't understand when they are pronounced, just try it once, and see what you think. He holds these receptions for the ambassadors who are sent to Washington. He also holds a reception for the Congress and one for the Supreme Court, among many others, and I want to say to you that the wife of the President has a tremendous burden. She had to receive all the visiting ladies . . . and many other people who come to Washington. The last year we were in the White House Mrs. Truman, by count, shook hands with 50,000 people. I shook hands with 25,000, but I dodged half of them, and she had to go ahead and do the job. That is a most important part of the President's office—the social end of it.

Now, I have enumerated to you six full-time jobs that one man has to fulfill. There isn't any way in the world under the Constitution of the United States for him to get out of those jobs. . . .

The records of his transactions are in his papers which are considered his private property. Washington set that precedent, and the Adamses established it, and it has been the custom ever since for the President to take his papers with him when

[9] Notes used by Harry S. Truman July 10, 1956, at the Chicago Library Luncheon. The notes are in Mr. Truman's personal papers and are printed here with his special permission.

RADIO ADDRESS OF THE PRESIDENT
FEBRUARY 23, 1942

MY FELLOW AMERICANS:

I chose tonight to talk with you for two reasons. First,
that the celebration of Washington's Birthday may serve as a
reminder to some people that General Washington led our nation
in a war which lasted eight years, and during that time was
defeated and last battles and key places more often than he
won battles or conquered strongholds. During most of that long
period he faced an important minority in each one of the thirteen
States that was constantly telling him to seek an honorable
peace. His supplies were short and, in a true sense, every
Winter was a Valley Forge. He had traitors in his own ranks --
not Benedict Arnold alone -- but many others whose petty
jealousies, whose personal selfishness, whose inability to
take punishment and whose back seat driving would have caused
a weaker and less honorable man to throw up the sponge in the
early part of the Revolutionary War.

The other reason I chose tonight to talk with you is
that I have been observing for several weeks -- and from
vast sources of information -- the temper of the American
people and their reactions to current events.

FIGURE 5. From Manuscripts of Franklin D. Roosevelt's Speech, Delivered February 23,
1942. The first pages of four of seven versions are included here.

DRAFT #3

RADIO ADDRESS OF THE PRESIDENT

FEBRUARY 23, 1942

The celebration of Washington's Birthday in the midst of our initial military and naval reverses in this world-wide struggle is a most appropriate occasion for us to talk with each other about things as they are today and things as we know they shall be in the future. What made Washington the predominant, symbolic figure of his time was not only his generalship, his philosophy, his physical courage or his devotion to the great cause he served. ~~sacrifice~~. It was something more important even than these — something which we refer to simply as character -- moral stamina.

General Washington led our first armed forces ~~colonies~~ in a war which lasted eight years. [During those years his armies were defeated and strategic positions were lost more often than he won victories or captured key strongholds.]

In those years, the continental army was faced continually with formidable odds and recurring defeats. Supplies and equipment were lacking. In a sense, every winter was a Valley Forge. Throughout the thirteen states there existed fifth columnists — witting or unwitting — selfish men, jealous men, fearful men, who proclaimed that Washington's cause was hopeless, that he

FIGURE 5. *(Continued)*

RADIO ADDRESS OF THE PRESIDENT

FEBRUARY 23, 1942

~~The celebration of~~ Washington's Birthday ~~in the midst of our latest military and naval reverses in this world-wide struggle~~ is a most appropriate occasion for us to talk with each other about things as they are today and things as we know they shall be in the future.

~~What made Washington~~ *Trait of Washington* the predominant, ~~symbolic figure of his time was not only his generalship, his philosophy, his physical courage or his devotion to the great cause he served. It was something more important even than these — something which we refer to simply as character~~ *was* -- moral stamina.

General Washington led our first armed forces ~~in a war which lasted eight years.~~

For eight ~~eight~~ years, ~~the~~ *his* continental army was faced continually with formidable odds and recurring defeats. Supplies and equipment were lacking. In a sense, every winter was a Valley Forge. Throughout the thirteen states there existed fifth columnists -- ~~scheming or plotting~~ -- selfish men, jealous men, fearful men, who proclaimed that Washington's

FIGURE 5. (Continued)

RADIO ADDRESS OF THE PRESIDENT

FEBRUARY 23, 1942

My Fellow Americans:

Washington's Birthday is a most appropriate occasion

for us to talk with each other about things as they are today

and things as we know they shall be in the future.

For eight years, General Washington and his Continental

Army were faced continually with formidable odds and recurring

defeats. Supplies and equipment were lacking. In a sense,

every winter was a Valley Forge. Throughout the thirteen

states there existed fifth columnists -- and selfish men, jealous

men, fearful men, who proclaimed that Washington's cause was

hopeless, that he should ask for a negotiated peace.

Washington's conduct in those hard times has provided

the model for all Americans ever since -- a model of moral stamina.

FIGURE 5. (Continued)

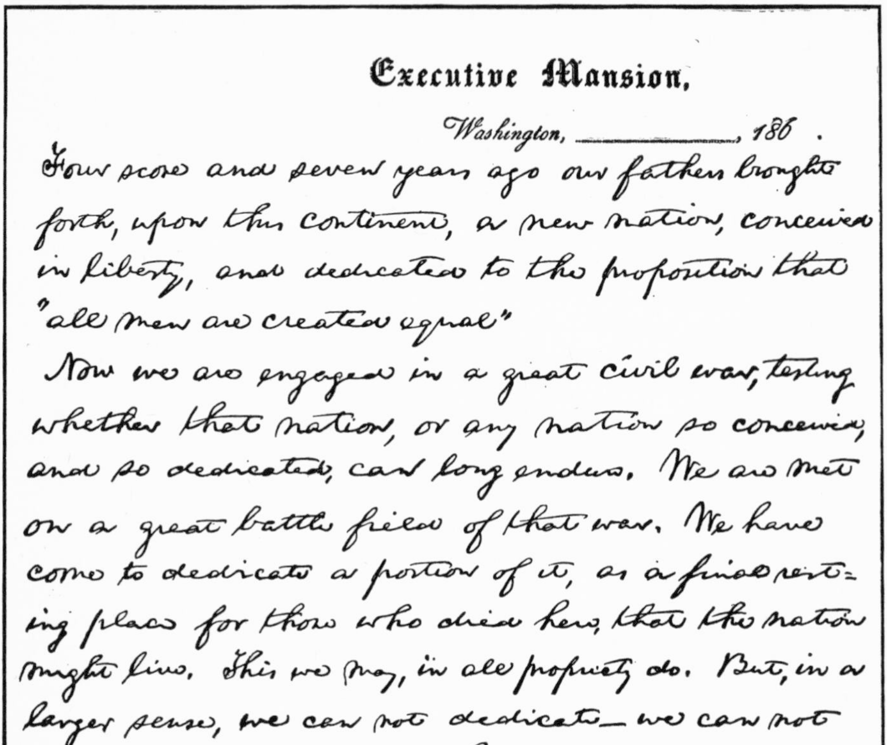

Executive Mansion,

Washington, ______, 186 .

Four score and seven years ago our fathers brought forth, upon this continent, a new nation, conceived in liberty, and dedicated to the proposition that "all men are created equal"

Now we are engaged in a great civil war, testing whether that nation, or any nation so conceived, and so dedicated, can long endure. We are met on a great battle field of that war. We have come to dedicate a portion of it, as a final resting place for those who died here, that the nation might live. This we may, in all propriety do. But, in a larger sense, we can not dedicate— we can not consecrate— we can not hallow, this ground— The brave men, living and dead, who struggled here, have hallowed it, far above our poor power to add or detract. The world will little note, nor long remember what we say here; while it can never forget what they did here.

It is rather for us, the living, we here be dedica ~~to stand here,~~

FIGURE 6. The Gettysburg Address. This is the first draft of this famous speech delivered by Abraham Lincoln, November 19, 1863.

ted to the great task remaining before us—
that, from these honored dead we take increased devotion to that cause for which
they here, gave the last full measure of devotion— that we here highly resolve these
dead shall not have died in vain; that
the nation, shall have a new birth of freedom, and that government of the people by
the people for the people, shall not perish from the earth.

FIGURE 6. (Continued)

he leaves the White House. Now, I am going to enumerate to you just a few instances of what has happened to Presidential papers. . . .

Washington took his papers to Mount Vernon. They stayed there for quite awhile, and then somebody came and got them and took them up to Massachusetts. They fooled around with them awhile and sent them back, and finally they got into the Library of Congress. Sol Bloom, who was a Congressman from New York, took it upon himself to go into the Washington situation and had Washington's papers assembled, indexed and printed. There were 150 volumes of them, and it's the most wonderful thing that Sol ever did. They tell a story about that incident. Sol was a Congressman from one of the districts in New York which never needed any help in the Congress, and Sol didn't have to work very hard at his job, but everybody in his district knew him. They were holding a meeting one time in his district on these Washington papers, and one of his constituents said, "Well, I know Sol pretty well, but . . . [who's] this fellow Washington he's always talking about?"[10]

The Speech Manuscript

Personal preference or the nature of the occasion sometimes influence a speaker to read from manuscript rather than to rely on an outline or notes. In preparing his manuscript, a speaker frequently makes extensive changes from one draft to the next. As you will recall from the Roosevelt and Eisenhower examples in Chapter II, the revision process is especially prominent in state addresses.

Roosevelt's 1942 Washington's Birthday Address provides a fine opportunity for observing the development of a speech through a comparison of several drafts. Seven drafts plus the original reading copy are available in the Roosevelt papers at Hyde Park. On pp. 40-43 are copies of the first page of drafts one, three, and four and of the final reading copy. You may find it interesting to trace the development of a phrase—such as "moral stamina"— through the several versions. For the story of how this speech was prepared, see pp. 17-20.

Perhaps the most famous presidential address in American history is Lincoln's Gettysburg address. The original and second versions are now in the Library of Congress. Of these drafts, a Library of Congress pamphlet states:

That Lincoln wrote the address on a rough bit of paper on the way to Gettysburg is an exploded but persistent legend. Actually, the first sheet of the first draft was written in Washington, on Executive Mansion stationery. The corrections and the second page were written in lead pencil, probably at Judge Wills' house in Gettysburg, where Lincoln spent the night of the 18th.

The second draft is believed to be the reading copy which Mr. Lincoln held in his hand at the dedication ceremony, and is assumed to have been written on the

[10] Transcript of speech by Harry S. Truman at the Chicago Library Luncheon, July 10, 1956. The transcript is in Mr. Truman's personal papers and is quoted here with his special permission.

morning of the 19th, between breakfast and the start for the cemetery grounds. There are a number of changes from the first version, some of them slight matters of punctuation, or of a single word. . . .[11]

A reproduction of the first draft appears on pp. 44-45. You may wish to compare it with the usual published version.

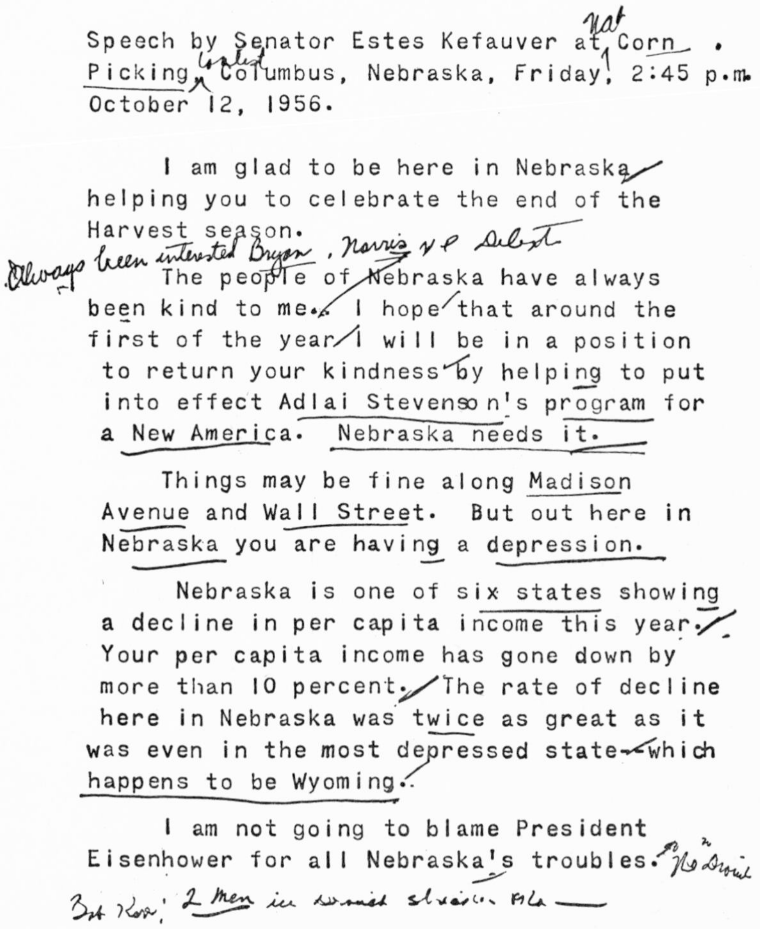

Speech by Senator Estes Kefauver at Corn . Picking, Columbus, Nebraska, Friday, 2:45 p.m. October 12, 1956.

I am glad to be here in Nebraska helping you to celebrate the end of the Harvest season.

The people of Nebraska have always been kind to me. I hope that around the first of the year I will be in a position to return your kindness by helping to put into effect Adlai Stevenson's program for a New America. Nebraska needs it.

Things may be fine along Madison Avenue and Wall Street. But out here in Nebraska you are having a depression.

Nebraska is one of six states showing a decline in per capita income this year. Your per capita income has gone down by more than 10 percent. The rate of decline here in Nebraska was twice as great as it was even in the most depressed state—which happens to be Wyoming.

I am not going to blame President Eisenhower for all Nebraska's troubles.

FIGURE 7. A Page from the Reading Copy of a Speech by Estes Kefauver, Senator from Tennessee and Democratic Vice-Presidential Candidate in 1956.

Senator Estes Kefauver of Tennessee is one of many speakers to develop his own particular system of marking a manuscript. A page from the reading manuscript of one of Kefauver's addresses is reproduced above. Notice especially the Senator's use of underlining, virgules, and hand-written interpolations.

The materials provided in this chapter on the preparation of notes and manuscripts are by no means exhaustive—merely suggestive. Seeing the techniques of other speakers should stimulate you to devise a system which meets your personal needs.

EXERCISES

1. The following article contains an interesting discussion of the purple martin and its habits. After a careful reading of the material, prepare outlines for speeches of the following types:
   a. An informative speech, using the deductive order (for material on the informative speech, see p. 120).
   b. A convincing speech using the inductive order (for information on the convincing speech, see p. 138).
   c. An actuating speech, using the motivated sequence (for information on the actuating speech, see p. 139).
   In all three outlines, label your proposition or central thought; in (a) and (b) label the introduction, discussion, and conclusion; in (c) label the steps in the motivated sequence: attention, need, satisfaction, visualization, and action.

WANTED: 10,000 NEW MARTIN HOMES[12]
by Leslie Lloyd

The shortage of homes which has plagued many families during the past fifteen years is a familiar problem to birds, especially those which nest in cavities. If disaster areas could be named in the bird world, surely the purple martin would be given a very high priority for new housing facilities.

When the white settlers came to America, martins were nesting in tree cavities or holes in rock cliffs. The virgin forests which furnished an abundant supply of nesting sites gave way rapidly to advancing civilization. Under present day economic conditions most decadent trees which would provide nest holes are quickly removed to make room for rapidly growing young trees. The occupation of nearly all of the few remaining cavities by English sparrows and starlings has left martins stranded with very few natural nesting sites. Recently in and around Baton Rouge they have been observed nesting in rural mail boxes, iron stand pipes, bridge superstructures and other equally hazardous places. With a little effort much can be done to alleviate this housing shortage.

Fortunately martins are a plastic species adaptable to changing conditions. Their acceptance of nest boxes illustrates how some wild birds have adjusted themselves to civilization. Since martins have become almost entirely dependent upon man-made houses for nesting sites, it is probable that the total population within their natural range is limited by the lack of houses. . . .

Martins are a welcome and colorful addition to any area of habitation. Their cheerful notes, which are unusually musical for swallows, consist of a variety of chirps,

[11] "Abraham Lincoln's Gettysburg Address, the First and Second Drafts Now in the Library of Congress," pamphlet published by the Library of Congress, 1950.

[12] Leslie Lloyd, "Wanted: 10,000 New Martin Homes," *Louisiana Conservationist*, January, 1955, pp. 8-9.

twitters and squeaky calls. Their graceful soaring, steep dives and powerful flight are a pleasant sight.

In addition to their esthetic value, martins are of considerable economic importance. Their food is taken in the air and consists entirely of insects. Only rarely in cold, rainy weather when no insects are flying do they feed otherwise. Under such circumstances food is picked from the surface of water or from the tops of weeds or bushes. Among the insects which are consumed are serious agricultural pests such as cotton boll weevils, strawberry weevils, mosquitoes, flies, squash bugs, stink bugs, tree hoppers, many beetles and other insects. Dragon flies may form a surprisingly large proportion of their food. Because of their aerial feeding habits, martins are not subject to the diseases of ground feeding birds. Fruits and berries are never eaten. Several people have reported that they are useful in sounding an alarm when hawks or crows approach their nesting area.

Martins spend the winter in Brazil and reappear in Louisiana from February to April. Although they nest from British Columbia to Prince Edward Isle, there is a progressive increase in the number of breeding pairs from north to south so that they are very common in Louisiana from the Arkansas line to the Gulf of Mexico.

The nest is constructed of bits of dry grass, weeds, twigs and leaves. Quite often mud and small pieces of gravel are added to the nest. Both sexes build the nest and both assist in feeding the young. Four or five pure white eggs are deposited in the nest; incubation requires about two weeks with the young remaining in the nest for 24 to 28 days.

Martins will occupy a great variety of nesting boxes. Since they are social birds with a fondness for the company of their own kind, they will live in large colonies. Complicated and expensive houses are not necessary. A very simple and inexpensive house which anyone can build can be made from a wooden apple box and two orange crates obtainable at the nearest grocery.

Any house with compartments which are approximately 6 x 6 inches, with entrances measuring 2½ inches in diameter, is suitable. Since martins have very short legs, the bottom of the entrance should be located not over 1½ inches above the floor of the house. Naturally the more durable the wood, the longer the house will last. Cypress is excellent for house construction because of its durability, lightness and ease of working.

. . . house construction from an apple box . . . is especially good since children can build it with a few inexpensive tools. Although this type of house is not as durable as one built of cypress, with proper care it will last four or five years. The outside should be painted with any color of paint which suits the builder's fancy. The house should be placed on a pole or an iron pipe about twelve to fifteen feet from the ground in a rather open area away from trees. Wooden poles should be "cat-proofed" by placing a two foot wide metal guard around them at an elevation of six feet.

2. Interview a local speaker (minister, lawyer, businessman, teacher) on his methods of organizing materials for a speech. Does he plan to accomplish certain ends at various places in the speech (i.e., gaining initial attention, or making a final appeal)? Does he speak from a full outline, key words, or a manuscript? If possible, bring to class a set of notes which he actually used for a speech plus a tape recording of the speech as he delivered it.

3. When a speaker divides his central thought or proposition into the main points which he intends to develop, he should always use a single principle of division. He should be sure that the main points are all-inclusive of the ideas necessary to

support his thesis and that at the same time the main points are mutually exclusive. Among the most usable methods of partitioning a subject are:

time	space
parties involved	operational procedures
fields of endeavor	component parts
problem-solution	causal relationships

For each of the following examples, determine whether there is a single principle of division. If so, identify the principle. Correct the faulty examples.

a. Grade school athletic competition deserves the support of all parents.
  (1) It promotes good physical development for participants.
  (2) It provides a healthy after-school-hours activity.
  (3) It encourages character development.
  (4) It fosters emotional adjustment to both success and failure.

b. Paratroop training consists of four consecutive stages.
  (1) Learning to pack the parachute properly.
  (2) Learning jump procedures in dummy planes.
  (3) Making actual parachute falls from training towers.
  (4) Jumping from an airplane in flight.

c. Al Jolson should be remembered because of his generosity.
  (1) He gave of his talent.
  (2) He gave of his physical strength.
  (3) He gave of his money.

d. Hawaii should be granted statehood.
  (1) There is a long history of the question.
  (2) Hawaii meets the usual criteria required of territories seeking statehood.
  (3) Hawaii's citizens want statehood.

e. Benjamin Franklin deserves recognition.
  (1) As an author.
  (2) As an inventor.
  (3) As a statesman.

f. Raw sugar can be produced from sugar cane through five broad steps.
  (1) Extraction of juice from cane stalk.
  (2) Clarifying or purifying the raw juice.
  (3) Evaporating water from the clarified juice.
  (4) Crystallizing solid sugar from the syrup.
  (5) Centrifugation of the sugar crystals.

g. John Smith deserves honor for his contributions to the Jamestown colony.
  (1) Smith's early life.
  (2) Smith was a great leader.
  (3) Smith's courageous nature.

h. William Jennings Bryan's career as a speaker.
  (1) Chautauqua and lyceum.
  (2) Secretary of State.
  (3) Political campaigns.
  (4) Legal.

i. The turn of the nineteenth century witnessed three different patterns of rural life in the United States.
  (1)The Northern farmer.
  (2) The Southern planter.
  (3) The Western frontiersman.
  (4) Modern agriculture owes much to these pioneers.

j. There should be uniform traffic regulations throughout the United States.
   (1) Citizens of the several states are travelling within the United States more than ever before in history.
   (2) Ignorance of the difference in traffic regulations from state to state causes many accidents.
   (3) Uniform traffic regulations in all states would solve this phase of our national safety problem.
4. The instructor will give each student one of the following assignments:
   a. Prepare a speech using the deductive order.
   b. Prepare a speech using the inductive order and stating the proposition.
   c. Prepare a speech using the inductive order and revealing the proposition through implication.
   As each speech is given, the other class members will write down what they consider the major points and the proposition. These notes will be given to the speaker in order that he may evaluate his own ability to communicate specific points to an audience.
5. Prepare a three- to five-minute speech in which you explain the operation of some apparatus. If possible, bring the apparatus to class for actual demonstration. Divide your explanation into three or four steps or points. Follow this procedure: after a brief introduction, give a preview of your points; as you present each point, write it on the blackboard; in your conclusion, review the points developed by pointing to them as you repeat them orally. Prepare a written outline, using the form below.

INTRODUCTION

I. How I intend to get an attentive hearing:
II. How I intend to relate my subject to the interests and wants (motives) of listeners:

   The Central Thought: ....

DISCUSSION

The first point is ....
   A.
   B.

The second point is ....
   A.
   B.

The third point is ....
   A.
   B.

CONCLUSION

Summary:
   1.
   2.
   3.

A check sheet for evaluating this speech appears on p. 53.

REFERENCES

Readings to Be Assigned with Chapter III

Baird, A. Craig, and Knower, Franklin H., *General Speech: An Introduction*, McGraw-Hill Book Company, 2nd ed., 1957, chap. 5, "Organizing and Outlining."

Brigance, William Norwood, *Speech: Its Techniques and Disciplines in a Free Society*, Appleton-Century-Crofts, Inc., 1952, chap. 11 "Organizing the Speech into Orderly Form"; chap. 12, "Beginning and Ending the Speech"; chap. 14, "Making the Outline."

Bryant, Donald C., and Wallace, Karl R., *Fundamentals of Public Speaking*, Appleton-Century-Crofts, Inc., 1953, chap. 12, "Outlining"; chap. 13. "Introductions, Conclusions, and Transitions"; chap. 23, "Organizing the Persuasive Speech"; chap. 24, "Speech Plans."

Crocker, Lionel, *Public Speaking for College Students*, American Book Company, 3rd ed., 1956, chap. 17, "Techniques of Structuring the Speech"; chap. 18, "Outlining the Speech."

Gilman, Wilbur E., Aly, Bower, and Reid, Loren, *The Fundamentals of Speaking*, The Macmillan Company, 1951, chap. 4, "Analyzing and Organizing Material"; chap. 5, "Adapting Material."

Gray, Giles W., and Braden, Waldo W., *Public Speaking: Principles and Practice*, Harper & Brothers, 1951, chap. 13, "The Introduction"; chap. 14, "The Discussion"; chap. 15, "The Conclusion."

McBurney, James H., and Wrage, Ernest J., *The Art of Good Speech*, Prentice-Hall, Inc., 1953, chap. 12, "The Organization of Speech."

Monroe, Alan H., *Principles and Types of Speech*, Scott, Foresman and Company, 4th ed., 1955, chap. 14, "Arranging and Outlining Points Clearly"; chap. 15, "Beginning and Ending a Speech"; chap. 16, "Organizing the Complete Speech: the Motivated Sequence"; chap. 17, "Outlining the Complete Speech Using the Motivated Sequence."

Oliver, Robert T., and Cortright, Rupert L., *New Training for Effective Speech*, The Dryden Press, 1951, chap. 9, "Organizing the Speech."

Thonssen, Lester, and Baird, A. Craig, *Speech Criticism, The Development of Standards for Rhetorical Appraisal*, The Ronald Press Co., 1948, chap. 14, "The Structure of Oral Discourse."

White, Eugene E., and Henderlider, Clair R., *Practical Public Speaking: A Guide to Effective Communication*, The Macmillan Company, 1954, chap. 4, "Making the Outline"; chap. 5, "Organizing the Discussion"; chap. 7, "Developing the Introduction"; chap. 8, "Developing the Conclusion."

Speech Evaluation Chart

NAME_____

	Inferior	Poor	Fair	Average	Above Average	Excellent	Superior
	1	2	3	4	5	6	7
CHOICE OF SUBJECT: appropriate to speaker, listener, assignment, time limit							
OPENING SENTENCES: relating to interests and wants of listener.							
CENTRAL THOUGHT: stated in simple sentence							
PREVIEW: statement of all main points							
DEVELOPMENT OF FIRST POINT							
DEVELOPMENT OF SECOND POINT							
DEVELOPMENT OF THIRD POINT							
SUMMARY							
CONTROL OF BODILY ACTIVITY: facial expression, eye contact, gestures, posture, movement							
VOICE AND PRONUNCIATION							
OVERALL EFFECTIVENESS							

SCORE_____

Chapter IV

THE SPEAKER MEETS THE AUDIENCE

THE Mr. Snarf of the platform, whether he is a college professor, the president of a corporation, the chairman of a civic group, or a wild-eyed agitator, is sometimes characterized by sentences like the following: "He knew his subject, but he just couldn't put it over," or "He tried hard, but he failed to make his point," or "He just went on and on. I thought he'd never stop." Snarf may bury his face in his manuscript with never a glance at the audience. He may dwell on minute details or remote points, forgetting that his listeners are not interested in elaborations. He may exceed his time limit at the expense of the other speakers. He may speak in sweeping generalities and meaningless jargon. He may exhibit a superior attitude which antagonizes the listeners. In short, the Snarfs forget their listeners. They think about themselves and their subjects and fail to consider the listeners.

Many speeches which are declared superior in a speaker's study, before the speaker's friends or before a captive audience, may fall flat in the open forum when the speaker meets the listeners. To blame the audience for not appreciating clever repartee or high-flown thoughts is no solution to the problem. The speaker must meet the listeners on their ground, at their level of understanding, in their language. He must consider their likes and dislikes, their level of comprehension, their attitudes and sentiments. *He must meet the audience.*

The present chapter gives some case studies of speakers who mastered difficult speaking situations. In each case the speaker planned carefully his approach to gain a favorable hearing. In every case the speaker attempted to establish (1) his right to speak and his good sense, (2) his good character, and (3) his good will toward his listeners.

In several of the speeches the speakers use strong emotional appeals to move their listeners to agree or to act. In Aristotelian terms, these speakers use ethical and pathetic appeals.

Women Speak to Important Male Audiences

Margaret Chase Smith, Senator from Maine, faced a challenging audience when she spoke to the Overseas Press Club Annual Awards Dinner in New York City, April 19, 1955. She was the first woman to address this important gathering of newspaper men. Senator Smith was well aware of the problems which a woman Senator often faces in speaking. On one occasion she explained: "I think it is wise to speak only when you have strong convictions. Then people listen. It's particularly important for a woman Senator. The minute a woman gets aggressive, speaks too much—she makes enemies."[1]

FROM SPEECH ENTITLED "IMPATIENCE AND GENEROSITY"[2]
by Margaret Chase Smith

1. There is the biblical saying of "The first shall be last and the last shall be first." That saying is most probably prophetic of this phase of your 1955 Awards Dinner. For I am told that I have the honor of being the first woman to ever give the principal address at this famous Dinner of yours. I shall probably be the last for I fear I shall be a disappointment to such a brilliant array of journalistic pundits and foreign correspondents. I beg of you not to let your disappointment prejudice you against having women speakers in the future.

2. Your very genial and affable President, Bob Considine—with whom I have served several times on the panel of "Who Said That?"—in extending to me the honor of addressing you tonight suggested that you might be interested in my observations from two recent trips I made overseas.

3. It is with considerable misgiving that I do so. For me to tell you of the overseas press what I saw and my impressions overseas is like Gravel Gertie telling Marilyn Monroe how to be glamorous—or Republicans telling Eisenhower how to win elections.

4. During the past six months, I made two overseas trips—the first last October, the second this past February and early March—to twenty-three countries covering fifty thousand miles. I made the trips in search of *first hand* knowledge—knowledge that I wanted to get with *my own* eyes and ears instead of through the eyes and ears of someone else. They were unofficial personal trips.

5. Perhaps it was the adopted strains of journalism in me—perhaps it was the fascination some politicians have for getting down to the grass roots and feeling the pulse of the public—but I wanted to try to get even a slight bit of that knowledge a Senator *can't get* on an official committee trip.

6. For example, I talked with a Communist leader in France because I wanted to try to find out *why* he, a former Catholic, became a Communist. I thought I could get a better insight of how great might be the danger of France going Communist *by talking* to this man than in *just receiving* the official briefings that a Senatorial Committee would ordinarily get.

[1] *Morning Advocate* (Baton Rouge, Louisiana), February 28, 1952.
[2] Complete text in *Vital Speeches of the Day*, May 15, 1955, pp. 1230-1233.

7. And in these past few years when *too many* of us have been afraid of our shadows and live in mortal fear that someone might call us a Communist or pro-Communist merely because we had known at some time anyone who was even slightly non-conformist, *what* chances are there of a Senatorial Committee officially talking to a French Communist? . . .

QUESTIONS FOR STUDY

1. After carefully reading the paragraphs quoted, make a list of problems which Senator Margaret Chase Smith probably thought she faced. How did the speaker attempt to meet these problems?
2. In the introduction, the speaker should attempt to gain (1) an attentive hearing, (2) a friendly hearing and (3) an intelligent hearing (for discussion see Gray and Braden, chap. XIII). To which of the three does the speaker give the most emphasis? Why?
3. In Par. 1 the speaker compliments her listeners by calling them "a brilliant array of journalistic pundits and foreign correspondents." In Par. 2 she speaks of "your very genial and affable President." In these remarks do you think the speaker was insincere? Are these compliments in good taste? What aspect of the occasion probably justifies this approach?
4. Speakers are often warned not to open a speech with apology. Does Par. 1 constitute an apology? Why do you believe the speaker considered it necessary to open with these sentences? Does the paragraph weaken or strengthen the speech? Give reasons for your answer.
5. How does the speaker attempt to demonstrate her modesty?
6. In what ways does she declare her good will toward her listeners?
7. In Par. 5 and 6, evaluate the purpose and effectiveness of the following phrases: "in search of first hand knowledge," "knowledge that I wanted to get with my own eyes and ears instead of through the eyes and ears of someone else," "getting down to the grass roots and feeling the pulse of the public," "to get even a slight bit of knowledge a Senator can't get on an official trip."
8. What eight specific facts does the speaker include to emphasize that she is qualified to discuss her subject?
9. In Par. 7, what traits of character does the speaker demonstrate? Why is this appeal selected for her immediate audience?
10. Does the speaker imply, without a direct mention, that she possesses certain traits of good character?
11. If you had prepared this introduction, what would you have changed? Why?

Another prominent woman speaker today is Oveta Culp Hobby. On October 8, 1954, she faced a difficult speaking assignment when she addressed the Executive Club of Chicago.

FROM A SPEECH ENTITLED "CITIZEN RESPONSIBILITIES"[3]
by Oveta Culp Hobby

1. Mr. Stripp, Ladies and Gentlemen, I am glad to be in Chicago. I am especially glad that the occasion is the first Ladies' Day of your new season.

[3] *Vital Speeches of the Day*, December 15, 1954, pp. 905-908.

2. At the risk of seeming just a little ungracious, I must be candid and admit that one reason for my pleasure at visiting here is because Chicago is so much closer to Houston than Washington.

3. And there's no question about the fact that the Capital of America's Heartland is much closer to the people of our country than Washington, D. C. ever can be.

4. As for Ladies' Day—well, I'm all in favor of bigger, better and more Ladies' Days. It is certainly an interesting commentary on our times to note that the first males to take official cognizance of the merits of Ladies' Day were the gentlemen who run big league baseball. I can't vouch for their motive in inaugurating this pleasant custom, but I suspect that—besides increasing attendance—it had something to do with obtaining womanly approval for a sport that ranked midway between pool rooms and dart boards in the estimation of a good many wives.

5. Certainly I dare not ascribe the same motive to the officers of the Executives' Club!

6. More power to the baseball men—and more power to male strongholds like the Executives' Club.

7. But I would not have you misunderstand me because I never marched in a bloomer parade or picketed the White House for woman's suffrage, and I didn't come to stump for feminism. I'm not a feminist in any sense of the word. I'm a citizen, with I hope a sense of responsibility.

8. At the present time I am an official of your government. In this capacity, I would like to speak to you about responsibility—your responsibility and my responsibility to our nation and to ourselves.

9. Responsibility itself is probably one of the most taken-for-granted concepts in the book and one of the most over-worked words in the English language. Our familiarity with the term has perhaps even bred some contempt for its meaning. I hope you will agree that it might be well worth our while, in these circumstances, to have a try at putting responsibility in a different setting. Perhaps we can give both the word and the concept new meaning—meaning appropriate to its significance at this point in our lives. . . .

QUESTIONS FOR STUDY

1. The successful speaker attempts to establish rapport, or a common bond of sympathy and understanding, between himself and his listeners. In what ways does Mrs. Hobby attempt to establish rapport?
2. What is the speaker's purpose in Par. 2? Is her remark intended as humor?
3. What is the speaker's purpose is emphasizing that "the Capital of America's Heartland is much closer to the people of our country than Washington, D. C. can ever be"?
4. In these paragraphs, do you find any evidence that the speaker attempted to appeal to women among her listeners?
5. Why do you think that the speaker emphasized that she had "never marched in a bloomer parade or picketed the White House for woman's suffrage?" Why does she say that she is "a citizen," not "a feminist"?
6. How does the speaker subtly compliment her listeners? Why?
7. What is the speaker's purpose in Par. 9?
8. Compare these paragraphs with those of the previous speaker. In what ways are they alike? Different? Which do you think shows the greater skill in audience adjustment?

A Politician Invades a University Campus

Politicians and university audiences are sometimes incompatible. The politician, accustomed to the hurly-burly of the stump, feels ill at ease in the presence of "eggheads" who may insist on asking embarrassing and theoretical questions. The university dweller, preferring his ivory tower, may regard the politician as trite and commonplace, as a kind of relic of the past, interesting to watch but of little real significance.

During the 1956 Presidential campaign, however, the leading contenders seemed more willing than usual to brave the rarefied campus atmosphere. One such visit was that of Adlai Stevenson, who spoke to the students and faculty of Yale University on October 5, 1956. Upon his arrival in New Haven, Connecticut, he was met by a student parade in which many "I like Ike" signs were displayed. He was well aware that many of his listeners were pro-Eisenhower supporters. Undaunted by a critical university audience, Stevenson made a pitch to win his egghead listeners.

The speech which Mr. Stevenson delivered to his Yale listeners was decidedly different from other speeches he delivered across the country. Joseph C. Harsh of the *Christian Science Monitor* stresses some of the differences in the following analysis:

When addressing a Yale University audience at New Haven, Conn., Adlai E. Stevenson employed three literary allusions which he could assume would be understood quickly and easily by that particular type of audience but which undoubtedly would go over the heads of the great majority of listeners at a nonacademic audience.

He referred to "the Macedonian cry," to Hans Christian Andersen's story of the Emperor's new clothes, and to George Orwell's dictum that "if you want to corrupt a people, first corrupt the words in which they express themselves."

Three other passages in the same Stevenson speech were equally suitable to an academic audience and equally unsuitable for a normal partisan political audience.

He quoted Chief Justice Earl Warren's remark that Republicans have "confused social progress with socialism."

He said that "victory is, after all, not an end in itself."

He stated that he did not consider himself blameless of overstepping the ground rules of political responsibility in a campaign.

The man who employed these literary allusions and those high-level references was a much happier, more relaxed, more assured public speaker than the man who for a number of days previous had been reading ghostwritten political speeches of a much more partisan nature to partisan audiences.[4]

[4] Joseph C. Harsh, "The State of the Nations," *Christian Science Monitor,* October 10, 1956, p. 1.

FROM A POLITICAL SPEECH[5]

by Adlai Stevenson

1. I feel that your reception has done altogether too much honor to a man whose previous undergraduate association was with a university which has often caused you acute embarrassment and me great joy on crisp autumn afternoons—namely Princeton!

2. I have also had some considerable association, personal and parental, with Harvard. So it is natural that I have always wanted to attend Yale, too, in one guise or another, but I never quite expected that it would be as an itinerant politician.

3. But your president is not only a man of warm hospitality and boundless tolerance, he is also an eminent historian, who knows that American life is made up of many strange things, and that even college students ought to be exposed to some of them. And one of the strangest is a man who runs for President; and a still stranger one is a man who runs for President twice.

4. Still, if I managed to circumnavigate only the wrong two of what used to be called the Big Three, I am relieved to say that I have a Yale man on the ticket with me, and I want to take this occasion to tell you how proud and happy I am about my running mate, an alumnus of your law school—Estes Kefauver.

5. I am particularly glad to be here at Woolsey Hall tonight because I always enjoy speaking at colleges. Now whenever I say this I can see most of my entourage wince—particularly those eggheads who surround me, all of whom are hardboiled now.

6. You know that word "egghead" is interesting. Some people think it means that you have a lot in your head, and some think it means that you have nothing on your head. In the latter respect I qualify as an egghead for obvious reasons.

7. But it is when I am deemed to qualify in the former that I am happiest. And curiously enough that is usually around universities, and especially university faculties, which I suppose proves something about the gullibility, credulity and innocence of the learned and the superior perceptions of their charges.

8. I said something like this about enjoying my occasional visits to universities in a speech at the University of Minnesota last March, and those eggheads on my staff acted as if this were the reason why I lost the primary.

9. But I would say to these great thinkers, the eggheads, that I really don't believe that they are as unpopular as they suppose; nor do I think that many Americans regard association with them as a criminal offense.

10. Now the fact that I enjoy talking at, to and with university audiences doesn't mean that I don't enjoy speaking at party rallies, too. What I like best perhaps is an evening that combines the best features of both—and I think we are going to have an evening like that tonight.

11. It has been an interesting campaign, and I welcome the opportunity Woolsey Hall provides to reflect for a moment about it. . . .

QUESTIONS FOR STUDY

1. Two recent critics have made the following observation about Stevenson's introductions: "His introductions are habitually apt—a reference to local history, a humorous anecdote or incident which occurred some place in the campaign, a

[5] *New York Times*, October 6, 1956, p. 10.

mention of a previous visit, or a mention of some family connection in the area."[6] In what ways is the present introduction typical? In what ways does it vary from the description given above?

2. In these paragraphs Stevenson gives at least six facts about his own background and associations which make him more acceptable to his listeners. Some of these facts are cleverly presented in an indirect way. Make a list of these facts.

3. Notice that Stevenson uses humor and some self-depreciating anecdotes in these paragraphs. What is his purpose in using these materials? What did he hope to accomplish?

4. Make an analysis of each paragraph quoted. Determine what was the speaker's purpose in each paragraph. How does each paragraph move the listener nearer the subject which Stevenson wishes to discuss?

5. Why does Stevenson comment about "eggheads"? What does he hope to accomplish by his good-natured ribbing of "eggheads"? In making fun of "eggheads" how does Stevenson in turn compliment himself?

6. In what ways does Stevenson make his listeners feel that he is one of them in his sympathies and aspirations?

7. Compare this introduction with other speech introductions which Stevenson used in the 1956 campaign (almost all of Stevenson's 1956 campaign speeches are quoted in the *New York Times*). In what ways is this introduction unique?

8. What is Stevenson's goal in these paragraphs? Is it to win (1) a friendly hearing, (2) an attentive hearing or (3) an intelligent hearing? Perhaps he was striving to achieve all three of these objectives. What evidence can you find that he was attempting to achieve all three? Which one receives the most emphasis? Which one receives the least emphasis?

General of the Army Douglas MacArthur Defends His Policies

Perhaps the most controversial speech of the past several years was the one General MacArthur delivered April 19, 1951, to a joint session of Congress on a nation-wide radio and television audience estimated at 20,000,000 to 30,000,000.[7]

This distinguished war hero had been dismissed from his command in the Far East because he had openly disagreed with the foreign policy of the Administration. Upon his return to this country he had been greeted by great ovations in the leading cities. In fact, the enthusiasm of the welcome had suggested that actually President Harry Truman and his Secretary of State, Dean Acheson, were on trial.

Nevertheless MacArthur faced a difficult speaking situation. He had violated the military code in speaking out against his Commander-in-Chief. Many thought him guilty of insubordination, unwise decisions, and warmongering.

[6] Windes and Robinson, "Public Address in the Career of Adlai E. Stevenson," *Quarterly Journal of Speech*, October, 1956, pp. 225-233.

[7] See *Christian Science Monitor*, April 20, 1951, p. 10.

Some even regarded him as vain and pompous. His critics thought that his speaking to Congress was highly inappropriate.

Time magazine described the occasion of the speech and his appearance as follows:

Across 8700 miles, through cheering crowds, clouds of black headlines and storms of angry argument, Douglas MacArthur had come to this podium to make his stand before the nation and to state his case to the world. . . .

As silence fell, he began to speak slowly, in a deep, resonant voice. . . . Douglas MacArthur spoke with a native eloquence that the nation had not heard in years, without bombast or gesture. The resonant voice sometimes rasped, sometimes sank almost to a whisper, but never rose from a low, confident pitch.[8]

FROM "ADDRESS TO CONGRESS"[9]
by Douglas MacArthur

Mr. President, Mr. Speaker and Distinguished Members of the Congress:

1. I stand on this rostrum with a sense of deep humility and pride—humility in the weight of those great architects of our history who have stood here before me, pride in the reflection that this home of legislative debate represents human liberty in the purest form yet devised.

2. Here are centered the hopes and aspirations and faith of the entire human race.

3. I do not stand here as advocate for any partisan cause for the issues are fundamental and reach quite beyond the realm of partisan considerations. They must be resolved on the highest plane of national interest if our course is to prove sound and our future protected.

4. I trust, therefore, that you will do me the justice of receiving that which I have to say as solely expressing the considered viewpoint of a fellow American.

5. I address you with neither rancor nor bitterness in the fading twilight of life, with but one purpose in mind: to serve my country.

6. The issues are global, and so interlocked that to consider the problems of one sector oblivious to those of another is to court disaster for the whole. While Asia is commonly referred to as the gateway to Europe, it is no less true that Europe is the gateway to Asia, and the broad influence of the one cannot fail to have its impact upon the other. There are those who claim our strength is inadequate to protect on both fronts, that we cannot divide our effort. I can think of no greater expression of defeatism. . . .

7. Efforts have been made to distort my position. It has been said in effect that I was a warmonger. Nothing could be further from the truth.

8. I know war as few other men now living know it, and nothing to me is more revolting. I have long advocated its complete abolition, as its very destructiveness on both friend and foe has rendered it useless as a means of settling international disputes.

9. Indeed, the second day of September, 1945, just following the surrender of the Japanese nation on the Battleship Missouri, I formally cautioned as follows:

[8] *Time*, April 30, 1951, p. 21.
[9] Delivered April 19, 1951, 1st session, 82nd Congress. *Congressional Record*, pp. 4123-4125.

Men since the beginning of time have sought peace. Various methods through the ages have been attempted to devise an international process to prevent or settle disputes between nations. From the very start workable methods were found in so far as individual citizens were concerned, but the mechanics of an instrumentality of larger international scope have never been successful. Military alliances, balances of power, leagues of nations, all in turn failed, leaving the only path to be by way of the crucible of war. The utter destructiveness of war now blocks out this alternative. We have had our last chance. If we will not devise some greater and more equitable system, our Armageddon will be at our door. The problem basically is theological and involves a spiritual recrudescence and improvement of human character that will synchronize with our almost matchless advances in science, art, literature, and all the material and cultural developments of the past 2000 years. It must be of the spirit if we are to save the flesh.

10. But once war is forced upon us, there is no other alternative than to apply every means to bring it to a swift end. War's very object is victory, not prolonged indecision.

11. In war indeed there can be no substitute for victory.

12. There are some who for varying reasons would appease Red China. They are blind to history's clear lesson, for history teaches with unmistakable emphasis that appeasement but begets new and bloodier wars. It points to no single instance where this end has justified that means, where appeasement has led to more than a sham peace. Like blackmail, it lays the basis for new and successively greater demands until, as in blackmail, violence becomes the only other alternative. Why, my soldiers asked me, surrender military advantages to an enemy in the field? I could not answer.

13. Some may say to avoid spread of the conflict into an all-out war with China. Others, to avoid Soviet intervention. Neither explanation seems valid, for China is already engaging with the maximum power it can commit, and the Soviet will not necessarily mesh its actions with our moves. Like a cobra, any new enemy will more likely strike whenever it feels that the relativity of military and other potentialities is in its favor on a world-wide basis.

14. The tragedy of Korea is further heightened by the fact that its military action was confined to its territorial limits. It condemns that nation, which it is our purpose to save, to suffer the devastating impact of full naval and air bombardment while the enemy's sanctuaries are fully protected from such attack and devastation.

15. Of the nations of the world, Korea alone, up to now, is the sole one which has risked its all against Communism. The magnificence of the courage and fortitude of the Korean people defies description. They have chosen to risk death rather than slavery. Their last words to me were: "Don't scuttle the Pacific."

16. I have just left your fighting sons in Korea. They have done their best there, and I can report to you without reservation that they are splendid in every way.

17. It was my constant effort to preserve them and end this savage conflict honorably and with the least loss of time and a minimum sacrifice of life. Its growing bloodshed has caused me the deepest anguish and anxiety. Those gallant men will remain often in my thoughts and in my prayers always.

18. I am closing my fifty-two years of military service. When I joined the army, even before the turn of the century, it was the fulfillment of all of my boyish hopes and dreams. The world has turned over many times since I took the oath at West

Point, and the hopes and dreams have all since vanished, but I still remember the refrain of one of the most popular barracks ballads of that day which proclaimed most proudly that old soldiers never die; they just fade away. And like the old soldier of that ballad, I now close my military career and just fade away, an old soldier who tried to do his duty as God gave him the light to see that duty. Good-by.

QUESTIONS FOR STUDY

1. One critic in evaluating this speech has said, "Rarely indeed have the American people heard a speech so strong in the tone of personal authority."[10] In what ways does Douglas MacArthur emphasize his "personal authority"?
2. In these paragraphs MacArthur openly states that he possesses several virtues (for example in the opening sentence he says, "I stand on this rostrum with a sense of deep humility and pride. . . ."). Make a list of the phrases which stress virtues and in each case give the virtue which is implied.
3. "No prominent speech of the post-war era," says Wilbur Samuel Howell, "has contained so strong an appeal to emotion as MacArthur's did."[11] Make a careful analysis of how the speaker appeals to emotion. Why did he select these emotions at a time when the United States was involved in the Korean conflict?
4. MacArthur's speech was broadcast to a nation-wide audience as well as being delivered to the Congress of the United States. Do you find any evidence of the speaker's attempt to include materials which would be particularly appealing to his greater audience?
5. What is the speaker's purpose in Par. 7, 8 and 9? Before giving your answer study carefully the paragraphs which follow (see Par. 10 and following).
6. Philip Wylie has said, "Unfortunately for him [MacArthur], the speech was immediately set in print where men could study it without emotion."[12] What elements would the delivered speech have which the printed speech would not have? On what basis shall we judge the speech—the delivered speech or the printed speech?
7. The close of this speech (Par. 17) aroused an intense debate as to its appropriateness. For example, one critic said, "The climax of 'old soldiers never die' was perhaps overdone for critics who heard the speech by radio. Some sneered at it as 'corn'. To those who saw it on television, however, it was emotionally effective, if not indeed spine-tingling and 'beyond the limits of ordinary present-day oratory.' "[13] Why do you think that some "sneered at it as 'corn' "? Why would those "who saw it on television" find it "emotionally effective"?

Winston Churchill Speaks to the French People

Winston Churchill, England's great Prime Minister, is probably the most eloquent man of his generation. His most stirring utterances were delivered during World War II when he was called upon to lead British resistance to

[10] Herbert A. Wichelns, *Quarterly Journal of Speech*, October, 1951, p. 329.
[11] See *Quarterly Journal of Speech*, October, 1951, p. 329.
[12] *Quarterly Journal of Speech*, December, 1951, p. 473.
[13] W. Norwood Brigance, *Quarterly Journal of Speech*, October, 1951, pp. 327-328.

the Nazi onslaught. In those dark days he gave his countrymen encouragement and inspiration through his oratory.

The summer of 1940 was particularly grave for the British people. Their armies had been driven from Norway and from the Continent. Daily the German Air Force dropped tons of explosives on English towns. On June 18, France, its armies defeated, asked Hitler for a separate peace. Now only Britain and the Commonwealths remained to challenge the Nazi forward push.

On June 17, 1940, Winston Churchill prepared the British people for the bad news in a terse short broadcast.

"A MESSAGE TO THE PEOPLE"[14]
by Winston Churchill

The news from France is very bad and I grieve for the gallant French people who have fallen into this terrible misfortune. Nothing will alter our feelings towards them or our faith that the genius of France will rise again. What has happened in France makes no difference to our actions and purpose. We have become the sole champions now in arms to defend the world cause. We shall do our best to be worthy of this high honor. We shall defend our Island home, and with the British Empire we shall fight on unconquerable until the curse of Hitler is lifted from the brows of mankind. We are sure that in the end all will come right.

QUESTIONS FOR STUDY

1. In "A Message to the People," determine the number of emotional appeals which this one paragraph contains. Why did Churchill select these appeals?
2. From the paragraph select the words which seem particularly impelling to you. Study the list carefully. How do you explain your choice of these words? How does your list compare with those of your classmates?
3. What was Churchill's purpose in the following sentence: "We shall do our best to be worthy of this high honor"?
4. Why did Churchill use the first person ("we" and "our") throughout the paragraph?

With France out of the way, the Nazi war machine could direct its full force at Britain. Bombing of English cities was a daily occurrence and the Nazi leaders promised an invasion soon.

One of Churchill's most dramatic speeches was delivered to the French people October 21, 1940. The British Prime Minister had much to win on this occasion. Could he keep the French from completely yielding to German pressure? The rumor persisted that Germany was urging the government of unoccupied France to make an open declaration of war against Britain. By this move the Germans hoped to influence wavering neutrals and to forestall the pro-British leanings of the French colonies.

Churchill chose to speak on a day after the R.A.F. had been particularly

[14] Broadcast June 17, 1940. From *Blood, Sweat and Tears* by Winston Churchill, copyright 1941 by Winston Churchill, G. P. Putnam's Sons, p. 301. Published in England by Cassell & Company Ltd.

active in bombing Berlin, northern Italy, and German "invasion" ports across the channel.

An announcer delivered the speech in French over B.B.C. Then Churchill spoke it in English. The English version was heard in France, but the French translation was jammed.

The speech was later broadcast at several wave lengths and transmitted overseas by short wave. Three networks carried the speech to listeners in the United States.

"TO THE FRENCH PEOPLE"[15]
by Winston Churchill

1. Frenchmen! For more than thirty years in peace and war I have marched with you, and I am marching still along the same road. Tonight I speak to you at your firesides wherever you may be, or whatever your fortunes are: I repeat the prayer around the *louis d'or*, "*Dieu protége la France.*" Here at home in England, under the fire of the Boche, we do not forget the ties and links that unite us to France, and we are persevering steadfastly and in good heart in the cause of European freedom and fair dealing for the common people of all countries, for which, with you, we drew the sword. When good people get into trouble because they are attacked and heavily smitten by the vile and wicked, they must be very careful not to get at loggerheads with one another. The common enemy is always trying to bring this about, and, of course, in bad luck a lot of things happen which play into the enemy's hands. We must just make the best of things as they come along.

2. Here in London, which Herr Hitler says he will reduce to ashes, and which his aeroplanes are now bombarding, our people are bearing up unflinchingly. Our Air Force has more than held its own. We are waiting for the long-promised invasion. So are the fishes. But, of course, this for us is only the beginning. Now in 1940, in spite of occasional losses, we have, as ever, command of the seas. In 1941 we shall have the command of the air. Remember what that means. Herr Hitler with his tanks and other mechanical weapons, and also by Fifth Column intrigue with traitors, has managed to subjugate for the time being most of the finest races in Europe, and his little Italian accomplice is trotting along hopefully and hungrily, but rather wearily and very timidly, at his side. They both wish to carve up France and her Empire as if it were a fowl: to one a leg, to another a wing or perhaps part of the breast. Not only the French Empire will be devoured by these two ugly customers, but Alsace-Lorraine will go once again under the German yoke, and Nice, Savoy and Corsica—Napoleon's Corsica—will be torn from the fair realm of France. But Herr Hitler is not thinking only of stealing other people's territories, or flinging gobbets of them to his little confederate. I tell you truly what you must believe when I say this evil man, this monstrous abortion of hatred and defeat, is resolved on nothing less than the complete wiping out of the French nation, and the disintegration of its whole life and future. By all kinds of sly and savage means, he is plotting and working to quench forever the fountain of characteristic French culture and of French inspiration to the world. All Europe, if he has his way, will be reduced to one uniform Boche-land, to be exploited, pillaged, and bullied by his Nazi gangsters. You will excuse my speaking frankly because this is not a time to mince words. It is not defeat that France will

---

[15] *Ibid.,* pp. 401-403.

now be made to suffer at German hands, but the doom of complete obliteration. Army, Navy, Air Force, religion, law, language, culture, institutions, literature, history, tradition—all are to be effaced by the brute strength of a triumphant Army and the scientific low cunning of a ruthless Police Force.

3. Frenchmen—rearm your spirits before it is too late. Remember how Napoleon said before one of his battles: "These same Prussians who are so boastful today were three to one at Jena, and six to one at Montmirail." Never will I believe that the soul of France is dead. Never will I believe that her place amongst the greatest nations of the world has been lost forever! All these schemes and crimes of Herr Hitler's are bringing upon him and upon all who belong to his system a retribution which many of us will live to see. The story is not yet finished, but it will not be so long. We are on his track, and so are our friends across the Atlantic Ocean, and your friends across the Atlantic Ocean. If he cannot destroy us, we will surely destroy him and all his gang, and all their works. Therefore, have hope and faith, for all will come right.

4. Now, what is it we British ask of you in this present hard and bitter time? What we ask at this moment in our struggle to win the victory which we will share with you, is that if you cannot help us, at least you will not hinder us. Presently you will be able to weight the arm that strikes for you, and you ought to do so. But even now we believe that Frenchmen, wherever they may be, feel their hearts warm and a proud blood tingle in their veins when we have some success in the air or on the sea, or presently—for that will come—upon the land.

5. Remember we shall never stop, never weary, and never give in, and that our whole people and Empire have vowed themselves to the task of cleansing Europe from the Nazi pestilence and saving the world from the new Dark Ages. Do not imagine, as the German-controlled wireless tells you, that we English seek to take your ships and colonies. We seek to beat the life and soul out of Hitler and Hitlerism. That alone, that all the time, that to the end. We do not covet anything from any nation except their respect. Those French who are in the French Empire, and those who are in so-called unoccupied France, may see their way from time to time to useful action. I will not go into details. Hostile ears are listening. As for those to whom English hearts go out in full, because they see them under the sharp discipline, oppression, and spying of the Hun—as to those Frenchmen in the occupied regions— to them I say, when they think of the future let them remember the words which Thiers, that great Frenchman, uttered after 1870 about the future of France and what was to come: "Think of it always: speak of it never."

6. Good night, then: sleep to gather strength for the morning. For the morning will come. Brightly will it shine on the brave and true, kindly upon all who suffer for the cause, glorious upon the tombs of heroes. Thus will shine the dawn. *Vive la France!* Long live also the forward march of the common people in all the lands towards their just and true inheritance, and towards the broader and fuller age.

QUESTIONS FOR STUDY

1. In the speech "To the French People," how did Churchill attempt to win a friendly hearing? How did he demonstrate his good will toward the French people?
2. In several places in the speech the speaker compliments the French people. Make a list of qualities suggested.
3. Notice that Churchill associates with "Herr Hitler" several bad qualities. What are these qualities? On one half page of notebook paper give the word, phrase, or

05572

sentence which suggests a quality. On the other half give the quality suggested.
4. In several places he attributes to the British people various good qualities. What are these qualities?
5. Make a list of the ways Churchill refers to Germany. Why does he not mention the German people?
6. What is the proposition of this talk? Why does he wait until the last of the speech to give the proposition?
7. In Par. 2 notice Churchill's reference to Italy. Why does he use this approach in referring to Italy? Is there anything in the background of the French people that would make this reference particularly telling?
8. Study the two references to Napoleon. Why does Churchill make these statements? What makes these references particularly telling?
9. Do you find any humor in the speech? Give the quotation. Do you think Churchill intended this statement as humor?
10. Why was the speech broadcast in the United States? What portions of it were directed toward his American listeners?
11. Are any portions of the talk directed to the listeners in the French possessions?
12. Study the final sentence. Why does Churchill choose to say, "Long live also the forward march of the common people in all the lands. . . ." Why did he not say, "the people of France"?
13. List the emotional appeals found in each paragraph. Why did Churchill select these appeals? Do the appeals in this speech, primarily addressed to the French people, differ from the appeals in the shorter message to his own people?

EXERCISES

1. Summary Exercise. After carefully studying all the selections quoted in this chapter, write a paper in which you compare how the various speakers attempted to meet the listeners. Limit your paper to a single aspect. You may wish to consider one of the following questions:
    a. How did the speakers use their reputations in gaining acceptance?
    b. How did the speakers attempt to establish that they were well informed on their subjects?
    c. How did the speakers attempt to establish their integrity? Compare direct and indirect attempts to show good character.
    d. What means were used to establish a common ground of understanding?
    e. How did the speakers attempt to demonstrate their good will toward their listeners?
    f. How did the speakers attempt to use emotional appeals?
    g. How did the speakers attempt to win and hold attention and interest?
2. Speaking Assignment. Deliver a five-minute talk on the analysis of the audience and the occasion. Analyze for your classmates how a speaker that you have heard (if possible, in a face-to-face situation) succeeded or failed because of good or poor adjustment. You may wish to speak on a topic similar to the following:
    a. How a poor audience analysis caused a speaker to fail.
    b. How on-the-spot adjustment to the speaking situation saved the day.
    c. How an unforeseen incident wrecked a speech.

    d. How an inappropriate subject embarrassed a speaker.

    e. How a speaker's appearance or platform department contributed to ineffectiveness.

    f. How a speaker made a difficult subject meaningful.

    g. A difficult subject that caused a speaker trouble.

    h. How courage scattered a mob.

    i. How a famous speaker coped with a difficult speaking situation.

    j. My "pet peeves" about speakers.

3. In each of the speeches listed below the speaker demonstrated unusual skill in the adaptation of his materials to his listeners. In studying the following speeches, analyze how the speaker met the problems which confronted him.

    a. Henry Ward Beecher's "Liverpool Address" found in William Norwood Brigance, *Classified Speech Models*, Appleton-Century-Crofts, 1928, pp. 40-65.

    b. William Jennings Bryan's "The Cross of Gold" found in A. Craig Baird, *American Public Address, 1740-1952*, McGraw-Hill Book Company, Inc., 1956, pp. 193-200; Wayland Maxfield Parrish and Marie Hochmuth, *American Speeches*, Longmans, Green and Company, 1954, pp. 492-500.

    c. Winston Churchill's "Blood, Toil, Tears and Sweat," found in *Blood, Sweat and Tears*, G. P. Putnam's Sons, 1941, pp. 275-276.

    d. George W. Curtis' "The Puritan Principle—Liberty Under the Law," found in Parrish and Hochmuth, pp. 359-364.

    e. Henry W. Grady's "The Race Problem," *Modern Eloquence* (1923 ed.) II, pp. 115-131.

    f. Henry W. Grady's "The New South," Baird, pp. 180-189; Parrish and Hochmuth, pp. 450-460.

    g. Patrick Henry's "Liberty or Death," Baird, pp. 29-31; Parrish and Hochmuth, pp. 91-94.

    h. Abraham Lincoln's "Cooper Union Address," Parrish and Hochmuth, pp. 284-304.

    i. Wendell Phillips' "The Murder of Lovejoy," Baird, pp. 138-143.

    j. Booker T. Washington's "Atlanta Exposition Speech," Baird, pp. 189-192; Parrish and Hochmuth, pp. 461-466.

4. Written Exercises.

    a. Find several examples of the following types of emotional appeals in the speeches quoted in this chapter: patriotism, reverence for God, fair play, fear, social approval, self respect, and adventure.

    b. After reading the complete MacArthur speech (found in *Age of Danger*, pp. 147-154), write a critique of his audience adaptation.

    c. Prepare a written analysis of a speaker whom you have heard in a face-to-face situation. Pay particular attention to how he uses his voice and bodily control in achieving his goal.

REFERENCES

Readings to Be Assigned with Chapter IV

Baird, A. Craig, and Knower, Franklin H., *General Speech: An Introduction*, McGraw-Hill Book Company, 2nd ed., 1957, chap. 7, "Adapting to the Audience and the Occasion."

Brigance, William Norwood, *Speech: Its Techniques and Disciplines in a Free Society*, Appleton-Century-Crofts, Inc., 1952, chap. 6, "The People to Whom You Talk."

Bryant, Donald C., and Wallace, Karl R., *Fundamentals of Public Speaking*, Appleton-Century-Crofts, Inc., 1953, chap. 20, "Partisans, Neutrals and Opponents."

Crocker, Lionel, *Public Speaking for College Students*, American Book Company, 3rd ed., 1956, chap. 21, "Analysis of the Audience."

Gilman, Wilbur E., Aly, Bower, and Reid, Loren, *The Fundamentals of Speaking*, The Macmillan Company, 1951, chap. 19, "Understanding the Audience."

Gray, Giles W., and Braden, Waldo W., *Public Speaking: Principles and Practice*, Harper & Brothers, 1951, chap. 5, "Occasion and Audience."

McBurney, James H., and Wrage, Ernest J., *The Art of Good Speech*, Prentice-Hall, Inc., 1953, chap. 11, "On the Audience and the Occasion."

Monroe, Alan H., *Principles and Types of Speech*, Scott, Foresman and Company, 4th ed., 1955, chap. 9, "Analyzing the Occasion and the Audience."

Oliver, Robert T., and Cortright, Rupert L., *New Training for Effective Speech*, The Dryden Press, 1951, chap. 10, "Adapting to the Audience."

Thonssen, Lester, and Baird, A. Craig, *Speech Criticism, The Development of Standards for Rhetorical Appraisal*, The Ronald Press Co., 1948, chap. 12, "Emotion in Speech"; chap. 13, "The Character of the Speaker."

White, Eugene E., and Henderlider, Clair R., *Practical Public Speaking: A Guide to Effective Communication*, The Macmillan Company, 1954, chap. 2, "Selecting the Speech Subject."

Chapter V

THE SPEAKER SUPPORTS HIS PROPOSITION

A GOOD speech begins with an idea which a speaker wishes to share with an audience. But the success of the speaker does not depend solely on the merit of his thought. It also rests at least in part on his ability to clarify, to amplify, or to prove that proposition for his listeners. Thus, to become an effective speaker, you should know the various forms of support and the means of using them. Among the most commonly used supporting materials are illustrations, examples, analogies, statistics, and authoritative quotations. These are the forms of support which will be considered in the speeches of this chapter.

Russell Conwell Lectures on "Acres of Diamonds"

One of the most popular lectures ever given by an American speaker was Russell H. Conwell's "Acres of Diamonds." He delivered the address to audiences from Maine to California; in fact, to audiences on four continents. The listeners never seemed to tire of the speech; some communities even invited him to deliver it as many as seventeen times. How did Conwell develop the proposition of his speech? The excerpt below will give you an idea of his method of supporting his thesis.

EXCERPT FROM SPEECH ENTITLED "ACRES OF DIAMONDS"[1]

by Russell H. Conwell

1. The "Acres of Diamonds" which I have mentioned through so many years are to be found in this city, and you are to find them. Many have found them. And what man has done, man can do. I could not find anything better to illustrate my thought than a story I have told over and over again, and which is now found in books in nearly every library.

[1] Text from "Acres of Diamonds: A Man, A Lecture, A University," undated pamphlet published by Temple University. The lecture in its entirety may be found in the several editions of *Modern Eloquence*.

2. In 1870 we went down the Tigris River. We hired a guide at Bagdad to show us Persepolis, Nineveh and Babylon, and the ancient countries of Assyria as far as the Arabian Gulf. He was well acquainted with the land, but he was one of those guides who love to entertain their patrons; he was like a barber that tells you many stories in order to keep your mind off the scratching and the scraping. . . .

3. I remember that toward evening he took his Turkish cap off his head and swung it around in the air . . . . Said he, "I will tell you a story now which I reserve for my particular friends!" So then counting myself a particular friend, I listened, and I have always been glad I did.

4. He said there once lived not far from the River Indus an ancient Persian by the name of Al Hafed. He said that Al Hafed owned a very large farm with orchards, grain fields and gardens. He was a contented and wealthy man—contented because he was wealthy, and wealthy because he was contented. One day there visited this old farmer one of those ancient Buddhist priests, and he sat down by Al Hafed's fire and told that old farmer how this world of ours was made.

5. He said that this world was once a mere bank of fog . . . and he said that the Almighty thrust his finger into the bank of fog and then began slowly to move his finger around and gradually to increase the speed of his finger until at last he whirled that bank of fog into a solid ball of fire, and it went rolling through the universe, burning its way through other cosmic banks of fog, until it condensed the moisture without, and fell in floods of rain upon the heated surface and cooled the outward crust. Then the internal flames burst through the cooling crust and threw up the mountains and made the hills and the valleys of this wonderful world of ours.

6. If this internal melted mass burst out and cooled very quickly it became granite; that which cooled less quickly became silver; and less quickly, gold; and after gold diamonds were made. Said the old priest, "A diamond is a congealed drop of sunlight."

7. . . . . And the old priest told Al Hafed that if he had a handful of diamonds he could purchase a whole country, and with a mine of diamonds he could place his children upon thrones through the influence of their great wealth.

8. Al Hafed heard all about diamonds and how much they were worth, and went to his bed that night a poor man—not that he had lost anything, but poor because he was discontented and discontented because he thought he was poor. He said: "I want a mine of diamonds!" So he lay awake all night, and early in the morning sought out the priest.

9. Now I know from experience that a priest when awakened early in the morning is cross. He awoke that priest out of his dreams and said to him, "Will you tell me where I can find diamonds?". . . . "Well," said the priest, "if you will find a river that runs over white sand between high mountains, in those sands you will always see diamonds.". . . Al Hafed said, "I will go.". . . .

10. He began very properly, to my mind, at the Mountains of the Moon. Afterwards he went around into Palestine, then wandered on into Europe, and at last, when his money was all spent, and he was in rags, wretchedness and poverty, he stood on the shore of that bay in Barcelona, Spain, when a tidal wave came rolling in through the Pillars of Hercules and the poor, afflicted, suffering man could not resist the awful temptation to cast himself into that incoming tide, and he sank beneath its foaming crest, never to rise in this life again.

11. When that old guide had told me that very sad story, he stopped the camel I was riding and went back to fix the baggage on one of the other camels, and I remember thinking to myself, "Why did he reserve that for his *particular friends?*"

There seemed to be no beginning, middle or end—nothing to it. That was the first story I ever heard told or read in which the hero was killed in the first chapter. I had but one chapter of that story and the hero was dead.

12. When the guide came back and took up the halter of my camel again, he went right on with the same story. He said that Al Hafed's successor led his camel out into the garden to drink, and as that camel put its nose down into the clear water of the garden brook Al Hafed's successor noticed a curious flash of light from the sands of the shallow stream, and reaching in he pulled out a black stone having an eye of light that reflected all the colors of the rainbow, and he took that curious pebble into the house and left it on the mantel, then went on his way and forgot all about it.

13. A few days after that, this same old priest who told Al Hafed how diamonds were made, came in to visit his successor, when he saw that flash of light from the mantel. He rushed up and said, "Here is a diamond—here is a diamond! Has Al Hafed returned?" "No, no; Al Hafed has not returned and that is not a diamond; that is nothing but a stone; we found it right out here in our garden." "But I know a diamond when I see it," said he; "that is a diamond!"

14. Then together they rushed to the garden and stirred up the white sands with their fingers and found other more beautiful, more valuable diamonds than the first, and thus, said the guide to me, were discovered the diamond mines of Golconda, the most magnificent diamond mines in all the history of mankind, exceeding the Kimberly in its value. . . .

15. Those Arab guides have a moral to each story, though the stories are not always moral. He said that had Al Hafed remained at home and dug in his own cellar or in his own garden, instead of wretchedness, starvation, poverty and death in a strange land, he would have had "acres of diamonds"—for every acre, yes, every shovelful of that old farm afterwards revealed the gems which since have decorated the crowns of monarchs. When he had given the moral to his story, I saw why he had reserved this story for his "particular friends." I didn't tell that old Arab I could see it. For it was that mean old Arab's way of going around a thing, like a lawyer, and saying indirectly what he did not dare say directly, that there was a certain young man that day traveling down the Tigris River that might better be at home in America. . . .

16. I told him his story reminded me of one, and I told it to him quick. I told him about that man out in California, who, in 1847, owned a ranch out there. He read that gold had been discovered in Southern California, and he sold his ranch to Colonel Sutter and started off to hunt for gold. Colonel Sutter put a mill on the little stream in that farm and one day his little girl brought some wet sand from the raceway of the mill into the house and placed it before the fire to dry, and as that sand was falling through the little girl's fingers a visitor saw the first shining scales of real gold that were ever discovered in California; and the man who wanted gold had sold his ranch and gone away, never to return.

17. I delivered this lecture two years ago in California, in the city that stands near that farm, and they told me that the mine is not exhausted yet, and that a one-third owner of that farm has been getting during these recent years twenty dollars of gold every fifteen minutes of his life, sleeping or waking. Why, you and I would enjoy an income like that!

18. But the best illustration that I have now of this thought was found here in Pennsylvania. There was a man living in Pennsylvania who owned a farm here and he did what I should do if I had a farm in Pennsylvania—he sold it. But before

he sold it he concluded to secure employment collecting coal oil for his cousin in Canada. . . . Now, you see, this farmer was not altogether a foolish man. He did not leave his farm until he had something else to do.

19. . . . . He wrote to Canada, but his cousin replied that he could not engage him because he did not know anything about the oil business. "Well, then," said he, "I will understand it." So he set himself at the study of the whole subject. He began at the second day of creation, he studied the subject from the primitive vegetation to the coal oil stage, until he knew all about it. Then he wrote to his cousin and said, "Now I understand the oil business." And his cousin replied to him, "All right, then, come on."

20. That man, by the record of the county, sold his farm for eight hundred and thirty-three dollars—even money, "no cents." He had scarcely gone from that farm before the man who purchased it went out to arrange for watering the cattle and he found that the previous owner had arranged the matter very nicely. There is a stream running down the hillside there, and the previous owner had gone out and put a plank across that stream at an angle, extending across the brook and down edgewise a few inches under the surface of the water. The purpose of the plank . . . was to throw over to the other bank a dreadful-looking scum through which the cattle would not put their noses to drink above the plank, although they would drink the water on one side below it.

21. Thus that man who had gone to Canada had been himself damming back for twenty-three years a flow of coal oil which the State Geologist of Pennsylvania declared officially, as early as 1870, was then worth to our state a hundred millions of dollars. The city of Titusville now stands on that farm and those Pleasantville wells flow on, and that farmer who had studied all about the formation of oil since the second day of God's creation clear down to the present time sold that farm for $833, no cents—again I say, "no sense."

22. But I need another illustration. . . .

QUESTIONS FOR STUDY

1. The illustration is one of the most widely used forms of support. Aesop's fables and Jesus' parables are narratives which have lasted through the centuries. Why do you think stories have so much audience appeal?
2. Does Conwell use illustrations to clarify, to amplify, or to prove his proposition? Be able to defend your point of view.
3. William Trufant Foster, author of a pioneer and classic text in argumentation, says of the illustration:

> A story introduced in argument for purposes of illustration is usually exceed-ingly effective or exceedingly flat. It is effective if it hits the point, directly and unmistakably, and if it is wholly subservient to its purpose. It is flat if it is vague or too long, and if it makes any pretensions at being the substance rather than the illumination of the argument.
>
> All kinds of illustrations are merely aids to the effective presentation of argu-ments, not themselves of evidential force. . . . Care must be taken not to use any kind of illustrations in place of proof.[2]

[2] William Trufant Foster, *Argumentation and Debating*, Houghton Mifflin Co., rev. ed., 1917, p. 258.

Do you think Foster would approve of Conwell's use of the illustration? Why does Foster say that the illustration is an aid to the effective presentation of arguments but is not proof?

4. Illustrations are either factual or hypothetical. Which kind does Conwell use? List the details within the illustrations which seem to authenticate them.

5. Evaluate Conwell's use of the illustration on the basis of the following questions:
   a. Are all essential details for a clear understanding of the illustration included?
   b. Are there digressions or unessential details which hinder comprehension?
   c. Do the illustrations agree with your knowledge of the facts involved?
   d. Is the desired conclusion the only point suggested by the illustration?
   e. Is the manner of telling the story interesting?

6. In your own words, tell a parable or a fable to the class. Keep a list of the stories told by your classmates for this assignment. Decide whether the original purpose of each tale was to clarify, to amplify, or to prove.

7. Invent a story of your own to illustrate a moral or ethical point.

A Student Uses Examples

During the 1954-55 school year Laura Ann Wilber, then a student at Mississippi Southern College, won several awards for her contest oration, "Without a Word." One section of her speech was especially well received:

EXCERPT FROM SPEECH ENTITLED "WITHOUT A WORD"
by Laura Ann Wilber

1. Look briefly with me at our United States today, and see, as I have seen, how our freedom of speech is being lost.

2. In Colorado a teacher was advised to discontinue a study of the Mexican laborers in beet-sugar fields because the subject was "too controversial." Fearing the criticism of local businessmen, a home economics teacher dropped a project in which her pupils tested certain nationally advertised brands of household appliances. An English teacher found it wise to remove John Steinbeck's books from the literature course. A biology teacher was forbidden to continue use of the film, "Human Growth." At an Illinois college teachers became suspect when they recommended that their students read Karl Marx in order to understand the philosophies of Communism and Mein Kampf to understand Fascism better.

3. Teachers find themselves under suspicion when they discuss Russian authors in World Lit. classes, even though many of these writers died before Marx was born. Professors of history, economics, political and social science must be careful if, when, and how they discuss Russia.

4. In Galesburg, Illinois, an alderman was irked because a college political science class was doing field research on the operation of the city government. The discussions he stirred up placed several members of the college faculty under suspicion of "Communistic leanings" by the townspeople. The stigma lingered even though the teachers were formally cleared and the alderman made to give a public apology.

5. The principal of a Rhode Island high school suspended one of the student clubs which called itself the "UNESCO Thinkers." Why? Why? Because a denominational paper had charged UNESCO itself (not the student club) with being under "atheistic control."

6. Is it any wonder that *Time* magazine in looking at youth today reported, ". . . the most startling fact about the younger generation is its silence—many students and teachers blame the lack of conviction on fear—the fear of being tagged subversive."

7. These are just a few examples, but they begin to show us the conditions existing in the United States today.

QUESTIONS FOR STUDY

1. Does Wilber use the examples primarily to clarify, to prove, or to amplify? Defend your point of view.
2. What point is Wilber seeking to establish? Are all of the examples related to the single point?
3. When examples are used to establish a generalization, the following questions should be asked to test the validity of the proof:
   a. Are the facts accurate?
   b. Is the example typical?
   c. Are there a sufficient number of similar examples to make a fair sample?
   d. Are there significant exceptions which need to be accounted for?
   e. In the light of other evidence, is it highly probable that the generalization is true?
   Do Wilber's examples meet these criteria?
4. An example is sometimes defined as a specific instance or an undetailed illustration. Develop one of the specific instances in the Wilber speech into a full-fledged illustration.
5. Make a generalization which you will defend before your class by offering examples. On the basis of the questions above, join the other members of the class in evaluating the various generalizations supported by your classmates.

The Analogy Serves as a Form of Support

If you work in a highly specialized field or have a comparatively technical hobby, you will occasionally face the problem of clarifying your job or interest to someone else. How does the chemist interpret his revolutionary process to the news reporter? Or the doctor clarify the blue-baby operation for the parent? Or the inventor explain the 3-D movie to a curious public?

The author of a 1957 Columbia University report on physics research answered his question by using analogies. Dr. T. D. Lee of Columbia University and Dr. C. N. Yang of the Princeton Institute for Advanced Study suggested certain physics experiments which challenged the concept of parity, a theory previously considered fundamental to nuclear physics. To explain to the layman the technical principles involved, the report included the following paragraphs:

PARITY[3]

Excerpt from a Columbia University Report

1. The concept of parity, although significant only in the realm of microscopic (atoms and particles) physics, has a well defined every-day definition. One way of describing this is as follows:

2. Suppose we are in communication with an intelligent civilization on another world and wish to determine whether their clocks run in the same sense as ours do—or again whether they mean the same thing by left-handed and right-handed as we do. We have always believed that communication of this idea, in the spirit of this analogy, is impossible. There was no absolute, universal sense to "handedness." However, the stranger's laws of physics are perfectly good—even if his definition is opposite to ours for, say, a left-hand screw and a right-hand screw.

3. The statement that the two worlds, one based upon a left-handed system and one based upon a right-handed system, have the same laws in physics is known as an "invariance principle," i.e., the laws of physics are said to be invariant or unchanged, if the right-hand and the left-hand convention are interchanged. The interchange is a reflection in the sense that a mirror image is a reflection in the plane of a mirror. Physicists refer to this reflection as a "parity operation." The Principle of Invariance to Reflection or to Parity Operation has been built into physical theories since 1925 and serves as a restriction on the types of laws predicted by those theories. It is this principle which has been destroyed by the recent Columbia experiments.

4. The main reason for this is that it has been discovered that elementary particles—neutrinos and mesons—possess a "handedness" as an intrinsic property. One must now speak of a left- or right-handed neutrino, for example. More precisely, these particles must now be considered to possess, in addition to charge, mass, spin, etc.—properties analogous to a screw—that is, a favored rotation (spin) and an advance along the axis of rotation, either in the right-handed or the left-handed manner. Another way of describing the situation is to compare an elementary (spinning) particle with a spinning bullet. If the shape of the bullet were a perfect cylinder, there would be no screw defined, or no "handedness," since the two ends of the bullet are identical.

5. The new concept of particles is now in analogy with a normal bullet (pointed nose) which differentiates one end of the spin from the other. Particles which "point" in one direction relative to the sense of rotation are called right-handed, etc. The fact that such particles exist on this world and on the other world now permits an absolute identification of right and left hand between the two worlds, in violent disagreement with previous concepts. No theory which has included the parity idea would have been successful. These experiments, brilliantly proposed by Lee and Yang, now at last open the way to a correct and unifying theory of elementary particles. Lee and Yang also point out that the over-all symmetry of the universe may still be preserved by assuming that, if our galaxy is essentially right-handed, some distant galaxy may be in turn left-handed. It may be that this assumed distant galaxy is identical to the hypothetical anti-matter, now a subject of intense

[3] The complete text of the report appears in the *New York Times*, January 16, 1957, p. 24.

speculation. This would represent an enormous simplification in our theoretical attack on the structure of the universe.

Technical concepts are not the only ideas which may be clarified by analogies. To explain her personal philosophy, Jocelyn Vandervoort, a student in Speech 31 at Mississippi Southern College, tried a technique similar to that employed in the Columbia report. Do you think her comparison is clear? When she gave the speech in her class, Mrs. Vandervoort used a deck of cards as a visual aid.

NO MAN IS AN ISLAND
by Jocelyn Vandervoort

1. There isn't one of you in this room who doesn't desire personal independence more than all other considerations. If you think you haven't already achieved it, then you're working to gain it.

2. Yet I say to you that personal independence is an illusion, a figment of the imagination. It doesn't really exist.

3. And I say: if you believe that personal independence and maturity are the same, you will never develop beyond the stage of adolescence.

4. Here in my hand is a pack of cards for a game of bridge, or for poker or canasta. Actually, these cards are useless—you couldn't even play a game of solitaire with them. One of the cards is missing.

5. Over there on the table is the missing card, the Ace of Spades, the top of its suit, the highest card in the deck. Yet, apart from the rest it loses all the values of a card and serves no useful purpose as a part of the deck. Neither this card nor this pack, separated as they are, can fulfill their intended functions.

6. So far, my development has been from a subjective point of view. Now let's take an objective look. Can the Ace ever truly separate itself from the deck? Say that God, or some all-seeing eye, were watching from the heavens: if this Ace were here in the United States, if these cards were spread all over Europe, and if the rest were scattered all over the face of the earth, even then the watcher in heaven would still see a deck just as you do here in this room. No matter where they are, no matter how impossible for us to see, the truth is the cards are still a deck simply because all 52 exist.

7. Since these cards have no will power or feeling, since they are inanimate, what I have just said is a very simple and understandable statement of fact. Suppose, now, that we complicate the situation. Suppose the cards are given the power of thought and of physical action, that they are granted intelligence and the illusion of self-determination. Would these new abilities change the pattern of the whole? Would the importance of the Ace be any the less relative? Even if the Ace willed to be separate, would it be any the less dependent on the other cards for its very identity? As long as the parts exist, the whole exists. And if you know the parts exist, you must acknowledge the existence of the whole.

8. The only time that you could consider yourself an Ace with all the properties of a card yet apart from the rest, is in your infancy. Your comfort and nourishment require no effort on your part. You receive sustenance from others without being required to contribute anything to anyone. You have the illusion of independence.

9. In early adolescence you grow up enough to become a part of a group—a Boy Scout, perhaps. In late adolescence, some of you become Made-in-Texas Texans, or

Insular New Yorkers, or First-Last-and-Foremost Mississippians.

10. Here, most of you stop. Some, I admit, might go on to the My-Country-Right-or-Wrong stage. Hitler went even further and became the promulgator of a theory of the super-race.

11. But I say: if your intellectual growth stops at any of these levels—if you become the Eternal Boy Scout, the Rabid States' Righter, or the Flag-Waving Nationalist—you stop at the level of sophomoric adolescence.

12. An Ace of Spades is not made except as a part of the deck. You, at the moment of your birth, become a part of Mankind, a part of all Mankind upon the earth. You are a part of Mankind for the span of your existence in the world. You will always be inter-dependent with the other parts to make the whole. You can deny it. You can disregard it. But remaining alive, you cannot alter the fact of your humanity.

13. And if your skin is as white as snow, as red as the Jack of Diamonds, or as black as the Ace of Spades, you are still an essential part of the whole. As the card is a part of the deck, man, no matter how he may wish to escape, is a part of Mankind. John Donne proclaimed this truth in the seventeeth century when he wrote:

> No man is an island, entire of itself; every man is a piece of the continent, a part of the main; if a clod be washed away by the sea, Europe is the less, as well as if a promontory were, as well as if a manor of thy friends or of thine own were; any man's death diminishes me, because I am involved in Mankind. And therefore never send to know for whom the bell tolls; it tolls for thee.

A third illustration of the use of analogy comes from an intercollegiate debate. The question is, Resolved: that strikes in public utilities be declared illegal. The speaker is Shoana Edgar of Middlebury College, who is upholding the negative.

EXCERPT FROM DEBATE ENTITLED "STRIKES IN PUBLIC UTILITIES"[4]

McGill University vs. Middlebury College
Shoana Edgar, First Negative Speaker

1. The Affirmative have been saying that they would eliminate strikes in public utilities by making them illegal, but they have completely failed to read their history and to notice what is going on in the world about them. For the inescapable truth that emerges from any study of attempts to make strikes illegal shows that rather than eliminating strikes, such attempts serve only to precipitate strikes. The entire attempt at such legislation in democratic countries shows that like the ill-fated attempt at prohibition, in 1918, all they accomplished was to aggravate the situation—in other words, to bring about the very conditions they are intended to cure.

2. Let us look at the record; let us see just what has happened when this has been tried. In New Zealand, where an act was passed in 1936 outlawing strikes—in 1937 there were 52 strikes, involving 11,411 workers; in 1939, 66 strikes, involving 15,682 workers. During the war, strikes were made a criminal offense in New Zealand with a heavy penalty for strikers. Yet strikes increased 73 per cent over the prewar average. Let us look at Australia, a classic example of the failure of compulsory arbitration to accomplish its purpose. There, relative to population,

---

[4] Complete text of debate may be found in Ruth Ulman (ed.), *University Debaters' Annual 1949-1950*, H. W. Wilson Co., 1950, pp. 203-227.

there are more strikes than in either the United States or Great Britain. In Great Britain, a munitions act was passed in 1915 which outlawed strikes in munitions industries, with heavy penalties. In the first thirty-three months after the act was passed, more than a million and a half munitions workers took part in illegal strikes, and only one-fifth of one per cent of those workers were ever prosecuted. Coming closer to this debate, let's turn to Canada, where there has been a law since 1908 requiring a period of investigation and delay before strikes can take place in public utilities or in the mining industries. In the period between 1908 and 1925, there were 435 illegal strikes in which the provisions of the act were completely ignored.

3. Finally, in our own United States, the Industrial Court Act of Kansas, in 1920, resulted only in incessant disturbance, turmoil, and unrest in the coal fields. These statistics prove conclusively that far from eliminating strikes in public utilities, outlawing strikes serves only to increase the number of strikes that take place. Outlawing strikes only precipitates the very conditions they are intended to cure. They aggravate the situation and create resentment and general unrest. All we would be doing, if we outlawed strikes, would be to create the situation in which labor, instead of striking against management alone, would be striking against government. All we could possibly hope to gain from such a step would be general disrespect for government, for its laws, and for its administration.

QUESTIONS FOR STUDY

1. An analogy is a comparison between two objects or events. If these objects or events are in different classes, the analogy is figurative; if they are of the same class, the analogy is literal. Classify each of the analogies in the three selections of this section.
2. How many different analogies are used in the explanation of parity? Which of the analogies is clearest to you? Do the other members of the class agree with your choice? What would be the purpose of using several analogies to clarify a single point?
3. Is the Vandervoort analogy internally consistent throughout the speech? (i.e., are Pars. 4 and 5 consistent with Par. 6? How does Par. 8 fit into the comparison? Are Pars. 9, 10, and 11 intended to be a part of the analogy?)
4. Are the last two sentences of Vandervoort's Par. 7 a valid generalization? Can you think of other analogies which would support the generalization? Or of analogies which would contradict it?
5. Evaluate the analogy from John Donne given in Par. 13 of the Vandervoort speech.
6. Can figurative analogies prove a point? What functions do they serve? (Use the figurative analogies in this section to illustrate your answer.)
7. What is the stated similarity on which Edgar bases the comparisons? (See the last sentence of Par. 1.) Is this similarity significant in determining the effect of laws prohibiting strikes? Can you think of differences between the United States and the British Commonwealth nations which would outweigh the similarity?
8. Edgar says that a "study of attempts to make strikes illegal shows that rather than eliminating strikes, such attempts serve only to precipitate strikes." The implication is that the laws cause the strikes. Are there factors, not mentioned by the speaker, which may have been equal or greater causes of strikes than the

laws? Do the examples show that the laws caused the strikes or that strikes occurred while the laws were in effect?

9. Try to verify the factual information given in Edgar's Par. 2. Keep a list of the reference books in which you attempt to locate the material.

10. Is Edgar justified in using the phrase "prove conclusively" in sentence two of Par. 3?

11. Write two paragraphs, one using a literal analogy to support the topic sentence and the other using a figurative analogy. You need not use the same topic sentence for both paragraphs.

The Director Measures the Effectiveness of the
United States Information Service

"Cut the foreign aid appropriations" was the rallying cry of several Congressmen seeking to reduce the federal budget in the spring of 1957. Each overseas agency requesting funds was understandably anxious to explain its function and program. Arthur Larson, Director of the United States Information Agency, was no exception. Speaking at the Public Affairs Luncheon of New York's Union League Club, he raised the question, "Just how effective is the U. S. Information Agency?" To answer this major question, he raised three subsidiary ones: (1) "Are we actually getting through to our audience?" (2) "Are we, in making these contacts, actually affecting people's minds and actions, and achieving the mutual understanding that is our goal?" and (3) "How can we increase and strengthen our impact?" Here is his answer to the first of these questions.

ARE WE MAKING CONTACT?
EXCERPT FROM SPEECH ENTITLED "THE UNITED STATES
INFORMATION SERVICE"[5]
by Arthur Larson

1. The first question, that always comes to mind here is: Are our radio broadcasts really getting through behind the Iron Curtain?

2. I have some fresh news for you on this point.

3. We have, until recently, generally been of the opinion that, while our broadcasts got through pretty well outside the cities in Russia, they were badly jammed in the cities.

4. However, we have lately had an unprecedented chance to talk with a very large number of people from Moscow, Kiev, Minsk, Stalingrad, Leningrad, Odessa, Tashken, and Samarkand, who have left the U.S.S.R., and we find that many of them have been listening to the Voice of America regularly. Their stories are confirmed by the fact that they give us specific quotes from our broadcasts and names of their favorite announcers.

[5] For complete text see *Vital Speeches of the Day*, June 1, 1957, pp. 492-495.

5. So far as the satellites are concerned, we have also had a fresh batch of cogent evidence. An independent research organization made a careful and elaborate survey of 1,000 Hungarian refugees. *Seven out of ten* said they listened to the Voice of America. Eight out of ten said that their principle source of news, including even their own papers, was western broadcasts.

6. We have also recently heard from another satellite that they have abolished the special police who checked on listening to free world broadcasts. There were so many people listening that the job was hopeless—and besides, the most avid listeners were the police themselves.

7. We can also gauge our impact somewhat by fan mail. The Voice got 326,000 letters from listeners last year.

8 Another kind of radio impact is seen in the fact that, in the last six months, we placed, for example, 333 hours of our programs on Greek radio stations and 817 on Iranian stations.

9. Now, as to our Wireless Press Service, which provides a specialized report every day for distribution to local papers, let me give just one example.

10. When President Eisenhower made his speech on the Mid-East proposals, we got the full text to the Cairo papers in time for their morning deadlines, and three morning papers carried the full text. Meanwhile, in Iceland the presses were being held in the two major papers for the same copy, which they also ran in their morning editions.

11. At the same time, our press and publication service was being visited by no less than 60,000 Egyptians, asking for our special pamphlet containing the full text. Fifty thousand more wrote in asking for details. Even the Cairo radio used our Arabic translation. All in all, more than a million pieces of literature explaining these proposals went out of our Cairo office.

12. In the magazine field, you all have heard how our magazine "America Illustrated" is a sell-out as soon as it hits the stands in Russia. One Russian told us we could sell a million and a half copies, rather than our agreed fifty thousand.

13. The two largest-circulation magazines in Southeast Asia are two USIS publications, "Free World" and "The World Today" (Chinese). The former appears in nine languages and has a circulation approaching 700,000 copies. We have noticed lately that in Karachi it is so popular that it is salvaged from wastepaper collection points and resold on the streets for 7¢ a copy.

14. As to films: our color film of Sukarno's visit to the United States quickly broke all records in Indonesia, and has already been seen by 10 million people. We estimate that half the population of Indonesia will eventually see it.

15. We produce regular newsreels supporting American policy, explaining the advantages of private capital investment, featuring United States aid, and depicting such special events as the Hungarian uprising. These are seen by millions all over the world, in commercial as well as private showings, and on television in 32 countries, and even in our mobile units that get into remote areas where films have never been seen.

16. Let me tell you a story of what a mobile unit can do. In Pakistan not long ago the rice crop was threatened by rice borers, and the government couldn't get the people aroused to take necessary action. We were appealed to, and went to work with a mobile film unit, quickly reaching 100,000 people in 120 key villages—and we were told that this indeed prevented a disastrous crop failure.

17. As to exhibits: our Atoms for Peace exhibit has been seen by 14 million people. People's Capitalism has already been seen by a half million.

18. Our 143 libraries are visited by 28 million people each year, and there are 11 million checkouts of our 3 million books. In Athens, almost any evening, you can see the children's section of the library filled with mustached adults, studying the brightly-illustrated books with the aid of a pocket dictionary.

19. These libraries are also the center of all kinds of cultural and educational activity. In fact, it has just been necessary to put on a policeman in front of our Addis Ababa center on Friday nights because of the crowd that wants to get into a feature program.

20. Our English teaching classes have about 90,000 students in any week. Our book translation programs help produce 709 translated books in a year, in 46 languages, with a total of 5½ million copies. Our low-priced book program, providing books mostly in the 10 and 15¢ range, will run to about 4 million copies.

21. In all of these ways, of which I have given you only random samples, and most important of all, through the everyday contacts that our employees keep up in 200 posts with local opinion-moulders, we believe we are achieving a good degree of success in the first step of actually reaching the people of other countries with our materials and message.

QUESTIONS FOR STUDY

1. How many do you consider "a very large number"? 50? 5000? 500,000? Give examples to illustrate that what may be "a large number" in one case would not be "a large number" in a different situation. What do you think Larson means by "a very large number" in Par. 4?

2. Should Larson identify the "independent research organization" mentioned in Par. 5? Is his personal proof, as Director of the United States Information Agency, sufficient to establish the reliability of any organization he refers to?

3. Check the figures to determine how many refugees left Hungary after the 1956 uprising and prior to March 1, 1957. Is 1,000—the number used for the survey mentioned in Par. 5—a fair sample?

4. What information in Par. 13 increases the significance of the circulation figure for "Free World"?

5. What is the population of Indonesia? Is 10 million a significant part of the population? Identify the phrases in Par. 14 which emphasize the significance of the number of people who have seen the film.

6. A frequent instruction on the use of statistics is "round them off." Locate the references where Larson has rounded off the numbers and the references where he has not. Why would he prefer the exact figures in the particular places where they are used?

7. Does the evidence given in the preceding paragraphs warrant the conclusion of Par. 21? Is there a balanced presentation of evidence to include all programs and all areas of the world? Support your answer by citing material in the speech.

8. In *Public Speaking*, Gray and Braden say: "*Avoid presenting too many statistics at a given time.* Their abstract nature requires that we give to them greater attention and concentration than to some other types of material. Long lists should be avoided. Thought breaks in the form of illustrations and humor should be included to ensure attention and interest."[6] What "thought breaks" has Larson included? Are they sufficient to insure that the audience will attend to the statistics?

[6] Giles W. Gray and Waldo W. Braden, *Public Speaking: Principles and Practice*, Harper & Brothers, 1951, p. 288.

9. The Statue of Liberty plus its pedestal is approximately 300 feet high. What comparisons could you draw to help an audience visualize this height?

10. Develop a paragraph through the use of statistics. Among the topics which are sometimes treated effectively through statistics are: sports, weather, the cost of living, and voter apathy. Be sure that your figures are a true index to what they are supposed to measure, in units familiar to your audience, reliable, and vividly expressed.

A Speech Teacher Urges Training for an Articulate Democracy

Davy Crockett, King of the Wild Frontier, was a national mania, appearing on radio, film, television, and in the nation's press, when Robert Gunderson spoke on "Davy Crockett's Tongue-Tied Admirers." Gunderson skillfully capitalized on a fad of the moment to stress a serious theme—America's need of training for an articulate democracy. The speech was delivered to the University of Virginia Institute for Teachers of English, Speech, and Drama. One outstanding feature of the address was the lecturer's repeated use of quotations to support his points.

EXCERPT FROM SPEECH ENTITLED "DAVY CROCKETT'S
TONGUE-TIED ADMIRERS"[7]
by Robert G. Gunderson

1. Pioneer Americans provide a refreshing contrast to the "beat" generation of today. They admired vigor in speech, bombast in oratory, hyperbole in humor, and no-holds-barred in politics. "I'm David Crockett, fresh from the backwoods, half horse, half alligator, a little touched with snapping turtle," proclaimed the newly-elected Congressman on his first trip to Washington. "I can wade the Mississippi, leap the Ohio, ride a streak of lightning, slip without a scratch down a honey locust, whip my weight in wildcats, hug a bear too close for comfort and eat any man opposed to Jackson." The irrepressible Representative from West Tennessee hardly needed to add, "I'll wear no man's collar." Like many Westerners, our hero was suspicious of the kind of pussyfooting now popular with many who today sing his praises. "Always suspect a man," he said, "who affects great softness of manner, or unruffled evenness of temper, or an enunciation studied and slow. These things are unnatural. . . . The most successful knaves are usually of this description, as smooth as razors dipt in oil, and as sharp. They affect the softness of the dove, which they have not, in order to hide the cunning of the serpent which they have." When a White-House functionary cried, "Make way for Colonel Crockett," Davy responded with a vigorous independence now alas out of fashion: "Colonel Crockett can make way for himself."

2. Foreign travelers invariably testified that nineteenth-century citizens were bold, articulate champions of democracy—convinced of their own stake in the American experiment—and of their own important role in it. Charles Dickens was dismayed because politics was the "national amusement." Count Adam Gurowski noted that

[7] Complete text in *Vital Speeches of the Day*, September 1, 1955, pp. 1462-1466.

"the thirst for knowledge" was a major "characteristic of the American mind." Though admittedly most citizens lacked formal education, de Tocqueville found "hardly a pioneer's hut" which did not "contain a few odd volumes of Shakespeare." Philip Hone, onetime mayor of New York, observed that an American blacksmith "would think meanly of himself if he could not argue a point of law with the village lawyer." James Bryce reported a kindly sense of "human fellowship" in which citizens valued the integrity of others and felt that citizenship itself constituted "a certain ground" for respect.

3. Though respecting each other as individuals, our ancestors did their own thinking. Since they enjoyed controversial talk, they spoke frankly—and often at great length—even when sometimes they had little to say. So eager were they for speech-making that they preferred it even to drama. "Lectures," complained the aristocratic Philip Hone in 1841, "are all the vogue, and the theaters are flat on their backs." Speakers displayed a remarkable laryngeal stamina, and listeners rewarded them with an even more remarkable patience, if not to say interest. A commentary of thirty minutes or an hour was hardly worthy of being called a speech. During the famous hard-cider canvass of 1840, for example, William C. Rives of Albemarle County made many speeches, some of which were over four hours' duration. A detailed analysis of these verbal marathons proves that they were informative as well as lengthy; a few, in fact, were outstanding. The solid intellectual content and the frequent classical allusions testify to the respect which speakers once accorded their listeners. As always, of course, there were those who said a lot about nothing. "Their tongues," said Congressman Crockett, "go like windmills whether they have grist to grind or not."

QUESTIONS FOR STUDY

1. Identify the individuals quoted by Gunderson. (If you are not already familiar with their careers, use an encyclopedia or biographical dictionary.) This speech was given to an audience of speech and English teachers. Do you think they would probably recognize and accept each person cited by Gunderson?
2. How does Gunderson indicate that the persons mentioned in Par. 2 probably spoke from first-hand knowledge? Verify from other sources that each of these individuals did have an opportunity of directly observing American conditions.
3. Does the quotation from Davy Crockett adequately support sentence 2 of Par. 1? Defend your opinion.
4. Do the quotations in Par. 2 establish the topic sentence? Defend your opinion.
5. Does Gunderson's position as Chairman of the Department of Speech of Oberlin College qualify him to make statements such as sentences 2, 4, 5, 7, and 8 of Par. 3? What additional means does he use to support each of the statements?
6. Develop a paragraph in which you support the topic sentence through appropriate quotations. To illustrate the wide range of possibilities, these four subjects are suggested:

Campus topic   —Should freshmen be allowed to bring cars on the campus?
Contemporary
    question   —Do doctors think smoking causes lung cancer?
Literary evaluation —Is *Huckleberry Finn* the great American novel?
Historical research —What were living conditions like in Southern cities during the Civil War?

Be sure that you select quotations from individuals who are competent to testify, who have first-hand knowledge of the subject, and who will be accepted by your classmates as authoritative. You may need to identify with an appropriate phrase or two some of the persons you quote.

A Student Speaker Combines Several Forms of Support to Establish His Proposition

A speaker rarely depends on a single form of support throughout his talk. In this section a student speech using several forms of support is printed for your analysis. The speech, "A Chance or a Policy?" is the work of Howard E. Kunzmann, Jr., a graduate of Mississippi Southern College. His talk was prepared for a class in persuasion.

A CHANCE OR A POLICY?
by Howard E. Kunzmann, Jr.

1. One day in June, 1940, a little girl was given seven cents to get candy. With the copper pennies clenched in her little fist, she ran excitedly toward the nearby grocery store. Across the street—up the block—then another street, the main thoroughfare. Barbara, only eight and not tall enough to see up the street over the parked cars, stopped for a split second, then began running across the street. One step, then a second, this one bigger than the first, then a—but there was no third step. A car hit her. Two hundred fifty feet of black tire marks later the car screeched to a halt. Little Barbara lay in a white bandaged heap in a hospital for the next four months, then at intervals for special operations over a period of two years. Her parents are still paying the bill. The whole family suffered. Why? Because the driver of the automobile didn't have a cent of insurance. He didn't own a home or any property. He could afford thirty-one cents for a gallon of gasoline, but nothing for insurance. A liability policy would have covered most of the expenses of the accident. Barbara had seven cents in her hand. That driver could have had a good policy for less than seven cents a day.

2. Maybe you're thinking my sister Barbara was one in a million. Well, more than one in a million are injured in vehicle accidents every year. The National Safety Council reports that 1,350,000 persons were injured on our highways last year. That's not one in a million. That's almost one in a hundred. I wish to speak to you tonight about this very important subject, to propose that automobile liability insurance should be mandatory in our state.

3. Most of us are aware that there is a statute on our law books entitled the "Safety Responsibility Act," which, in effect, says that you must have a minimum automobile liability policy of "five-ten-and-five." This means simply that up to five thousand dollars will be paid for each injury in any one accident, with the total cost of all injuries in any one accident not to exceed ten thousand dollars, and up to five thousand dollars will be paid for property damage.

4. But what of the person who does not have this insurance? The statute says

that he must deposit with the state treasurer a bond of fifteen thousand dollars in cash or securities. Unfortunately, in spite of the requirement, many people do not have either the insurance or the collateral. The law is actually little more than a piece of paper.

5. What happens when a driver without insurance or bond is the cause of an accident? When he reports the accident to the state highway patrol, he notes the fact that he does not have insurance or bond. The Safety Responsibility Bureau then gives him a certain number of days to get a policy. His driver's license is revoked for a period of one year, the registration of all vehicles in his name is forfeited, and he is obligated to pay all damages incurred in the accident under penalty of not getting another driver's license until he does so. That's all the law can do.

6. As I have previously pointed out, there are drivers who take a chance rather than a policy. Today the minimum liability insurance policy costs approximately seven cents a day or about twenty-five dollars a year. For another ten dollars you can buy almost twenty times as much coverage. That's how cheap insurance is. Yet many people in this state do not carry liability insurance. In a letter to me dated January 20th, George R. Saucier, Director of the Safety Responsibility Bureau of the Mississippi State Highway Patrol, estimated that only 60 percent of the registered vehicles in this state are covered with liability insurance. Are you among the uninsured 40 percent? Even if you do have property and savings sufficient to cover a court suit, why risk them all for a few dollars?

7. Perhaps a few more figures will show you how important this issue really is. In the city of Hattiesburg during 1955, there were a total of 528 vehicle accidents, resulting in injuries to 73 persons and in the deaths of eight others. The Hattiesburg police have no idea how much these accidents cost dollarwise. But the usual estimate is that every death alone causes an economic loss of $100,000 to the United States' economy.

8. Let's look at it another way. Let's say you have a home worth $15,000. That's just a modest home these days. Many people own homes worth that much money. You drive, own your own automobile, but have no liability insurance or bond. One day you have an accident. Where will the money come from to pay the damages awarded the victim? Well, if the court awards the victim $15,000, you may lose your home even though you have spent twenty years paying for it. For a few dollars you could have bought a liability policy that would have paid for the damages, thereby protecting your property. Also, the company insuring you would have had its own lawyer in court and would have taken care of court costs at no expense to you. I believe you will agree with me that it just doesn't pay to take a chance rather than a policy.

9. These statistics and examples I have used this evening point up the need for an even better safety responsibility act. I believe that a mandatory liability law can be put into effect in Mississippi without major complications.

10. What would a mandatory liability law entail? It would mean that every vehicle in the state would have to be insured. Every driver would have to take out and maintain an auto liability policy. Only persons showing proof of having a policy in force would be allowed to purchase new and used cars or license tags. City and state highway patrol units could enforce these regulations through spot checks of drivers.

11. What do the opponents of this plan say? They claim the cost would be too high. They point out, and I'd like to cite Mr. Saucier's letter again, that "the liability insurance coverage on a family car today for the minimum requirements is approxi-

mately thirty-five dollars per year. . . . [Mr. Saucier is] of the opinion that the same coverage would be one hundred thirty-five dollars if we had compulsory insurance. . . ." But other states do not have this trouble. Massachusetts has compulsory insurance, and the cost is nowhere near the figure Mr. Saucier suggests.

12. Another objection comes from some insurance companies who protest compulsory liability on the grounds that bad risks would hurt them. Here again many states have taken effective steps to prevent any one insurance company from getting all the bad risks. Virginia, for example, has an assigned risk plan in effect. All insurance companies operating in the state are pooled by the state insurance commission. Bad risks are assigned to one of the companies in the pool. And the assigned risk policies are not too high. They average thirty-two dollars per year for the minimum "five-ten-and-five" policy. Therefore, Mississippi could set up a similar assigned risk plan.

13. To further keep costs down, we need a statute on the books which will limit the amount of damages a person may seek for injuries received in an accident. Some states already have such statutes. May I again cite the state of Virginia? Virginia limits liability to $10,000 per injury per accident. No one can file suit for more than this amount. Such a law would help to keep the cost of liability policies down because companies would not be liable for larger damage suits.

14. Still another and most important way of keeping this insurance cost down would be to initiate a rigid driver's examination. One bad driver on the highway with hundreds of good drivers is as dangerous to the good drivers' safety and welfare as the proverbial rotten apple in the barrel of good apples. Dr. Elmer Hess, President of the American Medical Association, supports the necessity for examinations. According to an Associated Press release of January 24th, Dr. Hess declared to the sixteenth Annual Congress of Industrial Health: "No children less than eighteen should be allowed to drive after dark. . . . On the other end of the age scale, it is absurd to assume that merely because a person is licensed to drive when he's young, that he should hold the privilege for life. . . . Examinations . . . would weed out those physically and temperamentally unfit to drive."

15. I have shown you this evening that Mississippi's present safety responsibility law is inadequate, that many drivers take a chance rather than a policy, and that a mandatory liability law can be put into effect without major complications. Help put this compulsory liability law on the books by bringing the problem to your civic groups, by writing your state legislator to demand action, and by making sure that *you,* above all, have the necessary insurance.

QUESTIONS FOR STUDY

Identify each form of supporting material in the Kunzmann speech. Evaluate the speaker's use of supporting material. Back up your points by citing material from the speech. The following questions may help you prepare your evaluation.

1. Illustrations
   a. Are all essential details included for a clear understanding of the illustration?
   b. Are there digressions or unessential details which hinder comprehension?
   c. Do the illustrations correspond with your knowledge of the facts involved?
   d. Is the desired conclusion the only point suggested by the illustration?
   e. Is the manner of telling the story interesting?
2. Examples or Specific Instances
   a. Are the facts accurate?

b. Is the example a typical case?

c. Are there a sufficient number of similar examples to make a fair sample?

d. Are there significant exceptions which need to be accounted for?

e. In the light of other evidence, is it highly probable that the generalization based on the examples is true?

3. Analogies (literal)

a. Are the similarities between the two objects or events significant in determining the point to be established?

b. Are there differences which outweigh the similarities?

c. Are accurate facts used?

d. Is the analogy consistent with other known facts or other forms of reasoning?

4. Statistics

a. Are the statistics an index to what they are supposed to measure?

b. Are the units of measurement familiar terms for the audience?

c. Is the statistical information made vivid by relating it to matters familiar to the audience?

d. Is the source reliable?

e. Are the statistics rounded off to significant figures?

5. Authoritative Quotation

a. Is the person competent to speak in the particular field?

b. Is his information first hand?

c. What are his normal prejudices?

d. Will the audience accept him as an authority?

e. Is his testimony supported by other authorities and evidence?

EXERCISES

1. Classify the forms of supporting material used in the Sermon on the Mount (*The Gospel According to Matthew*, Chapters 5-7). Which kind is used most frequently.

2. Identify and evaluate the principal kinds of supporting material in each of the following excerpts.

a. The author of the famous chapter on "Snakes in Ireland" began it with this sentence: "There are no snakes in Ireland." And there the chapter ended. As a man of good sense, when he had exhausted his topic, he stopped. If I followed his example, I would tell you that in our over-taxed, over-regulated, over-governed world there are no free economies, and would then sit down— to our mutual satisfaction. But now that hair shirts have gone out of fashion, service club members seem to think it prudent to do penance by politely listening to luncheon speakers. And so, to our free economy, which, strictly speaking, is as unreal as a unicorn.[8]

b. The cost of one modern heavy bomber is this: A modern brick school in more than thirty cities.

It is: Two electric power plants, each serving a town of sixty thousand population.

[8] Glenn E. Hoover, "Our Free Economy: Reality or Cliché?" *Vital Speeches of the Day,* June 1, 1957, p. 506.

It is: Two fine, fully equipped hospitals.

It is some fifty miles of concrete pavement.

We pay for a single fighter plane with a half-million bushels of wheat.

We pay for a single destroyer with new homes that could have housed more than eight thousand people.[9]

c. History shows that . . . [compulsory government medical care] has not been more successful where it has been tried . . . than our present system. In Britain the industrial absenteeism because of illness was higher in the first year of the health program than ever before. There was an increase of sickness from July 1948 to 1949; the death rate went up rather sharply; and even the number of deaths was 72,125 more than the year before. This is what is evident under a system of compulsory medicine, whereas in the United States under a system of voluntary medicine the number of deaths is comparably low.[10]

d. How much is 140 billion dollars? Well, first it is the amount that we have sent to foreign countries to aid their fight against Communism. . . . But how much is 140 billion? I have no idea. I know it's $3.25 for every second since the death of Christ. I know that it would make a stack of silver dollars over 230 miles high. And I know that it represents a cost of $875 for every living American—a sum that some day must be transferred from the pants pocket of Joe Citizen to the Treasury vest pocket of Uncle Sam. And I know that $875 ought to be enough to equip the taxpayer with two additional ulcers, at no extra charge. But how much is 140 billion—it is a sum too large to imagine, too great to be counted, too huge to repay in your generation or mine. But that's the sum we have given away during the last few years.[11]

e. I would like to pose a question, which came up during the last war, when we were working under OPA. You see, when you control the price of goods, that's only half the problem. You've got to control the quality, because we learned, under OPA, if they control the price of a pair of shoes for children, at $5.00, and the price was fixed, but the quality of shoes wasn't fixed, and that pair of shoes would normally last six months, but then the manufacturer chiseled on the quality, and he put paper soles on instead of leather soles, they lasted only three months. So really while you were paying $5.00 for a pair of shoes, it wasn't the same pair of shoes. Now we plugged those holes in OPA; we worked hard at it. The present law specifically does not permit controlling quality standards. I want to know how you can make a law work that does not protect the consumer and guarantee that for the same price, he's getting the same quality of goods.[12]

f. What is the cause of the tremendous acceleration of scientific progress in the past thirty or forty years, after so many centuries of relatively static civilizations? The main factor has been scientific research, carried out on an expand-

[9] Dwight D. Eisenhower, "A Peace Program," in A. Craig Baird (ed.), *Representative American Speeches, 1952-1953*, H. W. Wilson Co., 1953, pp. 35-36.

[10] Helen Evans, "A National Medical Program," in Ruth Ulman (ed.), *University Debaters' Annual: 1949-1950*, H. W. Wilson Co., 1950, p. 155.

[11] Joe Greenlief, "Dykes," *Winning Orations of the Interstate Oratorical Association 1955*, a publication of the Interstate Oratorical Association, Kenneth G. Hance, Executive Secretary, p. 60.

[12] Walter P. Reuther, "How Can We Stop Rising Prices?" America's Town Meeting of the Air discussion, Harold F. Harding (ed.), *The Age of Danger*, Random House, 1952, p. 292.

ing scale. . . . In the early lifetime of many of us in this room, industry—at least in the United States—did practically no research. True, there were some pioneers in this field before 1920. General Electric, duPont, Eastman and a few others had already organized outstanding laboratories, which were largely responsible for making these companies so prominent. But most industrial progress up to 1920 resulted from the work of individual inventors. The telephone was developed by a teacher of the deaf, Bell; the telegraph, by a professor, Morse; radio, by another professor, Marconi. Edison and Steinmetz were regarded as freak geniuses, of whom we could expect to have only one or two in a generation.[13]

g. Wisdom and virtue cannot be forced from a crowd as eggs from chickens under electric lights.[14]

h. Speaking of success, I am always reminded of the story of a young Scottish businessman who went to London and made an enormous success of his business. One of his English friends asked him if he could explain why, at his age, he had made such an outstanding success. The Scotchman promptly replied, "I give all the credit to the Aberdonian kipper which I eat every morning. It's the finest brain food in the world. I'll send you one." The Englishman thanked him and in due time received a package with a small fish in it and a bill for one pound, which at that time was worth $5.00. The Englishman ate the kipper and after a few days met his Scottish friend at the club and said, "Jock, I appreciate very much prompt delivery of that kipper, but actually, I don't seem to be any smarter and certainly my firm hasn't apparently noticed any improvement in my work." The Scotchman said, "I'll send you another." In due time this came with another bill for one pound, and the same sequence of meetings and delivery of kippers went on for a couple of months. At the end of that time, the Englishman said to the Scotchman, "Jock, I do appreciate all the trouble you go to in sending me the small fish, but don't you think a pound is a pretty high price for a small kipper?" The Scotchman answered, "It's beginnin' to work."[15]

i. The interesting fact about . . . fear is that it has two faces. . . . It is our friend when it leads us to look up and down the street before stepping from the pavement. . . . [Or] when it leads us away from a disease. . . . But fear's other face is that of a foe. When fear leads us to look under the bed every night for a subversive agent, then it is our enemy. . . . Fear is like water; a certain amount is necessary for life—too much, however, and we drown. Or then again, fear is like electricity; it can bring comfort in our homes or death in a small room in Sing Sing. These are the two faces of fear, and the control of this Jekyll-Hyde emotion depends solely upon two things. Two factors can influence the role fear plays in our lives, *education* and *faith*.[16]

j. . . . the name "the humanities" has encountered difficulties . . . because some

---

[13] Robert E. Wilson, "Maintaining Scientific Progress in America," *Vital Speeches of the Day*, September 1, 1955, p. 1459.

[14] A. Whitney Griswold, "Balancing Moral Responsibility and Scientific Progress," A. Craig Baird (ed.), *Representative American Speeches, 1951-1952*, H. W. Wilson Co., 1952, p. 151.

[15] Robert A. Weaver, "Things and People," *Vital Speeches of the Day*, September 1, 1955, p. 1469.

[16] Bruce Thielmann, "Fear: Friend or Foe?" *Winning Orations of the Interstate Oratorical Association 1955*, p. 82.

quite important people object to it. For example, some years ago Ralph Barton Perry, eminent Harvard philosopher, wrote:

There has lately developed a practice of grouping departments under "divisions," a popular classification being: physical science, biological science, social science—and "the humanities." Now this is a most extraordinary arrangement. In an institution which professes to exist for the purpose of inculcating it, liberal culture is only one quarter of the whole; and a nondescript quarter, occupying the place of a sort of rearguard appointed to pick up the stragglers and misfits which find no place higher up in the procession.

In the same vein John Erskine has written that "I have no use for a definition of the humanities which excludes the sciences. Louis Pasteur is for me one of the greatest of humanists." In turn, Professor Gilbert Chinard of Princeton has declared that "humanism is not a subject which can be taught, but a state of mind and a discipline which permeates all human activities."[17]

k. Have you ever thought, for instance, that there has not been in history a great orator who has deeply moved the hearts of men, who was not himself inspired by some great cause into which he had flung himself with abandon? There was Demosthenes, rousing the people of Athens against Philip of Macedonia; Cicero, with his eloquent attacks upon Catiline and other enemies of the Roman Republic who were traitors; Patrick Henry, in his rousing challenge to the foes of American liberty; Daniel Webster, pleading for the maintenance of the American Union; Daniel O'Connell, with his crusade for Irish independence; John Bright, denouncing the evils of the Crimean War, and setting forth in alluring terms his vision of universal peace; and Winston Churchill, standing upon the embattled Isle of Britain and hurling defiance in the face of the tyrant aggressor. Not one of these men could have risen to half his stature had it not been for the cause into which he flung his life.[18]

3. Check the authenticity of Bonnell's references in the quotation above. Select one of the speakers he names and prepare a speech on the relationship of that speaker to the cause with which he is identified.

4. Prepare an oral evaluation of the use of supporting material in one of the following speeches:

Armstrong, James W., "Foundations for Manhood," Vital Speeches of the Day, December 15, 1953, pp. 153-155.

Bonnell, John Sutherland, "Making Life Worth Living," in A. Craig Baird (ed.), Representative American Speeches, 1952-1953, H. W. Wilson Co., 1953, pp. 169-174.

Brower, Charles H., "Curiosity and Discontent," Vital Speeches of the Day, December 15, 1953, pp. 157-158.

Casassa, Charles S., "The Freedom to Teach," Vital Speeches of the Day, December 15, 1953, pp. 143-147.

Cooke, Alistair, "Oh, Baby," Vital Speeches of the Day, August 15, 1937, pp. 661-663.

[17] W. H. Cowley, "The Heritage and Purposes of Higher Education," Vital Speeches of the Day, May 1, 1955, p. 1206.
[18] John Sutherland Bonnell, "Making Life Worth Living," Representative American Speeches, 1952-1953, op. cit., p. 173.

Cowley, W. H., "The Heritage and Purposes of Higher Education," *Vital Speeches of the Day*, May 1, 1955, pp. 1203-1207.

Crawford, H. D., "Bulwarks of a Vital Profession," *Vital Speeches of the Day*, January 1, 1954, pp. 189-192.

Crocker, Lionel, "Good Speech Is Good Business," *Vital Speeches of the Day*, March 1, 1953, pp. 298-301.

Dewey, Thomas E., "Man's Right to Knowledge and the Free Use Thereof," *Vital Speeches of the Day*, January 15, 1954, pp. 211-212.

Douglas, Paul H., "Five Great Americans," in A. Craig Baird (ed.), *Representative American Speeches, 1951-1952*, H. W. Wilson Co., 1952, pp. 85-90.

Evans, Louis H., "The Present Responsibility of Our Churches," *Vital Speeches of the Day*, July 15, 1954, pp. 602-608.

Gannon, Robert I., "The Want of the World," in A. Craig Baird (ed.), *Representative American Speeches, 1948-1949*, H. W. Wilson Co., 1949, pp. 229-233.

Gilmore, Eddy, "A Report on Russia," *Vital Speeches of the Day*, November 15, 1953, pp. 85-90.

Griswold, A. Whitney, "Balancing Moral Responsibility and Scientific Progress," in A. Craig Baird (ed.), *Representative American Speeches, 1951-1952*, H. W. Wilson Co., 1952, pp. 147-152.

Gunderson, Robert G., "Davy Crockett's Tongue-Tied Admirers," *Vital Speeches of the Day*, September 1, 1955, pp. 1462-1466.

Han, Pyo Wook, "The Importance of Asia," *Vital Speeches of the Day*, May 1, 1954, pp. 424-427.

Johnston, Eric, "Lifeblood of American Capitalism," *Vital Speeches of the Day*, December 1, 1953, pp. 126-128.

Lipscomb, Ed, "Pocketbook Politics," *Vital Speeches of the Day*, January 1, 1954, pp. 177-180.

Morrell, J. L., "Dilemmas for Decision," *Vital Speeches of the Day*, November 15, 1954, pp. 851-854.

Oliver, Robert T., "The Top Communist Weapon," *Vital Speeches of the Day*, May 1, 1955, pp. 1200-1203.

Pittman, R. Carter, "George Mason, the Architect of American Liberty," *Vital Speeches of the Day*, December 15, 1954, pp. 925-928.

Ritterbush, Philip C., "Vandalism and Juvenile Delinquency," *Vital Speeches of the Day*, March 1, 1954, pp. 302-305.

Sarnoff, David, "The Moral Crisis of Our Age," *Vital Speeches of the Day*, December 1, 1955, pp. 118-121.

Scott, John, "Will the Iron Curtain Lift?" *Vital Speeches of the Day*, December 1, 1955, pp. 113-117.

Scott, W. Kerr, "Don't Park Here," *Vital Speeches of the Day*, November 1, 1955, pp. 60-61.

Sheen, Fulton J., "The Changed Concept of Man," *Vital Speeches of the Day*, November 15, 1953, pp. 83-85.

Smith, Margaret Chase, "Impatience and Generosity," *Vital Speeches of the Day*, May 15, 1955, pp. 1230-1233.

Thorpe, Merle, "How to Promote a Depression," *Vital Speeches of the Day*, May 15, 1954, pp. 463-467.

Vining, Elizabeth Gray, "The Educated Heart," *Vital Speeches of the Day*, July 15, 1954, pp. 600-602.

References

Readings to Be Assigned with Chapter V

Baird, A. Craig, and Knower, Franklin H., *General Speech: An Introduction,* McGraw-Hill Book Company, 2nd ed., 1957, chap. 6, "Supporting Details."

Brigance, William Norwood, *Speech: Its Techniques and Disciplines in a Free Society,* Appleton-Century-Crofts, Inc., 1952, chap. 13, "Supporting the Ideas."

Bryant, Donald C., and Wallace, Karl R., *Fundamentals of Public Speaking,* Appleton-Century-Crofts, Inc., 1953, chap. 10, "Supporting Material"; chap. 22, "Evidence and Logical Patterns."

Crocker, Lionel, *Public Speaking for College Students,* American Book Company, 3rd ed., 1956, chap. 13, "Seven Techniques of Support"; chap. 15, "Three Kinds of Proof."

Gilman, Wilbur E., Aly, Bower, and Reid, Loren, *The Fundamentals of Speaking,* The Macmillan Company, 1951, chap. 16, "Persuading."

Gray, Giles W., and Braden, Waldo W., *Public Speaking: Principles and Practice,* Harper & Brothers, 1951, chap. 11, "Forms of Support."

McBurney, James H., and Wrage, Ernest J., *The Art of Good Speech,* Prentice-Hall, Inc., 1953, chap. 8, "The Content of the Speech"; chap. 9, "Amplification."

Monroe, Alan H., *Principles and Types of Speech,* Scott, Foresman and Company, 4th ed., 1955, chap. 12, "Supporting Main Points."

Oliver, Robert T., and Cortright, Rupert L., *New Training for Effective Speech,* The Dryden Press, 1951, chap. 8, "Selecting and Developing Ideas."

Thonssen, Lester, and Baird, A. Craig, *Speech Criticism, The Development of Standards for Rhetorical Appraisal,* The Ronald Press Co., 1948, chap. 11, "The Integrity of Ideas."

White, Eugene E., and Henderlider, Clair R., *Practical Public Speaking: A Guide to Effective Communication,* The Macmillan Company, 1954, chap. 6, "Discovering and Using the Supporting Materials."

Chapter VI

THE SPEAKER EXPRESSES HIS IDEAS

A SPEAKER must have something to say. However, his effectiveness is not determined by his idea alone: the way in which he phrases his thoughts may be of equal importance in winning audience approval. Thomas Wilson, sixteenth century author of the first comprehensive treatment of rhetoric in the English language, expressed the importance of style with these words: "But yet what helpeth it though we can find good reasons, and know how to place them, if we have not apt words and picked sentences, to commend the whole matter." Or, as the *New York Times* editorially approved the choice of Churchill for the 1953 Nobel prize, "words well chosen, uttered at the right time, bravely spoken, are the most powerful things in the world."

What Are the Characteristics of a Good Style?

First in importance is clarity. If what you say is not intelligible to your listener, you may as well stop talking. Why hide your meaning in the fuzzy phrasing of what Congressman Maury Maverick called "gobbledygook"? Which is easier and clearer to say? "Auditing your rhetorical attempts enables me to advance the prognostication for you of considerable achievement and probable meritorious accomplishment in the area of oral verbal proficiency in the years which lie ahead." Or, "I think you'll be a good speaker some day." To underscore the importance of clear expression, Moore declares, "The simplest, most direct way of saying something is always the best way."[1]

Clarity alone, however, will not produce a good style. The speaker's language should also be vivid and impelling. "Vividness," says Brigance, "is the *sine qua non* of spoken style."[2] A vivid style is one which is fresh and animated, one

[1] Robert Hamilton Moore, *Effective Writing*, Rinehart and Co., Inc., 1955, p. 189.
[2] William Norwood Brigance, *Speech Composition*, Appleton-Century-Crofts, Inc., 2nd ed., 1953, p. 218.

which evokes sharp and lifelike mental images. Consider the words of Winston Churchill immediately after Munich: "This is only the first sip, the first foretaste of a bitter cup which will be proffered to us year by year unless, by a supreme recovery of moral health and martial vigour, we arise again and take our stand for freedom as in the olden time." Churchill has taken an abstract idea, that Britain must recover her former virtues if she is to avoid further humiliations, and has clothed it in vigorous language.

The language of a speaker must have the additional quality of appropriateness. Thonssen and Baird point out: "What may be correct or clear before a certain group may be decidedly not so to another. These virtues reside partly in their propriety, in their being fitted to the special conditions of the moment. Thus we must look to appropriateness as an important stylistic quality. It is, indeed, the most functional aspect of the whole problem of style. . . ."[3] The speaker's style must be in keeping with his own personality, with the aims of the particular speech, with the occasion, and with the nature of the audience. Anne Morrow Lindbergh's description of a church service for Alaskan Eskimos provides a vivid illustration of the adaptation of language to make it appropriate for a particular audience. Mrs. Lindbergh writes:

. . . nothing distracted the congregation. Men, women, and children leaned forward earnestly watching the minister. Many could not understand English. Even those who had learned it in school were bewildered by psalms sung by a shepherd on a sun-parched hillside.

" 'We have gone astray like sheep,' " began the reading. Sheep, what did that mean to them? I saw stony New England pastures and those gray backs moving among blueberry bushes and junipers.

"Like the reindeer," explained the minister, "who have scattered on the tundras." The listening heads moved. They understood reindeer.

" 'Your garners will be filled.' " Big red barns, I saw, and hay wagons rumbling uphill. But the Eskimos? "Your meat cellars," the minister answered my question, "will be full of reindeer meat."

" 'Your oxen will be strong,' " read the next verse. "Your dogs for your dog teams will pull hard," continued the minister. " 'The Power of God.' " How could he explain that abstract word Power?

"Sometimes when the men are whaling," he started, "the boats get caught in the ice. We have to take dynamite and break up the ice to let them get out. That is power—dynamite—'the dynamite of God.' "

"For Thine is the Kingdom, 'the dynamite,' and the Glory forever and ever. Amen," I said over to myself.[4]

The fourth quality of good style is impressiveness[5] or that quality which

---

[3] Lester Thonssen and A. Craig Baird, Speech Criticism, The Ronald Press Co., 1948, p. 414.

[4] Anne Morrow Lindbergh, North to the Orient, Harcourt, Brace, and Co., 1935, pp. 106-107.

[5] Giles Wilkeson Gray and Waldo W. Braden, Public Speaking, Harper & Brothers, 1951, chap. XVIII.

stirs emotions and arouses deep feelings. Great speakers as well as poets seek to capture this quality in their words and sentences. They accomplish this end through careful selection of specific examples and through the use of figures of speech, allusions, and emotionally loaded words. They intensify the effect by subtle rhythms resulting from balanced sentences and parallel structure.

What Are the Techniques for Achieving a Good Style?

Cicero wrote, "All speech, then, is formed of words, which we must first consider singly, then in composition; for there is one merit of language which lies in single words, another which is produced by words joined and compounded."[6] Let us follow the injunction of Cicero and consider both words and sentences as elements of style.

AN AUTHOR DEFINES HIS SUBJECT

Every day we use general terms—college, personality, humanities, literature —which we would find difficult to define with precision. Neal W. Klausner, Professor of Philosophy at Grinnell College, explained the place of the humanities in American education in his inaugural lecture for the John Scholte Nollen Memorial Lectureship.

EXCERPT FROM "THE HUMANITIES: MIRRORS OF GENIUS"[7]
by Neal W. Klausner

1. The major interest we have in the liberal arts is with man and his achievement. But it is not the abstraction "man" that concerns us. For it was not man that wrote *Hamlet,* but Shakespeare; not man that composed *Don Giovanni,* but Mozart; not man that painted the "View of Toledo," but El Greco; not man that completed the *Summa Theologica,* but Thomas Acquinas. It is the human being together with his creation that draws and compels our admiration and study. The humanities, a general name for such studies, describe a sensitive, imaginative, reflective being, who is puzzled by his own existence, by its promises and frustrations; who reaches out for friendship and love; who is eager to try the powers which he feels moving within him. It is in the humanities we discover that a man can never be adequately understood merely by an examination of what he is at any given moment in history. He is what he was and what he wills to be. He is a being able to take the requisite action needed to transform the actual by reference to the ideal. His history can never be written perceptively in physical, physiological or sociological terms alone. Without the pertinent vocabulary of aspiration he is minimized, distorted and misconceived.

[6] Cicero, *De Oratore,* book III, chap. 37.
[7] For complete text see the *American Scholar,* Winter, 1954-1955, pp. 81-87. Also published in Richard M. Ludwig, (ed.), *Essays Today 2,* Harcourt, Brace and Co., 1956, pp. 78-82.

2. . . . the justification of the humanities . . . [does not lie] only in a psychological state called enjoyment, which may be induced by almost any slight titillation of the senses. If this were so, our culture would have reached its culmination in the comic book, the juke box, and the "art" calendar. But we know there is a difference between a surface manifestation of sorrow and mutual grief; between minor irritation and mutual hatred; between momentary attraction and mutual love; between effervescent gaiety and mutual joy. And this gives us the clue. A prolonged and comprehending study of the humanities may bring about an experience of mutuality between creator and perceiver so that the agony and joy of the creation is repeated again and again whenever the two meet in understanding. Here is the silver cord that unites man with man, nation with nation, past with present. This is why Plato is no longer an aristocratic Greek philosopher, nor Jesus a humble Jewish prophet, nor Dante an exiled Italian poet, nor Dostoevski a tormented Russian author, nor Beethoven a deaf German composer. They belong now to every mind that recapitulates their existence, or perhaps it is better to say they belong to any age in which they are rethought. This is the truth Emerson spoke in the lines:

> I am the owner of the sphere,
> Of the seven stars and the solar year,
> Of Caesar's hand, and Plato's brain,
> Of Lord Christ's heart, and Shakespeare's strain.

If I can think Plato's thoughts as he thought them, love my fellow men as Jesus loved them, hear Beethoven's music as he heard it, this is enough. I do not need to find a practical excuse for these aims. Indeed, is it not absurd to search for one, and a symptom of misunderstanding to feel the need of one?

QUESTIONS FOR STUDY

1. One rule for effective diction is to use specific and concrete words, wherever possible, rather than general and abstract words. A general word is a name for an entire class while a specific word names units within a class. Which phrases or sentences in Klausner's paragraphs are the most general? Which are the most specific? Find examples of general statements which are accompanied by specific examples. Do the specific examples clarify the style? Do they make it vivid? Do they make it impressive?
2. Sentence 3, Par. 1, could be paraphrased: "For it is not men who write plays, but individual authors; not men who compose operas, but individual musicians; not men who paint pictures, but individual artists; not men who create theological systems, but individual philosophers." Is the paraphrase or the original more vivid? Why?
3. Euphony refers to the choice of words which will produce a pleasant succession of sounds. Make a list of the phrases which you consider especially euphonious. Compare your list with those of other members of the class.
4. In discussing the nature of rhythm, Marguerite Wilkinson says: "Nothing is artistically worse than indignation waltzing, unless it is sorrow capering to the lilt of a tango or joy droning a dirge."[8] In your opinion, has Klausner fused thought and rhythm into an acceptable whole? Make a list of the phrases in which the sequence of the syllables especially fits the thought.

[8] Marguerite Wilkinson, *New Voices*, The Macmillan Company, 1920, p. 66.

5. The dictionary defines "titillate" as "to tickle; hence, to excite pleasurably." Why is Klausner's phrase, "any slight titillation of the senses," more effective than "any slight pleasant excitement of the senses"?

6. Sentence 3, Par. 2, contains a series of comparisons phrased in general terms. Rewrite and expand this sentence by finding specific examples for each part of the comparison (i.e., actual examples of a "surface manifestation of sorrow" and of "mutual grief").

7. What is the effect of the repetition of the "m" sound in sentence 3, Par. 2? Awkward or needless repetition of a word is considered a stylistic flaw; however, intentional repetition may be used to gain clearness and force. Is Klausner justified in his repeated use of "mutual" in this sentence?

8. Analyze the parallelism in sentence 7, Par. 2:

Plato	—aristocratic	Greek	philosopher
Jesus	—humble	Jewish	prophet
Dante	—exiled	Italian	poet
Dostoevski	—tormented	Russian	author
Beethoven	—deaf	German	composer

List additional examples of parallel structure. Evaluate their effectiveness.

9. "The Humanities: Mirrors of Genius" was originally published in the *American Scholar*. It was later reprinted in *Essays Today 2*, a collection planned to provide models of good composition for college students. Do you think the language is appropriate for both groups of readers? Analyze the appropriateness of the language from the viewpoint of a college student.

10. The quotation of poetry is sometimes suggested as a technique for increasing impressiveness. Does the quotation from Emerson heighten the effectiveness of Klausner's Par. 2?

11. Prepare your own definition of another concept or subject related to the collegiate life or curriculum. A few suggestions are: liberal arts, the university, literature, a college degree, group dynamics, western civilization, art.

A GENERAL CLARIFIES HIS IDEA OF LEADERSHIP

While he was Chief of Staff of the United States Army, General Maxwell D. Taylor was invited to speak to the students at The Citadel. For the cadets of this military school General Taylor chose the subject of leadership.

EXCERPT FROM SPEECH ENTITLED "SOME REFLECTIONS ON THE
SUBJECT OF LEADERSHIP"[9]
by General Maxwell D. Taylor

1. There are a great many fallacies expressed about leadership. For example, it is said that military leaders are born and not made. I do not believe that for a moment. Our entire Army school system is a testimonial to our belief that leadership can be taught, and the success of its officer graduates testifies to the fact that it has been taught. This school system begins at West Point, extends through the many service schools teaching the techniques of the arms and services, and culminates in the Army War College and the National War College, designed to cultivate the minds of the

[9] Complete text found in the *Congressional Record,* January 24, 1956, A695-A697.

future senior leaders of the military service. It was this school system which developed our leaders during the lean years between World Wars I and II when the Army had few units to command and little opportunity to gain tactical experience in leadership.

2. Another fallacy which one encounters is that leadership expresses itself in some mysterious way through flashes of genius. One hears of the intuitive genius of Napoleon which led to the concept of the maneuver of Austerlitz. One hears of the marvelous insight of Wellington in picking the moment to order, "Up guards, and at them" for the decisive counterattack of Waterloo. I believe that a careful analysis of such situations will reveal no stroke of revelation. The good general does not await a bright light, like that which appeared to Saul on the way to Damascus, to obtain a vision of the road to victory. If he has not behind him a life-time of professional study, if he has not brought to this campaign diligent preparation, careful anticipation of all possibilities, and a body of men believing in him as their leader, it is most improbable that he will receive a stroke of genius to bail him out in a crisis.

3. We hear sometimes that special gadgets or special formations—tricks, as it were—are responsible for successful leadership in battle. One reads of the magic of the double envelopment at Cannae as explaining the great success of Hannibal in annihilating the Romans. The military as well as laymen are taken in. The German strategists adopted the cult of the double envelopment before World War I and made it a fetish of their military doctrine. Similarly, the Theban phalanx of Epaminondas or the oblique order of attack of Frederick the Great are sometimes cited as examples of military formations with an intrinsic capability of assuring success. I believe that an analysis of these examples would reveal that success depended on different and more important things.

4. Putting aside these fallacies and related considerations of what leadership is not, let us take a positive approach and see if it is possible to agree on certain attributes which appear present in men who have evinced good leadership.

QUESTIONS FOR STUDY

1. Gray and Braden list the following methods for determining the meanings of words: explanation, classification and differentiation, context, synonym, etymology, purpose or effect, negation, and example.[10] Which of these methods does General Taylor employ to define leadership? Which does he use to clarify "flashes of genius"? How does he explain what he means by "special gadgets or special formations"?

2. Transitions are the glue which makes words, phrases, sentences, paragraphs and entire sections of speeches stick together in a coherent whole. List the transitions in each paragraph. Pay particular attention to the transitions which connect paragraphs. Which words in the first line of Par. 2 connect it with Par. 1? What connects Par. 3 with Pars. 1 and 2? What is the function of Par. 4?

3. Almost all of General Taylor's examples are drawn from military history. Are these appropriate for him? for his audience? for his subject?

4. In the part of his speech not printed here General Taylor discusses three positive attributes of leadership—human understanding, professional competence, and strong and independent character. Write a paragraph developing one of these characteristics.

[10] For a discussion of these terms, see Gray and Braden, *op. cit.*, pp. 398-403.

5. Prepare your own definition of leadership. How do the qualities which you include compare with those which General Taylor selects? Be able to justify your own choices.

A SPEAKER DISTINGUISHES RELATED CONCEPTS

Carter Davidson provides another example of a speaker seeking precision in the expression of his thoughts. In addressing a University of Buffalo audience Dr. Davidson distinguished between several pairs of frequently confused words in order to emphasize the importance of accuracy in thought and expression.

EXCERPT FROM SPEECH ENTITLED "COMMON CONFUSIONS"[11]
by Carter Davidson

1. When our friend, Alice, took her famous trip into Wonderland, she was more than commonly confused by the similarities joined with differences in the Tweedledums and Tweedledees of that looking-glass country. Lewis Carroll was no fool, but a learned professor of mathematics, attempting to show his readers what a vast amount of discrimination is needed to distinguish sense from nonsense. In this connection as an educator I always enjoy reading Alice's discussion with the Mock Turtle on the curriculum. He remarked that he had taken "the usual course," consisting of "Reeling, and Writhing, and Rhythmetic, in all four branches, Ambition, Distraction, Uglification, and Derision." These sounded so much like the real thing to Alice, that she was confused—and well she might be, for this was her first experience with the puzzling science of semantics, or the origins and meanings of words. Stuart Chase has written a book about "The Tyranny of Words," which convinces its readers that words are dangerous swayers of human opinion and destinies. . . .

2. In our economic thinking, we Americans tend to confuse Money with Wealth, putting our millionaires at the top of our social and political scale, and forgetting that often true wealth is not convertible into cash, but resides in the love and respect of our friends, the satisfaction which we derive from our work, or our store of experiences from which we can draw pleasant memories. Benjamin Franklin, one of our wisest Americans and also wealthiest in the satisfactions of life, advised that it is simpler to reduce our financial wants to a point below our income, than to increase our income to the point where we will have no unsatisfied cravings. Think over the list of men and women you like most, and ask whether their wealth is spiritual, intellectual, social, or merely financial. . . .

3. The confusion between Religion and Theology has caused more quarreling, dissension, war among men than any of the other confusions which I have mentioned. Yet the line is clear: religion deals with the standards by which a man lives and relates himself to his universe and society, whereas theology is the study of the theory of the universe and its creation. Theology is practically impossible of logical or scientific proof, religion is proved in practice every day. Theology with its variant theories tends to separate men into sects; religion by its very nature must bind men together. The hope of peace on earth and good will among men lies in a universal religion, but theologians in general are doing all they can to prevent

[11] For complete text, see *Vital Speeches of the Day*, August 1, 1947, pp. 614-617.

it; perhaps the true religion of the future will come from the hearts of the common men, instead of from the theological seminaries.

4. The trouble makers in our political world are also busy confusing our minds about Democracy and our Republicanism. They are not the same: democracy refers to the spirit which pervades a society, which insists upon the rights of individuals, our freedom personal and intellectual, religious, economic, political, and educations [sic]; our republic, on the other hand, refers to our form of government, which allocates responsibilities to executives, legislature, and judiciary, sets up checks and balances between the federal government, the states, the townships, and the citizens, and provides the machinery for effective social organization. The world has been full of tragic examples, during recent years, of countries which had republican forms of government without a democracy; on the other hand, England and the Scandinavian countries have achieved a democratic society under the forms of monarchy. Some critics of America have been arguing of late that the founders of our nation were interested in establishing a republic, but had no faith in democracy. I insist that the same men who wrote the Constitution also wrote the first ten amendments, the Bill of Rights for democratic freedoms; the genius of the United States of America is that it has successfully combined a republican form of government with a democratic free society almost unique in the annals of man. . . .

5. This should bring me to the conclusion . . . When we, like Alice in Wonderland, are confused and befuddled by the similarities of phrase which conceal a vast difference of meaning, or by the clever misinterpretations of propaganda, let us call a halt to sift the true from the false, to discriminate fairly, to apply our new senses of good taste and good humor.

QUESTIONS FOR STUDY

1. What methods of definition does Davidson use? Compare his techniques of definition with those of Klausner and Taylor.
2. Pars. 1 and 5 are the first and last paragraphs of Davidson's speech. They are the only paragraphs in which he refers to Alice in Wonderland. What purpose do these initial and final references serve?
3. Check the dictionary definitions of money, wealth, religion, theology, democracy, and republicanism. How do the dictionary definitions compare with Davidson's?
4. Look up the meanings of the following words in the dictionary: discrimination, semantics, dissension, variant, allocate, judiciary, annals, and propaganda. Where several meanings are given, decide which is the meaning Davidson intended to use.
5. Other "common confusions" which Davidson discusses in his speech are: size and importance, speed and progress, authority and wisdom, excitement and pleasure, education and training, preparation for life and preparation in life, and reading knowledge and reading for knowledge. Write a paragraph defining one of the pairs. After you have written your definition, compare your concept with Davidson's by checking the text of his speech.

A STUDENT EXPLAINS THE SIGNIFICANCE OF HIS PROFESSION

Joe Sanchez, a day employee of Standard Oil, spoke on the importance of the petroleum industry to his evening speech class at Louisiana State University.

He did not attempt to evaluate Esso in terms of its volume of business, its technical processes, or its number of employees. Instead he emphasized the usefulness of its products in everyday life.

OUR DAILY OIL

by Joe Sanchez

1. Did you ever stop to wonder why most people disapproved of cosmetics when grandma was a girl? It wasn't due to our Puritan heritage, as most people think—the Gay Nineties lived up to their name. No, it was because most store-bought cosmetics, in grandma's day, smelled bad—I should say, smelled like sin.

2. However, in 1890 an apothecary named V. Chapin Daggett hit upon the idea of substituting white mineral oil as a base for cold cream. The result was sensational. A whole new world opened up—Cosmetics from Petroleum!

3. I wonder if most of us realize how many contributions to our mode of life have been made by the Oil Industry. Just for the fun of it, let's run through a day in the life of one of you ladies to see what it would be like without these many contributions. Let's make believe it's Sunday morning, and we'll boycott all products made from or powered by petroleum.

4. If the Sunday you choose is cool, you will have to shiver without your oil burner. If it's hot, you mustn't turn on your electric fan. It would burn out its bearings in five minutes without lubrication.

5. Don't reach for that rayon dressing gown! It isn't in the closet any more. Oil derivatives went into its manufacture.

6. There's no use looking in the bathroom medicine cabinet for a nasal spray even though you are catching a cold. Nine chances out of ten, that spray had an oil base. For that matter, the whole bathroom is pretty much of a mess. The linoleum has vanished from the floor and the lacquer from the cabinets. Most, if not all, of the soap is gone, and so are the cosmetics. (You'll hear about this from your husband, too, when he looks in vain for his brushless shaving cream, rubbing alcohol, face lotion, and hair tonic.)

7. To keep the record absolutely straight, let me say here that many of the products I have mentioned and will mention *can* be made without the use of petroleum, but few of them *are* made that way these days. Now let me continue with the sad story of your oil-free Sunday.

8. When you return to your bedroom to dress, the prospect is not pleasing. The varnish has faded from the furniture. Your best Sunday frock is a dreadful mud color, now that its dye has disappeared. Even your comb is missing.

9. Gone are the plastic window screens you had put up the other day. Flies and mosquitoes are arriving in swarms, but don't reach for the DDT. It is just a useless powder in the bottom of the spray gun, now that its oil base is no more. Whatever else you do, don't look at your garden! Bugs, plant diseases and weeds are having a field day there; but you can do little about them without your insecticides, fungicides, and herbicides.

10. So put on what odds and ends of clothing remain, don your squeaky, unpolished shoes, and creep down to breakfast. Don't wait for your husband. He's having trouble—can't find his belt, which looked like calfskin but really was made of an oil product.

11. The orange juice is sour and tastes stale. Formerly your oranges had been

ripened by means of a petroleum gas and had been kept fresh and bursting with vitamins by means of a wax. The breakfast food is soggy because the container no longer has its moisture-proof oilpaper wrapping. Ants have invaded the marmalade jar, which had been sealed with paraffin. The jelly runs like syrup, minus its synthetic pectin.

12. You can't lift the coffee pot or turn on the stove, now that their plastic handles are things of the past. The morning paper provides no refuge—it is just one expanse of white, since printing ink has carbon black in it. (That, too, stems from petroleum.) If you turn to the radio, it leers at you, naked, unashamed and useless, bereft of its plastic case, tuning knobs, and synthetic rubber insulation.

13. After you have wiped off the greasy dishes—washing them is next to impossible without your petroleum-derived detergent—you decide to take a picture of the wreckage. But it's no good. The film, made with an oil ketone, is worthless.

14. Maybe you ought to send your husband on a little fishing trip to take his mind off his troubles. No! The fish line and lures are made of plastic and the reel won't spin without lubrication.

15. How about a walk, then? That won't do either. The street is no longer smooth asphalt, but only a ribbon of loose rock. Maybe you could negotiate that rock pile to a nearby church, but it has started to drizzle and your synthetic rubbers and raincoat are gone.

16. Is your cold getting worse from all this? A bit of fever, maybe? No use phoning for the doctor. The telephone case is made of plastic, in the first place. Naturally the doctor's car won't run without gasoline, oil, or tires. And his medicine cabinet is half empty. He has no allyl chloride left with which to relieve a cold, sinusitis, or hay fever, or to stop bleeding if an operation should become necessary. In the latter case he would have to resort to old-fashioned and uncertain anesthetics for a lack of the new and harmless cyclopropane. And, if you show signs of a nervous breakdown—which may be expected by this time—he won't be able to treat you with allonal, the drug which worked wonders during the war.

17. Let's call this crazy experiment off. I'm sure you can now see that the oil industry has made tremendous contributions to the health and happiness of every American. We tend to overlook these contributions because they are such an intimate part of our lives, but we would be hard-put, indeed, to do without them.

18. Because of this progressive and dynamic economy of ours, the oil industry cannot stand still; the oil industry will not stand still. It will continue research not only to improve the quality of existing products but also to find new products with which we may live a more enjoyable life.

QUESTIONS FOR STUDY

1. Some of the most frequently mentioned characteristics of oral style are:
    a. instant intelligibility
    b. personal elements of address
    c. contractions
    d. rhythm and smoothness to promote ear-appeal
    e. careful adaptation to the particular audience, occasion, and speaker
    f. simple words and sentences
    g. variety in sentence length
    h. many imperative, interrogative, exclamatory and fragmentary sentences.
    i. much repetition and restatement

Evaluate "Our Daily Oil" in terms of its oral quality.[12]

2. Imagery in language is a verbal appeal to one or more of the senses. The speaker tries to make his listeners see, hear, smell, feel, or taste what he is describing. Identify each kind of imagery Sanchez uses. Which type does he use most often? What effect does imagery have on his speech style?[13]

3. Select a vocation in which you are interested. Prepare a speech on that vocation showing its importance to the community.

TWO ORATORS PRAISE OUR FOREFATHERS

One of the most noted stylists among American speakers is Robert G. Ingersoll. The passage below comes from an address made in Elmwood, Illinois, in 1895.

EXCERPT FROM SPEECH ENTITLED "REUNION ADDRESS"[14]
by Robert G. Ingersoll

1. When I look about me to-day, when I think of the advance of my country, then I think of the work that has been done.

2. Think of the millions who crossed the mysterious sea, of the thousands and thousands of ships with their brave prows toward the West.

3. Think of the little settlements on the shores of the ocean, on the banks of rivers, on the edges of forests.

4. Think of the countless conflicts with savages—of the midnight attacks—of the cabin floors wet with the blood of dead fathers, mothers, and babes.

5. Think of the winters of want, of the days of toil, of the nights of fear, of the hunger and hope.

6. Think of the courage, the sufferings, and hardships.

7. Think of the homesickness, the disease, and death.

8. Think of the labor; of the millions and millions of trees that were felled, while the aisles of the great forests were filled with the echoes of the ax; of the many millions of miles of furrows turned by the plow; of the millions of miles of fences built; of the countless logs changed to lumber by the saw; of the millions of huts, cabins, and houses.

9. Think of the work. Listen, and you will hear the hum of the wheels, the wheels with which our mothers spun the flax and wool. Listen, and you will hear the looms and flying shuttles with which they wove the cloth. . . .

10. Think of the many thousands still passing toward the West, passing over the Alleghanies to the shores of the Ohio and the Great Lakes—still onward to the Mississippi, the Missouri.

11. See the endless processions of covered wagons drawn by horses, by oxen—

[12] For a discussion of the differences between written and oral style, see: Brigance, *Speech Composition, op. cit.*, pp. 200-204; Andrew Thomas Weaver and Gladys Louise Borchers, *Speech*, Harcourt, Brace and Co., 1946, pp. 141-146; Eugene E. White and Clair R. Henderlider, *Practical Public Speaking*, The Macmillan Company, 1954, pp. 261-271.

[13] For a discussion of imagery, see Gray and Braden, *op. cit.*, pp. 415-423.

[14] Complete text found in Ashley H. Thorndyke (ed.), *Modern Eloquence*, Modern Eloquence Corporation, 1923, vol. 10, pp. 269-279.

men and boys and girls on foot, mothers and babes inside. See the glimmering camp fires at night. See the thousands up with the sun and away, leaving the perfume of coffee on the morning air, and sometimes leaving the new-made grave of wife or child. . . .

12. Think of the inventions that went hand in hand with the work; of the flails that were changed into threshers; of the sickles that became cradles, and the cradles that were changed to reapers and headers; of the wooden plows that became iron and steel; of the spinning-wheel that became the jenny, and the old looms transformed to machines that almost think; of the steamboats that traversed the rivers, making the towns that were far apart neighbors and friends; of the stages that became cars; of the horses changed to locomotives with breath of flame, and the roads of dust and mud to highways of steel; of the rivers spanned and the mountains tunneled. . . .

13. Think of all that has been wrought, endured, and accomplished for our good, and let us remember with gratitude, with love and tears, the brave men, the patient, loving women who subdued this land for us.

14. Then think of the heroes who served this country; who gave us this glorious present and hope of a still more glorious future; think of the men who really made us free, who secured the blessings of liberty, not only to us, but to billions yet unborn. . . .

15. To-day we remember the heroic dead, those whose blood reddens the paths and highways of honor; those who died upon the field, in the charge, in prison pens, or in famine's clutch; those who gave their lives that liberty should not perish from the earth. And to-day we remember the great leaders who have passed to the realm of silence, to the land of shadow. Thomas, the rock of Chickamauga, self-poised, firm, brave, faithful; Sherman, the reckless, the daring, the prudent, and the victorious; Sheridan, a soldier fit to have stood by Julius Caesar, and to have uttered the words of command; and Grant, the silent, the invincible, the unconquered; and rising above them all, Lincoln, the wise, the patient, the merciful, the grandest figure in the Western world. We remember them all to-day, and hundreds of thousands who are not mentioned, but who are equally worthy, hundreds of thousands of privates deserving of equal honor with the plumed leaders of the host.

16. And what shall I say to you, survivors of the death-filled days? To you, my comrades, to you whom I have known in the great days, in the time when the heart beat fast and the blood flowed strong, in the days of high hope—what shall I say? All that I can say is that my heart goes out to you, one and all. To you who bared your bosoms to the storms of war; to you who left loved ones to die, if need be, for the sacred cause. May you live long in the land you helped to save; may the winter of your age be as green as spring, as full of blossoms as summer, as generous as autumn; and may you, surrounded by plenty, with your wives at your sides and your grandchildren on your knees, live long. And when at last the fires of life burn low; when you enter the deepening dusk of the last of many, many happy days; when your brave hearts beat weak and slow, may the memory of your splendid deeds—deeds that freed your fellow-men; deeds that kept the flag of the Republic in the air—may the memory of these deeds fill your souls with peace and perfect joy. Let it console you to know that you are not to be forgotten. Centuries hence your story will be told in art and song, and upon your honored graves flowers will be lovingly laid by millions of men and women now unborn.

17. Again expressing the joy that I feel in having met you and again saying farewell to one and all, and wishing you all the blessings of life, I bid you good-bye.

The second speaker is Franklin Knight Lane, Secretary of the Interior during the Wilson administration. The speech printed here was delivered at the opening of the Panama-Pacific Exposition, San Francisco, February 20, 1915.

EXCERPT FROM SPEECH ENTITLED "THE AMERICAN PIONEER"[15]
by Franklin Knight Lane

1. The sculptors who have ennobled these buildings with their work have surely given full wing to their fancy in seeking to symbolize the tale which this exposition tells. Among these figures I have sought for one which would represent to me the significance of this great enterprise.

2. Prophets, priests, and kings are here, conquerors and mystical figures of ancient legend; but these do not speak the word I hear.

3. My eye is drawn to the least conspicuous of all—the modest figure of a man standing beside two oxen, which look down upon the court of the nations, where East and West come face to face.

4. Towering above his gaunt figure is the canopy of his prairie schooner.

5. Gay conquistadores ride beside him, and one must look hard to see this simple, plodding figure.

6. Yet that man is to me the one hero of this day.

7. Without him we would not be here.

8. Without him banners would not fly, nor bands play.

9. Without him San Francisco would not be to-day the gayest city of the globe.

10. Shall I tell you who he is, this key figure in the arch of our enterprise?

11. That slender, dauntless, plodding, modest figure is the American pioneer.

12. To me he is, indeed, far more; he is the adventurous spirit of our restless race. . . .

13. He landed at Plymouth Rock and with his dull-eyed oxen has made the long, long journey across our continent. His way has been hard, slow, momentous.

14. He made his path through soggy, sodden forests where the storms of a thousand years conspired to block his way.

15. He drank with delight of the brackish water where the wild beasts wallowed.

16. He trekked through the yielding, treacherous snows; forded swift-running waters; crept painfully through rocky gorges where Titans had been at play; clambered up mountain sides, the sport of avalanche and of slide; dared the limitless land without horizon; ground his teeth upon the bitter dust of the desert; fainted beneath the flail of the raw and ruthless sun; starved, thirsted, fought; was cast down but never broken; and he never turned back.

17. Here he stands at last beside this western sea, the incarnate soul of his insatiable race—the American pioneer.

18. Pity? He scorns it.

19. Glory? He does not ask it.

20. His sons and his daughters are scattered along the path he has come.

21. Each fence post tells where some one fell.

22. Each farm, brightening now with the first smile of Spring, was once a battle-field, where men and women fought the choking horrors of starvation and isolation.

23. His is this one glory—he found the way; his the adventure. . . .

[15] *Ibid.*, vol. 7, pp. 226-229.

24. His sons are they who have cut these continents in twain, who have slashed God's world as with a knife, who have gleefully made the rebellious seas to lift man's ship across the barrier mountains of Panama.

25. This thing the sons of pioneers have done—it is their prayer, a thing done for man.

26. And here, too, these sons of the pioneer will tell of other things they do—how they fill the night with jewelled light conjured from the melting snows of the far-off mountains; how they talk across the world in their own voices; how they baffle the eagles in their flight through the air and make their way within the spectral gloom of the soundless sea; how they reach into the heavens and draw down food out of the air to replenish the wasted earth; how with the touch of a knife they convert the sinner and with the touch of a stone dissolve disease.

27. These things and more have they done in these latter days, these sons of the pioneer.

28. And in their honor he has fashioned this beautiful city of dreams come true. . . .

29. In blue and gold, in scarlet and purple, in the green of the shallow sea and the burnt brown of the summer hillside, he has made the architecture of the centuries to march before their eyes in column, colonnade, and court. . . .

30. Here, too, in this city of the new nation the pioneer has called together all his neighbors that we may learn one of the other.

31. We are called to live together side by side for all time.

32. The seas are but a highway between the doorways of the nations.

33. We are to know each other.

34. Perhaps strained nerves may sometimes fancy the gesture of the pioneer to be abrupt, and his voice we know has been hardened by the winter winds.

35. But his neighbors will soon come to know that he has no hatred in his heart, for he is without fear; that he is without envy, for none can add to his wealth.

36. The long journey of this slight, modest figure that stands beside the oxen is at an end.

37. The waste places of the earth have been found.

38. But adventure is not to end.

39. Here in this house will be taught the gospel of an advancing democracy—strong, valiant, confident, conquering—upborne and typified by the independent, venturesome spirit of that mystic materialist, the American pioneer.

QUESTIONS FOR STUDY

1. Make a list of the pioneer characteristics praised by Ingersoll and a second list of those emphasized by Lane. Which qualities appear on both lists? Select a virtue common to both speeches and compare the ways in which the two speakers develop it.

2. In either speech is there much factual material with which you were previously unacquainted? If you find little new information and nothing novel about the theme, why do you think the editor of *Modern Eloquence* selected them?

3. Compare the use of imagery in the two speeches.

4. Note the use of alliteration in each speech. Does alliteration promote or reduce euphony in the speeches? Support your opinion by rewording the phrases which have marked alliteration.

5. Evaluate the sentence patterns in the two speeches, including such items as:

length, structure (simple, compound, complex, compound-complex), thought (declarative, interrogative, imperative, exclamatory), and types (loose, periodic, balanced).

6. Analyze the speakers' use of repetition.

7. Herbert Read says that "a Metaphor is the swift illumination of an equivalence. Two images, or an idea and an image, stand equal and opposite; clash together and respond significantly, surprising the reader with a sudden light. This light may either illuminate or decorate the sentence in which it is found; and perhaps we may divide all metaphors into the *illuminative* and the *decorative*. . . . only the illuminative metaphor will be found appropriate in pure prose style."[16]

Do you think Read would consider Ingersoll's Par. 16 "pure prose"? Find other examples of Ingersoll's use of figurative language. What do you think he hoped to achieve through figurative language?

8. Notice the verbs which Lane uses in Par. 16. Are they clear? vivid? appropriate? impressive?

9. Both speeches contain several series of words or phrases which give a sense of progress (i.e., Ingersoll's "huts, cabins, houses"). List these series. Are they appropriate to the theme and mood of the speeches?

10. Study the way in which Ingersoll uses Pars. 13 and 14 to get from one point to the next. Find other transitional devices used by the speakers.

11. Read Brigance's discussions of "The Effective Phrase" and "Nuance Words" in *Speech Composition* (*op. cit.*, pp. 228-232) and Gray and Braden's discussion of "Loaded Words" in *Public Speaking* (*op. cit.*, pp. 457-458). Do Ingersoll and Lane use any phrases which are clichés? What use do they make of loaded or nuance words?

12. Read the speeches aloud. In which paragraphs is a strong rhythm most noticeable?

13. Styles in oratory vary. What one generation approves the next generation may abhor. A style appropriate to one speaker may be ludicrous on the tongue of the copyist. The occasion, the audience, and the speaker's purpose also influence style. The Ingersoll and Lane addresses are the oldest speeches in this chapter. How does their style compare with those of other speeches in the chapter? Do you think audiences today would enjoy their style? Why or why not? Ingersoll and Lane were both making commemorative talks. Was their style influenced by the nature of the occasion?

14. Prepare a short speech on a patriotic or historical theme. Try to achieve freshness and vitality in wording your ideas.

A COLLEGE PRESIDENT ENCOURAGES CONVERSATION

President A. Whitney Griswold of Yale is, according to A. Craig Baird, "a vivacious lecturer, always communicative, humorous, but also 'irrepressibly concerned' with important ideas."[17] "On Conversations—Chiefly Academic" is the speech which President Griswold delivered at the opening convocation of Brown University's 191st academic year in September 1954.

[16] Herbert Read, *English Prose Style*, Beacon Press, 1952, p. 25.

[17] A. Craig Baird (ed.), *Representative American Speeches, 1951-1952*, H. W. Wilson Co., 1952, p. 148.

EXCERPT FROM SPEECH ENTITLED "ON CONVERSATIONS—
CHIEFLY ACADEMIC"[18]

by A. Whitney Griswold

1. Conversation in this country has fallen upon evil days. The great creative art whereby man translates feeling into reason and shares with his fellow man those innermost thoughts and ideals of which civilization is made is beset by forces which threaten its demise. It is forsaken by a technology that is so busy tending its time-saving devices that it has no time for anything else. It is drowned out in singing commercials by the world's most productive economy that has so little to say for itself it has to hum it. It is hushed and shushed in dimly lighted parlors by television audiences who used to read, argue, and even play bridge, an old-fashioned card game requiring speech. It is shouted down by devil's advocates, thrown into disorder by points of order. It is subdued by soft-voiced censors who, in the name of public relations, counsel discretion and the avoidance of controversy like so many family physicians breaking the news gently and advising their patients to cut down on their calories. It starves for want of reading and reflection. It languishes in a society that spends so much time passively listening and being talked to that it has all but lost the will and the skill to speak for itself.

2. I wonder how many of us are aware of this predicament and interested in its possible consequences. It was conversation, reaching its orderly and exalted climax in the dialogues of Socrates, which, in an age without books or their latter-day substitutes, laid the foundation of the civilization we are dedicated to defend. It was conversation of which the New Testament, the greatest teaching ever recorded, was composed. It was conversation, among small groups of university scholars still in a bookless world that revived learning at the end of the Dark Ages. "I am a great believer in conversation," said Whitehead toward the end of his life. "Outside of the book-knowledge which is necessary to our professional training, I think I have got most of my development from the good conversation to which I have always had the luck to have access." . . . Conversation is the handmaid of learning, true religion, and free government. It would be impossible to put too high a price on all we stand to lose by suffering its decay.

3. How then do we account for the symptoms of decadence? Are they the result of a sinister softening-up process such as preceded the dictators of recent history not to mention Big Brother of 1984? Or are they our own fault? Are we being softened up or are we merely softening? In either case, what can we do about it? Ladies and gentlemen, I think that the present predicament of conversation in America is our own fault, and I take courage from the thought. For what is our own fault lies within our power to correct. I think there are a number of things we can do about it, and I propose to suggest a few that are already going on right here in this University and that ought to be encouraged and capitalized for the benefit of the nation.

4. Let me first defend the thesis that the predicament from which we suffer is our own fault and not something slipped over on us by conspiracy. . . . I rest my case on a cardinal principle of American business. The principle is, the customer is always right. If he wants fatter, more expensive cars, he shall have them. If he wants bubble gum and comics, he shall have them too. And if he wants to spend his time looking

[18] Complete text found in A. Whitney Griswold, *In the University Tradition*, Yale University Press, 1957. The speech also appears under the title, "This Tongue-Tied Democracy," in *Vital Speeches of the Day*, November 1, 1954, pp. 828-832.

and listening without ever discussing with his friends the meaning of what he sees and hears, that, too, is his prerogative. No, ladies and gentlemen, we look in vain for scapegoats in this quarter. The trouble here is toys, not traitors.

5. I would argue the same of scapegoats in general. Orderly conversation in its parliamentary sphere, the sphere essential to free government, has been much abused of late . . . stirring up strife all over the country. The effect of this strife has been to inhibit conversation . . . and some critics have found individuals responsible for the phenomenon. I do not agree with them. On the contrary, I think we are responsible for the individuals. I think we are responsible because we, the people, elected and appointed such individuals to represent us, and that is exactly what they are doing. They are representing our fears and suspicions.

6. This, I think, constitutes a real peril to the country, but not of the kind commonly deplored by the critics of such individuals. Bacon told us long ago that believing a rumor was as bad as starting a rumor. He said,

> "Suspicions amongst thoughts are like bats among birds, they ever fly by twilight. Certainly they are to be repressed, or at least well guarded, for they cloud the mind. . . . They dispose Kings to tyranny, husbands to jealousy, wise men to irresolution and melancholy. There are defects not in the heart but in the brain. . . . There is nothing makes a man suspect much, more than to know little; and therefore men should remedy suspicion by procuring to know more. . . ."

Suspicions arouse passions. If we become creatures of passion the individuals who represent us will represent passion. The danger is not that one or another of them may attempt to make himself dictator: I have enough faith in this country to believe that such an attempt would inevitably fail, all European analogies to the contrary notwithstanding. The danger is that we ourselves allow passion to blind us to things we should see with clear eyes and calculate with cool heads and so lead us to a Pearl Harbor compounded of hydrogen. In either case—the hypothetical one of a foreign-style *coup d'état* or the imminent danger that passions may . . . bring us to disaster— the remedy is "procuring to know more" ourselves, not hunting scapegoats to blame for our own shortcomings.

7. By this path I return to this University and the extraordinary opportunity that is yours who are about to enter it. Can you think of a better place for "procuring to know more" or for conversation to prove itself as a means to that end? Where else save Elysium itself is life so congenial to this combination as it is in a residential liberal arts college? Where else does conversation play so vital a part in the central purpose of the institution? Where else, though hard pressed from without, does it yet survive so stubbornly and hold out so much hope to those who would encourage it? Whitehead is but the most distinguished of educational philosophers . . . to testify to its value in his own education. Our civilization and our sacred liberties can be offered as potential evidence of its value to ours.

8. How then, shall we make the most of it? Shall we have courses in conversation? Perish the thought. Let us have conversation in courses but no courses in conversation. By conversation in courses moreover, I do not mean whispering at lectures. I mean as much give and take between teacher and student as is possible in this day of soaring enrollments, teacher shortages and financial deficits. . . . At its best, teaching is a two-way process, an exchange of thought between teacher and student, by which both profit and the thought exchanged becomes ennobled in the transfer. I do not see how we can make very great compromises with this principle without dashing our hopes for conversation and for higher education as well.

9. This is a hard row to hoe and we must have help with it. . . . Where then shall we look for help? Where better than to our own students . . . ? Here is potential relief from the teacher shortage that would cost nothing, that is present in every liberal arts college worthy of the name, and that needs only to be galvanized to prove its value. I say galvanized, not organized. Organization would kill it. . . . Undergraduate assistants to professors on the model of hospital nurses aides would find ideas harder to handle than . . . bed pans and finish by proving that teaching is a profession. But undergraduates who resisted the distractions of their elders and, in their own time and place, gave themselves over to conversation that tested and distilled into wisdom the knowledge derived from lectures and books would do honor to the disciples of Socrates and give our universities and our civilization a new lease on life.

10. To a certain extent this is already happening at Brown and Yale. Yet in relation to capacity the reserves of power have scarcely been tapped. They should be. Here is the strength of the residential liberal arts college waiting to be called upon, the principle of self-education waiting to be demonstrated. Both liberal education and the residential college were founded upon that principle, the liberal arts to train men and women to think for themselves, to learn by themselves, to go on educating themselves for the rest of their lives; the residential college to initiate and foster that process not as a club or hotel but as a corporate society of teachers and scholars. Only part of the process can be accomplished through formal instruction. The other, and not always the lesser part, is accomplished in the social life and intercourse of students outside the classroom.

11. British educators have made much of these principles—the liberal arts and the residential. . . . They say, in effect, that they would rather have a group of adult students living together as a residential community for two weeks than they would individually attending night school or taking correspondence courses for two years. . . . In the judgment of a people whose educational experience goes back nearly eight hundred years and from whose universities our own are lineal descendants, the residential principle is neither a whim nor a luxury but a vital necessity.

12. This is in keeping with the character of the American liberal arts college. . . . With its predominantly residential system of higher education, the United States is favored beyond any other nation in having ready to hand the very means which others emulate and strive to develop with scant resources. Our undergraduate students do not know their own strength. They do not realize the educational benefits they might confer upon all of us . . . by refinement and more extensive practice of the art of conversation.

13. The forms such conversation should take and the rules it should follow are of course important. Like all art it cannot be formless and it must show obedience to certain classic principles. Jargon is not conversation. Plain English, the purer the better, is essential. . . . Small talk and gossip are not conversation. Neither is indictment, with which I include any and all one-way processes of insinuation, invective, diatribe, denunciation, excoriation, anathema, and so on, notwithstanding their current popularity. Conversation is an exchange of thought that leaves all parties to it a grain the wiser. It implies progress. Though it may begin anywhere, even in the realm of the trivial, it should try to get somewhere and carry everyone with it as it goes.

14. The basic principles of conversation were established by Socrates both by example and by precept more than two thousand years ago. One of the most important of these was that conversation should take place among friends, in a congenial atmosphere, with common interests at heart. Best of all would be one common interest,

namely wisdom. . . . Wisdom to Socrates, was "the one true coin for which all things ought to be exchanged . . . and only in exchange for this, and in company with this, is anything truly bought or sold, whether courage or temperance or justice. . . ." Such were his last words to his disciples just before he drank the hemlock. . . . Again, in an earlier dialogue, Socrates declares:

> "Some things I have said of which I am not altogether confident. But that we shall be better and braver and less helpless if we think that we ought to enquire, than we should have been if we indulged in the idle fancy that there was no knowing and no use in seeking to know what we do not know;—that is a theme upon which I am ready to fight, in word and deed, to the utmost of my power."

Where could we find a better motto for higher education? These are, it is true, the utterances of a consecrated teacher and philosopher rather than merely a gifted conversationalist. Yet they tell us much about both learning and conversation. If Carlyle could define a university as a collection of books, Socrates might well have defined it as a conversation about wisdom. In any event we may conclude from what he did say that conversation about wisdom is true conversation.

15. To facilitate conversation of this kind, to keep it moving and make it truly productive, Socrates established one practical rule that has served both conversation and learning well ever since. This was his separation of the hypothesis and its consequences into two distinct questions. The hypothesis was first assumed as true. Then the consequences of the hypothesis were deduced, those which agreed with it being accepted as true and those which disagreed rejected as false. The hypothesis was never taken as axiomatic or self-evident and if called into question was debated in its turn. By this method the parties to a conversation were brought onto common ground, unity and relevance were ensured for their discussion, and the whole range of human knowledge was infinitely expanded. What a boon it might be to our troubled world that wastes so much time and temper arguing at cross purposes if we could apply this rule more generally to the discussion of human affairs today. Criticism would have to be answered on its merits rather than by attacks on the critic. Concealed or unstated premises would be brought out into the open. It might even become possible to discuss our foreign policy without raising our voices and accusing one another of treason. Who knows what enlightened dispensations in the national interest might not result? But I am afraid that for such exalted conversation as this we should either have to bring Socrates back to earth or wait as he did in the conviction that the ideals of men were laid away in heaven.

16. Even supposing we did bring him back to earth and summoned his thought to the matter at hand—the revival of conversation among students in residential colleges of the liberal arts—he might not find the going so easy at first, particularly at this season of the year. I can see him now returning . . . from a meeting of the Association of Colleges in New England. . . . On the train he has encountered graduates of two of the member institutions whose names, with apologies to Owen Johnson and J. P. Marquand, are Dink Stover and Bojo Brown. They engage Socrates in a discussion of education and arrive with the utmost despatch at the following proposition:

> Bojo: I don't like this new Ivy League Agreement.
> Dink: Neither do I. All this business about spring practice and recruiting players!
> Socrates: Players? What is the Ivy League, a group of actors?
> Bojo: No, a group of colleges.
> Socrates: Ah, and they have just agreed to recruit actors?

Dink: No, they have just agreed not to recruit football players.

Socrates: But why should they wish to recruit football players? I thought colleges were for students. At first I thought you were talking about players in the sense of actors or possibly musicians, who would entertain the students and recreate them after their studies. But why football players?

Bojo: Well, you see, a lot of colleges award football scholarships . . .

Socrates: But what has football got to do with scholarship?

Bojo: Well, I see what you mean, but that's what they call them.

Socrates: That may be what they call them, but what *are* they?

Dink (interrupting): They're grants of financial assistance . . .

Socrates: Financial assistance? You mean money? You mean young men are paid money to play football in college?

Bojo: In some cases, yes, but not in the Ivy League. Although by the way, Dink, a friend of mine in Greenwich told me. . . . Of course I don't believe it . . . that a Princeton man in his office told him that he knew for a fact that a group of your alumni had offered . . .

Dink: I deny that! And anyway, what about that fellow up in Buffalo who was registered in our Freshman Class and then a group of your alumni grabbed him. . . .

Bojo: Oh, that old chestnut! I . . . .

Socrates: Gentlemen, all this talk about football and chestnuts! I thought we were discussing education.

Dink and Bojo, testily, and in unison: WE ARE!

17. No, ladies and gentlemen, even with the help of Socrates we should have work to do before the art of conversation in our colleges came into its own. We should have to ensure our students a proper subject of conversation. Fortunately we have this, too, ready to hand in our liberal arts curriculum. This is the educational birthright of undergraduates at Brown and Yale. Its currency has never been devalued: it is still at par with the currency of Socrates' one true coin. . . . As a source of great conversation it has never been equalled. I do not decry vocational training. In some form or other it is essential for most of us and has something to offer all of us. What I do decry is vocational training masquerading as liberal education and usurping its place. The demand of society for the immediate and the utilitarian is unremitting. The Sophists answered it in Socrates' day. . . . Education can always cash in on this demand, nor do I criticize the educational institutions that do. I just hope Yale and Brown won't.

18. Is this a pious hope, visionary and impractical in this practical world? I ask you what might have happened if we had started cashing in on the demand when it was first felt. Let us take the timely case of television. It is said to be revolutionizing American life and we are urged to introduce courses in it in our curriculum. There have been several such inventions that were thought by contemporaries to be revolutionary agents of change in American life. The first was the telegraph. . . . Next came the telephone, then movies, then radio, and finally TV. Each one of these inventions, speedily put into mass production and consumption, was fraught with no less revolutionary consequences for our society and accompanied by no less apocalyptic prophecies than those which accompany television today.

19. Suppose, in view of this, Yale had added courses in the techniques and uses of each to its liberal arts curriculum. I can imagine an entering Freshman with the Course of Study Catalogue in his hand. He finds courses in telegraphy, telephony, cinematography, radiotelegraph and telephony and—words fail me to describe the

science of television. Then come the influence courses, the influence of the telegraph on the telephone, the influence of the telephone on radio, the influence of radio on the movie, and so on. Then the influence of influence courses, e.g., the influence of radio and telephonic techniques on communication and its impact on the American family. The Freshman reads on in despair. He is looking for a course in English. He can't find one. He goes to the Dean. "English?" says the Dean. "Oh we don't bother with that any more. We have developed more effective means of communication."

20. The most important thing about any form of communication is what is communicated. The most important thing about what is communicated is its valuation in the currency of Socrates' coin. The utilitarian skills and techniques of each generation are soon outmoded. The search for wisdom and virtue never is. Not all the technological triumphs of history have satisfied man's need for these, nor displaced or even approached them as the most inspiring and fruitful of all subjects of human conversation.

21. We must manage to present this subject to our undergraduates in such a way as will inspire them to help revive conversation in this tongue-tied democracy that has such good ideas yet cannot speak its own mind.

QUESTIONS FOR STUDY

1. Do you think the Baird comment could apply to this speech as well as to Griswold's earlier one?
2. Generally, the study questions on each previous speech excerpt have emphasized one or two aspects of style. For the Griswold speech try to analyze all stylistic techniques. The outline below will help you remember some important considerations.
    I. Choosing expressive words
        1. Specific?
        2. Clear definitions?
        3. Imagery?
        4. Active voice?
        5. Transitions?
        6. Figures of speech?
        7. Loaded words?
        8. Clichés?
    II. Wording effective sentences
        1. Oral style?
        2. Direct discourse?
        3. Euphony?
        4. Rhythm?
        5. Parallelism?
        6. Variety in sentence structure (simple, compound, complex, compound-complex)?
        7. Variety in sentence types (loose, periodic, balanced)?
        8. Variety in sentence thought (declarative, imperative, interrogative, exclamatory)?

EXERCISES

1. Cicero attempted to analyze style through three classifications—the plain, which was pure and unornamented; the middle, which was smooth and charming; and the

grand, which was embellished, ornate, and copious. Imagine that these three terms are points of a continuum.

Plain   Middle   Grand

Where would you locate each of the speech excerpts in this chapter? How does your style continuum compare with those of your classmates?

2. List the transitional words and phrases found in the speech excerpts in this chapter. Which are used most frequently? Do you know any additional transitions in common use which do not appear in these speeches? Add them to your list.

3. Use the outline given with the questions on Griswold's speech as a guide to analyze the style of the following speeches found elsewhere in this book:

Brown, Kenneth I., "Men and Women with Antennae," pp. 132-135.
Carleton, William G., "Effective Speech in a Democracy," pp. 153-155.
Churchill, Winston, "To the French People," pp. 65-66.
Conwell, Russell H., "Acres of Diamonds," pp. 70-73.
Kennedy, John F., "The Education of an American Politician," pp. 123-126.
MacArthur, Douglas, "Address to Congress," pp. 61-63.
Roosevelt, Franklin D., "Address to Congress, December 8, 1941," pp. 146-147.
Stevenson, Adlai, "A Political Speech," p. 59.

4. Printed in the parallel columns below is a student speech on "Civil Defense." The left-hand column is the original. Seeing this version, a teacher commented: "The goal is worthwhile; the choice and arrangement of material good. But the speech is dull! Perhaps because the style is too generalized." The right-hand column shows the revised speech. What are the kinds of changes that have been made? Have these changes improved the style? What other changes could be made?

CIVIL DEFENSE

Original Speech

1. When the first atomic bomb was dropped on Hiroshima during World War II, everyone was shocked at the destruction which was wrought by a single bomb. The shock was increased when an even more powerful device was tested in the Pacific in 1952. This was a hydrogen test explosion and was not as powerful as a hydrogen bomb. The radius of total destruction caused by the test weapon was three miles. This is equivalent to an area about twenty-eight times that normally considered as the L.S.U. campus or equivalent to an area about one-third the area of Baton Rouge. Moderate damage was done as far as ten miles from the center of the blast.

2. The Russians are known beyond any

Revised Speech

1. When the first atomic bomb was dropped on Hiroshima during World War II, we were shocked at the destruction wrought by a single bomb. We were again shocked by the even more powerful hydrogen test explosion at Eniwetok Atoll in the Pacific in November, 1952. The radius of total destruction caused by the test weapon—a weapon not as potent as the hydrogen bomb—was three miles, an area equivalent to about twenty-eight times the L.S.U. campus or one-third of Baton Rouge. Even as far as ten miles from the center of the blast, there was moderate damage.

2. The Russians are believed to possess

Original Speech	*Revised Speech*
doubt to possess a growing stockpile of atomic weapons and what is believed to be hydrogen bombs. Even the small atomic bombs like those dropped on Hiroshima and Nagasaki make one airplane able to deliver as much destruction as can be carried by a thousand planes using conventional bombs. Beyond any doubt the Russian air force would be capable of delivering their stockpile of atomic weapons.	a growing stockpile of atomic weapons, including hydrogen bombs. Even the small atomic bombs like those dropped on Hiroshima and Nagasaki make one airplane more destructive than a thousand planes carrying conventional bombs. We know that Russia has an air force capable of making an atomic attack.
3. An aggressor who was determined could deliver atomic or hydrogen bombs by plane to Baton Rouge and other cities once he decided to attack because no absolute military defense exists today or is likely to exist in the foreseeable future. It is probable that you think that this is impossible due to the Air Defense Command, the radar networks, and all of the other military forces which are charged with our protection. However, I learned that such an attack is possible while I was working with atomic weapons in the Strategic Air Command. This fact has been proved by the Strategic Air Command, for on practice missions it has made successful raids on Washington, Chicago, New York City, Baton Rouge, and similar cities.	3. A determined aggressor could drop atomic or hydrogen bombs on Baton Rouge and other cities of the Gulf area because no absolute military defense exists today or is likely to exist in the foreseeable future. You are probably thinking that a sneak attack is impossible with the Air Defense Command, the radar networks, and all of the other military forces to protect us. However, while I was working with atomic weapons in the Strategic Air Command, I learned that such an attack is possible. The Strategic Air Command has proved this possibility by its successful practice missions over Washington, Chicago, New York, and our own Baton Rouge.
4. It is a well-known fact that a tremendous amount of industry is concentrated in the north Baton Rouge area, and it is growing at an ever-accelerating rate. This industry is vital to our nation in time of peace or war. Esso's plant is one of the largest refineries in the United States; Ethyl's plant is the largest producer of anti-knock compounds for use in aviation and commercial gasolines; Kaiser's plant is a major contributor to aluminum production; the Solvay, General Chemical, Nagatuck, Gulf States Utilities, U.S. Rubber, and other similar plants produce products which are vital to the nation. This leads us to but one conclusion. Baton Rouge is a prime target area in the event of war with Russia.	4. We all know that a tremendous amount of industry is concentrated in north Baton Rouge and that it is growing at an accelerated rate. Esso is one of the largest refineries in the United States; Ethyl is the largest producer of the anti-knock compounds necessary for aviation and commercial gasolines; Kaiser is a major contributor of aluminum; Solvay, General Chemical, Nagatuck, Gulf States Utilities, U.S. Rubber, and other smaller industries are vital to the nation. There is but one conclusion: in the event of war with Russia, Baton Rouge is a prime target.

Original Speech

5. Knowing that it is possible for Russia to drop such weapons as atomic and hydrogen bombs on Baton Rouge leads us to this question: "How could we survive such an attack?" The answer to this question lies in a well-organized civil defense program. Civil defense organizations are composed of individuals like you and me and are organized on federal, regional, and local levels. Civil defense provides the public with information on survival procedures. It wants to help you learn how to survive in case we are attacked. What you do before the explosion can save your life and what you do after the explosion can also save your life.

6. The procedures which are so vital for you to follow before the attack are: learning the air raid signals and learning what to do when you hear them. You should know what to do if you heard the blast of an air raid siren right now. If the siren signal were a long steady blast of three to five minutes, it would mean that you should leave at once and follow an evacuation plan for your area. If there were no time to evacuate, another signal would be given so that suitable shelter could be found. After the explosion there would be other important instructions and procedures to follow. You should know how to obtain safe food and water, how to maintain sanitation, and how to decontaminate an area.

7. The Civil Defense Administration not only provides the public with this information but also trains its members to help the public carry out these instructions. Among other services offered by this organization to aid in survival is the engineering service. It is primarily responsible for emergency housing, restoration of vital utilities, and demolition of unsafe buildings and other hazards. Other services include such functions as fire fighting, rescue, medical aid, welfare, and communications.

8. To best provide all of these services,

Revised Speech

5. Knowing that it is possible for an aggressor to drop atomic and hydrogen bombs on Baton Rouge, we ask: "Could we survive such an attack?" The answer lies in a well-organized civil defense program, composed of many ordinary citizens like you and me.

6. What would you do if you heard the blast of an air raid siren right now? Do you know that a long steady blast of three to five minutes means you should immediately follow the evacuation plan for your area? Do you know what the plan is? If there were no time to evacuate, where would you seek suitable shelter? After the explosion, what would you do? Do you know how to obtain safe food and water? How to maintain sanitation? And how to decontaminate an area?

7. The Civil Defense Administration will provide you and your neighbor with the answers to these questions. It will also train you to help your community carry out these procedures. In case of disaster, emergency housing, restoration of vital utilities, and demolition of unsafe buildings are responsibilities of Civil Defense. Its other functions include fire fighting, rescue, medical aid, welfare, and communications.

8. To best provide these services, Civil

Original Speech	*Revised Speech*
Civil Defense utilizes existing groups such as hospital staffs, fire departments, plant maintenance and construction groups, and public utility employees. Not only are these groups utilized but individuals like you and me are trained to supplement these groups. Each such individual is trained in an area where his own skills are best utilized. With the necessary members trained to provide such specialized assistance, a Civil Defense program will appreciably reduce the loss of life and property. It will help us get back on our feet faster and maintain our will to win. Nothing could be more important to us in time of war.	Defense uses existing hospital staffs, fire departments, plant maintenance and construction groups, and public utility employees. But individuals like you and me are needed to supplement these groups. With well-trained citizens, a Civil Defense program can appreciably reduce unnecessary loss of life and destruction of property. In case of a sneak attack, a Civil Defense program can help us get back on our feet faster and maintain our will to win.
9. Because of its great importance everyone should help our local organization in its struggle for a bigger and better Civil Defense program. No one should depend on the other person to provide his safety. He should do something about it himself. He should join his local Civil Defense Administration now. If anyone will give me his name and mailing address tonight, I will personally see that he is mailed the necessary forms for joining. If anyone prefers to do so, he may contact Mr. W. H. Perkins directly at 3044 Belmont Avenue. His telephone number is 4-9102.	9. Realizing the importance of these services, won't you help develop a better Civil Defense program? Don't sit back and let others worry about your safety. Join your local Civil Defense Administration now. Give me your name and address tonight and I will personally see that you receive the necessary forms to join. If you prefer, you may contact W. H. Perkins at 3044 Belmont Avenue, telephone number 4-9102.
10. In conclusion, let me summarize briefly. Remember that the sole purpose of Civil Defense is to insure the survival of the United States. Assistance is needed by the local Civil Defense Administration. Everyone should join tonight to do his share for Civil Defense.	10. The sole purpose of Civil Defense is to insure your survival and the survival of your country. Your assistance is needed. Join tonight! Do your share for Civil Defense.

5. Read a speech in *Vital Speeches of the Day, Representative American Speeches,* or a similar collection. Prepare a five-minute summary of the speech. The purpose of this exercise is to help you achieve clarity and conciseness of expression.

6. Write an evaluation of the style of the speech which you read for exercise 5. Cite specific passages from the speech to support your opinion.

7. Prepare a three- to five-minute speech illustrating a language failure or success. The general topics below may help you think of an appropriate subject.

  A speech that failed because the language was not clear (why? too generalized? too much verbiage? nonoral style? inappropriate for the audience? essential definitions omitted?)

A misunderstanding between friends because of a language failure

How faulty directions spoiled the cake (or made us miss the kick-off, or caused some other disappointment)

A comparison of two ways of treating the same event (one newspaper headlined a story "U.S. Forces Overseas To Be Reduced"; another covered the same news with "Thousands of G.I.'s To Come Home")

How a speaker used language effectively (a convocation speaker adapts to a college audience)

8. Keep a list of all new words you read or hear. Each week go through the list and make sentences using each word correctly.

9. Locate two or more translations of the *New Testament*. (Among the most widely circulated versions are the King James, the Douay, the Moffatt, the Revised Standard, and the Phillips; the last is especially interesting for comparative purposes.) Compare the translations of a narrative passage such as an event in the life of Christ or a parable; compare translations of an expository passage such as one of Paul's doctrinal discourses. From a stylistic point of view, what are the virtues of each translation? the limitations?

REFERENCES

Readings to Be Assigned with Chapter VI

Baird, A. Craig, and Knower, Franklin H., *General Speech: An Introduction*, McGraw-Hill Book Company, 2nd ed., 1957, chap. 9, "Using Effective Language."

Brigance, William Norwood, *Speech: Its Techniques and Disciplines in a Free Society*, Appleton-Century-Crofts, Inc., 1952, chap. 15, "Using Words."

Bryant, Donald C., and Wallace, Karl R., *Fundamentals of Public Speaking*, Appleton-Century-Crofts, Inc., 1953, chap. 15, "Language."

Crocker, Lionel, *Public Speaking for College Students*, American Book Company, 3rd ed., 1956, chap. 19, "Effective Language in Speech"; chap. 20, "Techniques of Humor."

Gilman, Wilbur E., Aly, Bower, and Reid, Loren, *The Fundamentals of Speaking*, The Macmillan Company, 1951, chap. 6, "Composing the Speech."

Gray, Giles W., and Braden, Waldo W., *Public Speaking: Principles and Practice*, Harper & Brothers, 1951, chap. 16, "Using Language for Clarity"; chap. 17, "Using Language for Vividness"; chap. 18, "Using Language for Impressiveness."

McBurney, James H., and Wrage, Ernest J., *The Art of Good Speech*, Prentice-Hall, Inc., 1953, chap. 17, "Language and Style."

Monroe, Alan H., *Principles and Types of Speech*, Scott, Foresman and Company, 4th ed., 1955, chap. 18, "Wording the Speech."

Oliver, Robert T., and Cortright, Rupert L., *New Training for Effective Speech*, The Dryden Press, 1951, chap. 11, "Developing a Speech Style."

Thonssen, Lester, and Baird, A. Craig, *Speech Criticism, The Development of Standards for Rhetorical Appraisal*, The Ronald Press Co., 1948, chap. 15, "The Style of Public Address."

White, Eugene E., and Henderlider, Clair R., *Practical Public Speaking: A Guide to Effective Communication*, The Macmillan Company, 1954, chap. 12, "Using Language in Delivering the Speech."

Chapter VII

TYPES OF SPEECHES

THE previous chapters have approached speech practices from the point of view of various phases of speech making, namely preparation, organization, audience adjustment, forms of support, and style. This chapter seeks to give examples of the various types of speeches.

The Informative Speech

The informative talk is the order of the day in a variety of situations. For example, the city engineer explains to his assistants how to eliminate a hazardous corner with drawings on a blackboard of the proposed construction. A county agent, standing in a gullied field, discusses methods to prevent soil erosion. In a briefing session, the base commander instructs the bombing crew about the raid. The foreman demonstrates for his men the operation of a new tool. In History 107, Professor Sidney Jones lectures on life in Athens in the fifth century B.C. With her eager cub scouts about, the den mother lays out plans for the coming "cook out." The imparting of information is a frequent occurrence in our daily lives.

Below is a summary of several principles of the informative talk.

1. The goal of this type is to make clear, to give understanding, and to insure retention.

2. The speech outline is simple and easy for the listener to follow.

3. The points are few in number, preferably not more than five.

4. The speech plan is often deductive, i.e., the central thought or subject sentence is stated in the introduction, followed by the main points in the discussion.

5. The speech purpose is made clear in the opening sentences. The speaker may say, "My purpose is to explain the operation. . ." or "My goal is to give you information. . . ."

6. The speech makes use of a preview, sign posts ("My first point. . . .",

"My second point. . . ."), obvious transitions, restatement of important points and a complete summary.

7. The speech is frequently developed around a time pattern, a space pattern or topical pattern.

8. The supporting materials include definitions, illustrations, examples, comparisons, statistics and visual aids.

9. The oral presentation may be supplemented by a demonstration or even performance on the part of the trainees.

10. The listeners are encouraged to ask questions and at times to supplement the speaker's presentation with their own observations.

11. The rate of presentation is determined by the listener's comprehension rate.

12. The speaker's language is selected for its definiteness and exactness.

Many of these principles are well illustrated in the excerpts quoted below.

EXCERPT FROM A STUDENT SPEECH, "ON REPORTING THE WEATHER"[1]
by H. D. Sumrall

1. Today, collecting facts and disseminating information about the weather is one of the most important jobs of the meteorologist. Here in my hand I have a report on the weather conditions which comes through on the teletype machine every hour. Let me explain to you the various symbols.

```
BHM  M32Φ120Φ10 191/52/29↑‹15/009
ANB  E120Φ15 196/45/34↩10
ATL  20Φ250Φ7 220/42/38↩3/018
NCQ  25Φ250Φ4K 217/44/35↩6
LGC  E70Φ4K 210/38/36C
CSG  E140⊕5K 220/45/40↩9/017/BINOVC
MGM  M90⊕12 213/42/35↩6/015/BINOVC W
MEI  E120Φ10.180/56/51↑10/005
EVR  E50Φ100⊕15 200/48/41↩‹5
```

2. Now the letters on the left hand side of the page are the station call or identification letters.

3. For example, let's take ATL which stands for Atlanta, Georgia.

4. The next symbols you see are 20 and a circle with a line through it. This is a cloud report which means that there is a low cloud at 2000 feet, covering less than six-tenths of the sky. The weatherman reports the extent of clouds in tenths. Ten-tenths would be complete overcast.

5. The next symbols, 250 and a circle with a line through it, indicate another cloud at 25,000 feet which also covers less than six-tenths of the sky.

6. The 7 denotes the visibility on the ground in miles.

7. The 220 is the air pressure measured in milibars. Milibars are just another way the weatherman has of indicating atmospheric pressure.

[1] Presented in Speech 60 at Mississippi Southern College.

8. The 42 is the temperature, and the 38 is the dew point. The dew point is the amount of moisture in the air. Although the weatherman figures the relative humidity and records it in his records, he uses the dew point in plotting the weather map.

9. The little arrows you see next tell the direction of the wind, which in this case is east northeast.

10. The 3 is the velocity of the wind in miles per hour.

11. The 018 is the atmospheric pressure again, but in this form it is called an altimeter setting which is reported mainly for pilots.

12. Teletype reports of this type are sent out every hour, twenty-four hours a day, seven days a week, to aid the meteorologist. . . .

EXCERPT FROM A STUDENT SPEECH ENTITLED "PARTY GAMES"[2]
by Peggy Taylor

1. Old style fun-making still survives in many sections of back country of Arkansas. This institution is strictly American, and democratic in the broadest sense of the word.

2. Sometimes these frolics are held in the district school house, more often at a home or in a vacant cabin. The back rooms are provided for the very old or the very young; the fore-room is cleared of all furnishings and rugs, and the walls are lined with chairs and benches. Fun-makings usually begin after sundown as soon as the chores are done. They last sometimes until sunup, and very often the folks get home just in time to begin the chores again. These activities take strong constitutions, for during the frolic season a young man or young woman may go for as long as a week with little sleep.

3. One type of play party is a square dance without fiddles or other instrumental music. The merrymakers sing their own songs and provide their own mirth as they go along.

4. A play party usually opens with a compromising and simple game—one that everyone can play. Then, when the festive spirit livens, they burst out in unexpected and lively good ole' Arkansas hoe-downs.

5. There are dozens of play party games, with intricate steps and turnings.

6. However, I'd like to tell you about one which is called the "Juniper Tree." This game is played in a circle with a girl sitting in the center. An old hat is tossed up for snatch grab. Whatever boy gets hold of that is "reckoned as being lucky," for reasons that will soon become apparent.

7. The dancers march around the girl, singing:

> Rise up my dearest dear,
> Present me to your Paw,
> And we'll go off together,
> To the state of Arkansas.
>
> So keep your hat on,
> Hit'll keep your head warm,
> And take a sweet kiss,
> Hit'll do you good I'm shore, I'm shore.

At the command of "keep your hat on," the lucky man puts the hat upon the head

[2] Presented in Speech 60 at Mississippi Southern College.

of the girl and claims his kiss. The girl claims her successor . . . and so a good time is had by all.

8. Not too long ago, the fun-makings were havens for the dudes of the hills, who "dressed fit to kill." We no longer see the stiff collars and loud ties. We no longer hear those ivory cuff buttons clicking in celluloid cuffs either. And it once was the sign of a real "cat" to see the trouser legs tucked down into the top of the boots.

9. The recreation of the folk people is free and spontaneous. Their stories and songs have luckily been passed on to us for our enjoyment.

QUESTIONS FOR STUDY

1. Textbooks in public speaking usually list as the materials of the informative speech the following: definition, analysis, classification, demonstration, analogy, examples and illustrations, statistics, visual aids, interpretation, criticism, and authority. List each use of these materials. Which appears most often in these speeches? Are any of the kinds of materials not used at all in these two speeches?
2. What important factors of these speeches cannot be presented on the printed page, but can be presented orally?
3. These speeches were presented to a class of liberal arts majors. Is the material presented at their level of understanding? How could the speakers have made the speeches clearer?
4. Compare the plan of organization in these two passages. Does the speaker aid you in understanding his material by his plan of development?
5. Which of the two passages is the more interesting? Why? Do the interest factors contribute to your understanding? Explain your answer.
6. What is the central thought or subject sentence of the second excerpt? Prepare an outline of this selection.
7. Frequently in beginning public speaking classes the teacher gives a criticism like the following: "You should use more specific details in your speech." Can this criticism be made of these two excerpts? Why or why not?
8. Gray and Braden say, "Vividness has its primary basis in imagery, which in turn arises from concrete experiences. This imagery may be visual, auditory, motor, thermal, and so on, or any combination of them. The more definitely your language recalls such imagery, the more vivid it will be."[3] Study the imagery used in the selection on "Party Games." How many types of imagery do you find in the selection?
9. Prepare an informative talk in which you use either a chronological or spatial order of development.

EXCERPT FROM "THE EDUCATION OF AN AMERICAN POLITICIAN"[4]
by John F. Kennedy

1. It is a great if somewhat awesome honor to be here this evening with what is probably the greatest collection of brainpower any politician has ever addressed. More important, your are undoubtedly one of the most powerful audiences in the

[3] Giles W. Gray and Waldo W. Braden, *Public Speaking: Principles and Practices,* Harper & Brothers, 1951, p. 394.
[4] Delivered at the Annual Convention of American Association of School Administrators and National School Board Association, Municipal Auditorium, Atlantic City, New Jersey, February 19, 1957. Found in the *Congressional Record* (Daily Edition), vol. 103, February 21, 1957, pp. 2096-2097.

world—powerful not in terms of the national and international policies you control or manipulate, but powerful because in your hands the future leaders of this Nation, the most powerful nation in the world, are being shaped. Your responsibilities consequently are in many ways far greater than those of us who serve in national policymaking bodies.

2. My announced topic for this evening was "The Education of an American Politician." It was a title which frankly I thought might stimulate some interest— for the simple reason that most Americans, including educators, are not accustomed to thinking of us politicians as educated men. We may be experienced, or cynical, or skillful, or shrewd or even fluent—but no more education is required for this kind of success than that provided by smoke-filled rooms and back-stage deals. . . .

3. This disdain for the political profession in our schools and communities did not matter quite as much in the days when active participation in the political affairs of the Nation was limited to a select few. But today, the implications of national policy necessarily make politicians of all of us. Today, every citizen, regardless of his interest in politics, holds office; every one of us is in a position of responsibility; and, in the final analysis, the kind of Government we get depends upon how we fulfill those responsibilities. We, the people, are the boss, and we will get the kind of political leadership, be it good or bad, that we demand and deserve. . . .

4. Thus the American politician of whom I speak today, and with whose education I am concerned, is in effect potentially each and every American citizen. His opinions, his votes, and his efforts define the limits of our policy, provide its guideposts, and authorize its implementation. In Lincoln's words, that man on the street, the average citizen, the educated voter, "makes statutes possible or impossible to execute." His attitude toward taxation and selective service, foreign aid and alliances, the United Nations, imports, immigration, even his attitude toward members of minority groups in his own country—all of these have an impact upon foreign policy far beyond his knowledge. Without his indispensable support and loyalty, no American foreign policy in times such as these can suceed. . . .

5. "To inform their discretion by education." That is your task and the task of every teacher in every city and village in America—the education of American politicians, of all, or nearly all, Americans to serve as politicians in making public policy. But what kind of education will you offer? What kind of training is necessary to prepare young Americans for a more active and enlightened role in the political affairs of their Nation? Permit me to offer a few suggestions from my vantage point in the political arena.

6. First, I would emphasize that we need not an over-concentration upon civic and political affairs, but the development of a broad range of talents. We do not need men like Lord John Russell, of whom Queen Victoria once said that he would be a better man if he knew a third subject—but he was interested in nothing but the Constitution of 1688 and himself. We need instead men with the education of Thomas Jefferson, described by a contemporary as "A gentleman of 32, who could calculate an eclipse, survey an estate, tie an artery, plan an edifice, try a cause, break a horse, dance a minuet, and play the violin." We need men like Daniel Webster, who could throw thunderbolts at Hayne on the Senate floor and then stroll a few steps down the corridor and dominate the Supreme Court as the foremost lawyer of his time; like John Quincy Adams, who, after being summarily dismissed from the Senate for a notable display of independence, could become Boylston professor of rhetoric and oratory at Harvard and then become a great Secretary of State. (These were the happy days when Harvard professors had no difficulty getting

Senate confirmation.) We need men like Missouri's first Senator, Thomas Hart Benton, the man whose tavern brawl with Jackson in Tennessee caused him to flee the State, and yet whose education was described with these words in his obituary: "With a readiness that was often surprising, he could quote from a Roman Law or a Greek philosopher, from Virgil's Georgics, the Arabian Nights, Herodotus, or Sanchez Panza, from the Sacred Carpets, the German reformers or Adam Smith; from Fenolon or Hudubras, from the financial reports of Necca or the doings of the Council of Trent, from the debates on the adoption of the Constitution or intrigues of the kitchen cabinet or from some forgotten speech of a deceased Member of Congress."

7. Secondly, I would emphasize that we need scholarship fitted for practical action, for something more than merely discussing political issues and deploring their solutions with learned phrases, intellectual achievements fitted for more than the delights of abstract discourse. . . .

8. It is not enough, therefore, that our schools merely be great centers of learning, without concerning themselves with the uses to which that learning is put in the years that follow graduation. Indeed, care must be taken to see that it is not left behind upon graduation. . . .

9. Third, I would emphasize the importance, in teaching students about public affairs, of avoiding the confusion of political idealism with political fantasy or rigidity. We need idealism in our public life; we need young men and women who will stand for the right regardless of their personal ambitions or welfare. But let us not permit them to carry that idealism to the point of fantasy—to the point where any compromise or concession is regarded as immoral. For politics and legislation are not matters for inflexible principles or unattainable ideals. Politics, as John Morley has acutely observed, "is a field where action is 1 long second best, and where the choice constantly lies between 2 blunders"; and legislation, under the democratic way of life and the Federal system of government, requires compromise between the desires of each individual and group and those around them. Henry Clay, who should have known, said compromise was the cement that held the Union together:

"All legislation . . . is founded upon the principle of mutual concession. . . . Let him who elevates himself above humanity, above its weaknesses, its infirmaties [sic], its wants, its necessities, say, if he pleases, 'I never will compromise'; but let no one who is not above the frailities of our common nature disdain compromise." . . .

10. Fourth, I would emphasize the importance, in teaching students about public affairs, of avoiding the confusion of national patriotism with national mythology. Instillation of a sense of patriotism, of national pride, of awareness of gratitude for the liberties and opportunities that are ours as Americans—these are precepts which, of course, it is hoped every student shall grasp. But at the same time let us recognize the necessity of clearing away these false axioms and myths which, however comforting to our sense of security or appealing to our sense of patriotism, impair a realistic view of our Nation's role in the world. I refer to those myths, among others, that are based upon the untouchability of national sovereignty; the existence of inherently good, bad, or backward nations; the emphasis of governmental economy over national security; or the impairment of an aggressor's power by refusing him our diplomatic recognition.

11. Many Americans persist in the myth that the scientific skill of the United States cannot be duplicated in any other country; that the democratic way of life, inasmuch as it is the best way, will inevitably be the victor in any struggle with an alien power; that the United States can never lose a war, or that its shores can

never be attacked. Many still hold to the belief that our allies owe homage and gratitude to the United States and to all of its views at all times. There are those who believe the United States can still halt aggression by the arrival of a few American gunboats and marines. There are those who oppose assistance to or cooperation with our allies, those who reject bargaining or diplomatic pressure as a method of dealing with international disputes. Education for citizenship, for increased participation in American political life, must dispel these myths, if it is to avoid the description once furnished by Lord Bryce of a political education "sufficient to enable them to think they know something about the great problems of politics, but insufficient to show them how little they know."

12. Fifth and finally, I would emphasize that this kind of education requires quality as well as quantity. I realize that education cannot fulfill its responsibilities when nearly a million boys and girls are deprived by the classroom shortage of full-time schooling, when millions more are held back in unwieldy classes of 40 or more and when the Nation is short 135,000 qualified teachers. . . .

13. Of one thing we can be sure—the graduates of our schools and of our universities will be expected to play an increasingly important role in American political affairs. . . . They are expected to offer leadership and guidance for all. It was Prince Bismarck who said that one-third of the students of German universities broke down from overwork; another third broke down from dissipation; but the other third ruled Germany. (I leave it to each of you to decide which third attends conventions in Atlantic City.)

14. Those who are to be among the rulers of our land, in the sense that all thinking citizens must of necessity become political leaders, will not lack problems to which their education can be applied—increasing farm foreclosures, for example, in the midst of national prosperity—record small business failures at a time of record profits, pockets of chronic unemployment and sweat-shop wages amidst the wonders of automation, the care of the chronically and mentally ill, monopoly, race relations, taxation, international trade. . . . If those whom you send to solve these problems are truly educated politicians, as I have described that education this evening, if they can ride easily over broad fields of knowledge, if they can be, as Goethe put it, hammers instead of anvils, then there is no limit to the contribution they can make to the society which gave them that education.

15. There is considerable talk these days of the educational world's need for assistance from the political world. I am confident that assistance will be forthcoming. But I have also stressed to you tonight the assistance which the world of politics needs from the world of education; and to that end I ask your thoughtful attention to the task of uniting our two worlds still further.

16. "Don't teach my boy poetry," an English mother recently wrote the provost of Harrow. "Don't teach my boy poetry; he is going to stand for Parliament." Well, perhaps she was right, but if more politicians knew poetry, and more poets knew politics, I am convinced the world would be a little better place to live on this 19th day of February 1957.

QUESTIONS FOR STUDY

1. "Circumstances may determine the purpose a speech serves with some or all of the hearers. . . . A speech on the civil service may be informative to new government employees but persuasive to career-minded seniors in high school."[5] Can

[5] Wilbur E. Gilman, Bower Aly, and Loren Reid, *The Fundamentals of Speaking*, The Macmillan Company, 1951, p. 290.

you think of other illustrations of this principle? In light of this principle analyze the present speech. To what groups would this speech be informative? To what groups stimulating? To what groups persuasive?

2. After reviewing the characteristics of the informative speech given on page 120, decide whether this talk is a typical informative speech. In what ways is it not typical?

3. This speech was delivered to an audience of educators and persons interested in education. Senator Kennedy demonstrates that he understands the importance of audience adjustment. Consider the following questions:

   a. How did the speaker attempt to gain attention and to establish his right to speak?

   b. Of what attitudes is he attempting to dispose in Par. 2 and 3? What is his method?

   c. In Par. 3 what is his purpose in pointing out that "the implications of national policy necessarily make politicians of all of us."?

   d. Point out phrases and sentences which are worded pointedly for his immediate listeners.

   e. What motive appeals do you find in this speech? What are the purposes of these appeals?

4. What devices does the speaker use to insure retention?

5. The speaker uses two excellent means to make his main point stand out. What are they?

6. What types of supporting material does the speaker use? In each case, why do you think he chose the material?

7. Do you find any argumentative material in this talk? On what bases did you decide it was argumentative material?

8. Study the speaker's development of his fifth point (Par. 12-14). How is the development of this point different from that of the other points?

9. Develop a speech around a sentence or idea from this speech.

EXCERPT FROM "HOW TO IMPROVE CLASSROOM LECTURES FIFTY PERCENT"[6]
by Loren D. Reid

1. This paper will discuss four categories of improvement chosen in part from personal observation and in part as a result of informal interviews with seventy-five students who received college instruction on twenty different campuses.

2. In his *Rhetoric*, Aristotle states that the speaker's character is one of his most effective agents of persuasion. Listeners believe men of good sense, good moral character, and good will more readily than they do men of opposite traits. When I asked students, "What are the characteristics of the best classroom lectures that you have heard?" or "What are the reasons explaining why certain lectures are ineffective?" the answers often reflected opinions about the character and personality of the lecturer.

3. The good lecturer, these students pointed out, shows that he has the interest of his listeners at heart. At the beginning of the lecture, for example, good teachers use many methods of arousing the interest of their students. Instead of plunging coldly into the topic, the lecturer might open by commenting upon a chapel talk that all had heard. He might refer to some campus or national incident. He might mention

[6] Elmer Ellis, (ed.), "Toward Better Teaching in College," *The University of Missouri Bulletin*, vol. 55, May 1, 1954, pp. 19-24. Used by special permission.

a pertinent clipping that he had run across, or a new book he had received. He might begin with a summary or forecast. He might tell a story. All of these methods start the student thinking, in as painless a way as possible, about the subject before the group. Some of my informants had observed that experienced teachers were more likely to do these things than were younger faculty members. The younger teachers, they reported, are often too serious, solemn, and dignified.

4. The personality of the lecturer is further shown by the way he answers questions. Good teachers welcome questions from the floor and answer them with some completeness, often bringing in rare details that otherwise might not have come into the discussion at all. A few teachers seem unhappy when a question is asked, blurting out such brief and inadequate answers that students hate to offend by further inquiries. Some teachers say, in chilling tones, "I discussed that last hour." Others use the familiar dodge, "I'll take that up later on." In some instances, "later on" may actually be the logical time to consider the question; but experienced teachers know that important items can be successfully repeated two or three times anyway, and the question provides a good motivation for one of the repetitions.

5. In many lesser ways, a teacher can show good will towards his listeners. It may help if he says, "Now this is a complex principle; I'm going to try to make it clear, but I want you to feel free to ask questions about any point that you do not understand." It shows good spirit for him to say, "We've had to spend a long time on this classification, but another half-hour will see us over the worst of it." Or his personality may express itself in entirely different ways; instead of using gentleness and patience, he may use humor, challenge, praise, mock seriousness, or some other approach.

6. Students are sometimes embarrassed when the teacher begins his lecture by apologizing for his inexperience. The chairman of the, let us say, Sanskrit department, who has grown white-haired in the pursuit of knowledge, and who has achieved renown for his scholarship, may in all truth open a class by saying, "I do not know anything about Sanskrit." Such a declaration would express the humility that comes to a scholar who has long pursued a difficult topic. If, however, a beginning instructor makes such a statement, students will take it at face value and wonder why they are so unfortunate as to have to study under an ignoramus. A teacher need not reveal the full scope of his ignorance on the first day of the course.

7. If teachers will treat a student simply as they would a colleague, they will have the proper mental attitude for good lecturing. If one thinks of his listeners as fellow scholars, he is less likely to scold, heckle, bait, or patronize them.

QUESTIONS FOR STUDY

The faculty of the College of Arts and Sciences of the University of Missouri planned a symposium on improving teaching in college. Several professors presented talks on such subjects as improving morale, the use of discussion, the problems of motivation, recognition of reading skills, teaching values, using audio-visual aids, preparing tests and improving grading. Dr. Elmer Ellis, at the time Dean of the College,[7] summarized difficulties facing these speakers when he said, "Trying to tell a group of fellow teachers how to teach might well be classified as a hazardous occupation." One of the outstanding speeches of the series was presented by Loren D. Reid, Professor of Speech.

[7] At present Dr. Ellis is President of the University of Missouri.

1. "People absorb information more easily when it is made interesting. Hence a secondary purpose of such a speech is to create an interest in the information. But although the secondary purpose is important, it must never be made the primary object."[8]
   a. What methods does Dr. Reid use to make his speech both interesting and informative?
   b. Make a list of the "characteristics of the best classroom lectures." Make a second list of the methods the lecturer employs to make these suggestions more acceptable to his listeners.
   c. Why does the speaker state his information is "in part from personal observation and in part as a result of informal interviews with seventy-five students . . . on twenty different campuses."?
2. Below are several types of informative speeches: description, narration, exposition, criticism, demonstration, critical interpretation, lecture and report. Under which of these heads does the talk fall?
3. Does the advice given by Professor Loren Reid apply to other types of informative talks?
4. If you were preparing a similar talk for a group of ministers, what would you say?
5. Prepare a five-minute speech illustrating one of the points which Dr. Reid makes. Include in your talk several examples from your own observation of teachers.
6. Prepare a five-minute analysis of the lecture methods of one of your teachers. Support your point with specific illustrations.

EXCERPT FROM A SENATE SPEECH[9]
by Paul Douglas, Senator from Illinois

1. With the forebearance of Senators, I should like to analyze the importance of these areas. I have placed two maps behind me. One is a large map of the entire Middle Eastern area, and the other is a smaller map dealing with the immediate sections of Arabia and the Middle East.

2. Virtually all of the oil of the Middle East comes from the middle and northern sections of the Persian Gulf, and, in the case of Iraq, also from the valleys of the Tigris and Euphrates. Those rivers empty into the Persian Gulf.

3. This oil from the Persian Gulf area, which comprises three-fourths of the known oil resources of the world, and which furnishes more than two-thirds of the oil which Western Europe consumes daily—namely, 2 million out of 3 million barrels—can be taken to Western Europe in 2 different ways.

4. Approximately 1,200,000 barrels can come around the Arabian Peninsula, up the Red Sea, and through the Suez Canal by tanker; then the tankers continue their course through the Mediterranean and in some cases into the Atlantic.

5. There were also three pipelines from Saudi Arabia and Iraq which led to ports in Lebanon. Now, as we all know, the Suez Canal has been blocked by the sinking of ships on the part of Egypt, and 2 of the 3 pipelines have been blown up by

[8] Alan Monroe, *Principles and Types of Speech*, Scott, Foresman and Company, 4th ed., 1955, p. 388.

[9] This excerpt is from a speech delivered during the debate over the U. S. foreign policy in the Middle East. The question under discussion was whether the United Nations should punish Israel for not withdrawing from Egyptian territory in compliance with U. N. instructions. Found in *Congressional Record* (Daily Edition) February 1, 1957, pp. 1262-1264.

Syrian troops. Therefore, there is only one pipeline taking oil from Saudi Arabia to the Mediterranean port of Sidon.

6. So, the direct connections formerly relied upon for the shipping of 2 million barrels of oil have been cut down probably to not more than three or four hundred thousand barrels a day through the one pipeline which remains.

7. If we look at the maps in detail, we find that there is a possible supplementary or alternative route to the Suez Canal, and one also which can be supplementary or an alternative to the pipelines which have been blown up. That would be a pipeline from the Israeli port of Elath, at the head of the Gulf of Aqaba at the southernmost point of Israel, across Israel and to a port such as Haifa or Jaffa. There is no reason why this pipeline route should be confined to one pipeline. There could be two or more pipelines. Under those conditions the oil would move entirely through the State of Israel, and would not be subject to the difficulties which come from pipelines running through Syria. I wish to emphasize again that two of those pipelines have been blown up.

8. Furthermore, such a pipeline would not be under the control of Egypt.

QUESTIONS FOR STUDY

1. "Whenever a speech critic sets about the selection of speeches with the purpose of classifying them according to the general speech purposes—to inform, to entertain, or to persuade—he is certain to experience great difficulty as between the first and the third purpose. Many speeches that appear at first to be *informative* turn out on closer examination to be persuasive, in that the informaion presented actually leads directly toward establishment of a particular point of view or specific proposal."[10] How does the excerpt from Senator Douglas's speech illustrate this point?
2. In what paragraph does the speaker reveal that his purpose is persuasive, not informative? Point out the specific sentence in which the change occurs.
   a. Study carefully the verbs which Senator Douglas uses.
   b. What shift in verb form do you notice in the sentence in which he reveals an argumentative purpose?
   c. Why does Douglas state his point in a negative form?
3. In this section on the informative talk are included four excerpts from speeches. Compare them on the following bases:
   a. Method of development.
   b. Types of supporting material used.
   c. Use of motivation to hold interest.
   d. Audience adaptations.
   e. Attention factors.
   f. Language.
4. Write a 500-word theme in which you evaluate one of the items listed in Exercise 3.
5. Prepare an argumentative talk in which you use an expository development.
6. Is it possible to prepare an expository or informative speech by using argumentative materials? Explain your answer.

[10] Robert Oliver, *The Psychology of Persuasive Speech,* Longmans, Green, and Company, 1956, 2nd ed., p. 218.

Readings on Informative Speaking

Baird, A. Craig, and Knower, Franklin H., *General Speech: An Introduction*, Mc-Graw-Hill Book Company, 2nd ed., chap. 15, "Informative Speaking."

Bryant, Donald C., and Wallace, Karl R., *Fundamentals of Public Speaking*, Appleton-Century-Crofts, Inc., 1953, chap. 10, "Supporting Materials."

Gilman, Wilbur E., Aly, Bower, and Reid, Loren, *The Fundamentals of Speaking*, The Macmillan Company, 1951, chap. 15, "Informing."

Gray, Giles W., and Braden, Waldo W., *Public Speaking: Principles and Practice*, Harper & Brothers, 1951, chap. 8, "The Informative Speech."

McBurney, James H., and Wrage, Ernest J., *The Art of Good Speech*, Prentice-Hall, Inc., 1953, chap. 13, "The Methods of Inquiry"; chap 14, "The Methods of Reporting."

Monroe, Alan H., *Principles and Types of Speech*, Scott, Foresman and Company, 4th ed., 1955, chap. 20, "The Speech to Inform."

White, Eugene E., and Henderlider, Clair R., *Practical Public Speaking: A Guide to Effective Communication*, The Macmillan Company, 1954, chap. 14, "Speeches to Inform."

The Stimulating or Inspirational Speech

On December 22, 1820 the Pilgrim society assembled at Plymouth, Massachusetts, "to commemorate the landing and to honor the memory of the intrepid men who first set foot on Plymouth rock." The two hundredth anniversary of this revered event made a speech in order. And Daniel Webster, already well-known for his eloquence, was indeed a proper choice to voice the sentiment of those assembled and if possible to intensify their admiration for their forebears. Webster put his speech purpose as follows: "We have come to this Rock, to record here our homage for our Pilgrim Fathers; our sympathy in their sufferings; our gratitude for their labors; our admiration of their virtues; our veneration for their piety; and our attachment to those principles of civil and religious liberty. . . ." "Homage," "sympathy," "gratitude," "admiration," and "veneration" are words which characterize the purpose of ceremonial talks or what the Greeks called speeches of "praise or blame."

The goal of this type of speech is to arouse, to rekindle, and to heighten the appreciation of the listeners for a man, an institution, a virtue, or an issue.

Some well-known stimulating talks are the following:

Daniel Webster's "Bunker Hill Monument Address."

Abraham Lincoln's "Gettysburg Address."

Wendell Phillips' "The Lost Arts."

Robert G. Ingersoll's "At His Brother's Grave."

Theodore Roosevelt's "The Man with the Muckrake."

Russell Conwell's "Acres of Diamonds."

William Jennings Bryan's "The Prince of Peace."

Woodrow Wilson's "What the Flag Means."

Dwight Eisenhower's 1956 "Acceptance Speech."

The stimulating or inspirational talks have many subtypes.

The eulogy commends the character and actions of a deceased person.

The commendation shows affection and admiration for a living person.

The commemorative address celebrates a significant day or an important event.

Some common characteristics of this type of speech are the following:

1. The speaker and the listener are in essential agreement on the speaker's proposition.

2. The outline of the speech is likely to be concealed; the development progresses without calling attention to it.

3. The supporting materials include vivid examples, figurative analogies, appeals to imagery, and amplification.

4. The language is carefully selected to stir feelings, emotions, and sentiments. The sentences are constructed with great care, striving for balance and rhythm.

5. The delivery is polished, stately, dignified, and restrained.

Below you will find two types of stimulating talks quoted. Each one makes use of many of the principles just mentioned.

"MEN AND WOMEN WITH ANTENNAE"[11]

by Kenneth I. Brown, Executive Director, Danforth Foundation

1. I am indebted to a friend for the phrase that I have used for the theme of this commencement address. We happened to be together some months ago in a college situation far away from the continental limits of the U.S.A. Both of us had concern for the man who had recently come to the presidency of the college where we were visiting.

2. As a new administrator, he was embarking bravely upon an ever difficult job. We were there long enough to know that his efforts were praiseworthy, and that his direction was progressively sound. So far as we could see, the future augured well; and yet the new leader seemed to be stumbling. There were comments spoken in an undertone which were not complimentary. Even when words praised, the speaker's eyes did not underscore the praise.

3. My friend and I learned that the new administrator was thoughtless, or said to be thoughtless of those who had labored in the situation long years before his coming. Like so many new administrators, he was prone to change the date of creation to coincide with the beginning of his own administration. Some faculty leaders whose counsel might have been useful he seemed purposely to ignore, and there were bruised feet, many bruised feet where he had trodden without care. One

[11] Delivered at LeMoyne College, Memphis, Tennessee, May 28, 1956, and at Nebraska Wesleyan University, Lincoln, Nebraska, June 5, 1956. Found in *Vital Speeches of the Day*, August 15, 1956, pp. 666-667.

day in speaking together of the situation that we were trying to analyze my friend said these words: "Good man, but a man without any antennae." The phrase has lingered in my mind.

4. No man is an island, neither can he live within an all-inclusive government of one. He needs that sensitiveness to the incipient emotions and heart-longings of others if he is to live as a responsible member of the human race. He needs a special competence in those media of communication which are more difficult than the spoken language—the troubled eye, the quivering mouth, the withheld presence. Love is not alone the giving of self, even though that giving be generous and abundant. Love is the giving of self to another's need, and that need of the other can be learned not from generalizations about mankind nor from text books on psychology, but through the sensitive outreach of a human spirit touching gently another human spirit.

5. Our friend the new administrator may succeed, I do not know. But ruthlessness has its price, and also its consequences, and the wise man knows both in advance. The man without any antennae is the man who never quite comes into contact with his fellow human beings. He never sizes up the whole situation. He makes love into a self-thing because being without antennae he never touches the soul and the spirit of another.

6. There is something essentially tragic about the man who is unaware of the music in the air which he is not hearing, of the pictures in the air which he is not seeing. There is something essentially tragic about the man whose armor of personality prevents the subtle delicate shafts of human understanding that come from another, from penetrating into his own mind and heart.

7. One of the functions of education is to make us aware of the possibility of such understanding. Perhaps education is a process of building within us, according to the latest models, antennae which will allow us to move into direct contact with the spirit and the heart and the mind of another. I suppose that comes through the multiple and varied experiences of learning and living and loving. I am sure it comes in part through the human outreach that through understanding and compassion touches those around us.

8. Not only, however, do we need to be men and women with antennae. There is surging demand today that nations be nations with antennae, and with our concern for our beloved country, let us interpret this by saying, our United States needs especially to be a nation with antennae, catching the cries of the spirit, the suppressed longings of the other nations, large and small, in prosperity or in underprivilege.

9. For example, you don't build faith in democracy by believing the man opposing you to be an ignoramus or a scoundrel. We Americans are so often guilty of a parochialism of a high order. We are so convinced that we have the best form of national government—and so we have—that we fail to realize sometimes some of the very great strengths of the British Government. And the British in turn are so convinced that they have the best form of government—and perhaps they have for themselves—that they fail to realize the strengths of our organization.

10. In similar fashion we are persuaded that we have the best culturally, the best intellectually, the best philosophically, the best religiously in the whole world, and that kind of intellectual chauvinism can produce some exceedingly dangerous results. For example, it can produce a judgment that we in America have no need to know and to understand what other countries have—no need for antennae selfishly used—since obviously they have nothing to compare with our achievements, and why should we concern ourselves with lesser things.

11. Now it is one thing to know thoroughly ourselves as a nation and as a great

people, and to appreciate our achievements in comparison with similar achievements in other countries. But it is a quite different thing, out of sheer ignorance and in chauvinistic arrogance to believe ourselves best, and it is that kind of sheer ignorance that we as Americans have sometimes been guilty of.

12. We know India as a country of poverty, and no one who has seen India will for a moment deny India's devastating poverty. But let it be said that one of the very great revolutions taking place in India today with the Indian government and the Ford Foundation working handsomely together is in this area of village life where standards have been unspeakably low. What the average American does not know is the prosperous side of India, the cultural, intellectual, educational side of India. What the average American does not know, and presumably does not have too much interest in knowing, are those areas in which India has much to offer us.

13. When I came back from our trip last November I was having luncheon with one of my college-graduate friends who has traveled widely, but not outside of our own country. He said to me: "How did you travel in India?" I told him that we traveled by plane between the large cities, and in the cities themselves by car.

14. My friend showed obvious surprise. "But do they have automobiles in India?" I laughed and said that the home where we were staying had three cars at its front door, and we were welcome to make use of any of them.

15. My friend's face showed his amazement: "But what do you drive on when you drive in a car?" I smiled and told him that we were in New Delhi, one of the most beautiful cities in the world, patterned after our own Capital of Washington, with its government buildings and its gorgeous home built for the viceroy but now occupied by the Indian president, with its converging streets and its great circles of traffic. His answer was, "But I never knew that India had cars or had roads like those."

16. A second consequence is that intellectual arrogance can also persuade us that all other countries are sitting in passionate envy for everything we have, wanting nothing so much as to be exactly like us in government, in material prosperity, and in all the other facets of life. When you ask the man what he thinks the world envies us for most, he will probably answer, "Our automobiles, there are none better." (The Europeans, especially the Germans, would dispute that.) Or, "Our roads, there are none better." (When I was in Berlin in 1938, I saw some of the great autobahns that Hitler was building and they certainly looked mighty attractive to the non-engineering eye.) Or "Our plumbing." Ah yes, our plumbing, that is supposed to be the thing that the world envies us for most. We can grow ecstatic over our plumbing.

17. Have you ever stopped to notice that all the things we expect others to envy us for, are *material* advantages? And yet when the world shouts "Materialist" at us—as they do frequently and loudly—we are angry; we protest we are not materialists. We demand that the world see that there is a deeply religious and spiritual side to our culture and our civilization, and yet it is back to those materialistic advantages of our culture that we go when we list the things that the world stands most in envy of.

18. I am a child of my own culture and I admit my dependence on the automobile. I like our plumbing; I am happy to have enough to eat, with jam on the bread and a bit of whipped cream on the jam; I like it. In honesty I've got to admit that I am to that extent a materialist, putting body comforts, and physical ease, and technical advantages very, very high in the scale of living. I sometimes am afraid that when I put these materialistic advantages so high that inevitably there is a corruption in my spirit and a deterioration in my soul that says, "These are the things that are important in life, not courage, and integrity, and compassion, and faith, and love."

19. There are lonely men and women in American life today—of all ages, and of skins of all hues. And whether they be young or old, and whether they be Negro or white, they are reaching out in their loneliness to those with antennae who can catch their distress signals of loneliness and will come to their relief.

20. There is need abroad today—stark, desperate, yawning, colossal need—some of it the physical need for bread, and some of it the mental need for intellectual understanding, and some of the spiritual need for human friendship and divine forgiveness, a need for man and for God. And it will be men and women with this capacity for human outreach and deep compassion who will first be aware of the existence of such need, and recognizing it will take their part in satisfying such need.

21. To you in the flush of your academic success on the occasion of your commencement, I can find no more important word to bring to you than the word: Be men and women with antennae.

QUESTIONS FOR STUDY

1. What is the speaker's specific purpose in delivering the talk? Why does he consider it unnecessary openly to announce his purpose?
2. What is the proposition of the talk? How many times and in how many different forms does the speaker restate it? Rewrite the proposition in your own words.
3. Divide the speech into its parts: introduction, discussion-proper, and conclusion. What proportion is devoted to each? How does this compare with other speeches?[12]
4. What does the speaker hope to accomplish in the introduction? What does he hope to accomplish in the conclusion?
5. Reduce the organization to a simple outline. What is the plan of organization? How did the speaker's purpose influence his plan of organization? Is there any evidence that the audience attitudes influenced the speaker in arranging the speech?
6. After carefully reading the characteristics of a stimulating talk given on p. 132 decide in what ways the speech is typical and not typical.
7. The stimulating speech frequently makes use of emotional appeals. What emotional appeals do you find in this speech?
8. Many of the supporting materials of stimulating talks are used for amplification.[13] What types of amplifications are used in this speech?
9. You find many figures of speech in this talk. Analyze the types used. Why does the speaker use these figures of speech?
10. How does the speaker achieve vividness and impressiveness[14] in his use of language?
11. How does the speaker attempt to establish his ethical appeal in this speech? Make a list of the ways in which he established that he was well qualified to discuss the topic. What traits of character does he reveal?
12. Write a 500-word theme on one of the questions given above. Be sure to illustrate your discussion with quotations taken from the speech.
13. Investigate the nature of the Danforth Foundation and the accomplishments of the speaker. Is the speech what you would expect from a person with Brown's background and position?

[12] See Edd Miller, "Speech Introductions and Conclusions," *Quarterly Journal of Speech,* April, 1946, pp. 181-183.
[13] See Gray and Braden, pp. 302-305 or McBurney and Wrage, Chap. 9.
[14] See Gray and Braden, Chaps. 17, 18.

14. Build a stimulating speech around a striking sentence selected from the speech. For example, you may speak upon an idea like one of the following:
  a. "No man is an island, neither can he live within an all-inclusive government of one."
  b. "Love is giving of self to another's need."
  c. "There is surging demand today that nations be nations with antennae."

Ceremonial speeches are frequently the order of business in the Congress of the United States. On March 4, 1957 thirteen Senators delivered short speeches in honor of Sam Rayburn, the Speaker of the House. Quoted below are four of these speeches:

SPEECHES DELIVERED AT FORTY-FOURTH ANNIVERSARY OF CONGRESSIONAL SERVICE OF SPEAKER SAM RAYBURN IN THE UNITED STATES SENATE, MARCH 4, 1957[15]

Mr. Lyndon D. Johnson, Senator of Texas. Mr. President, this is a day of many anniversaries. But the one that is closest to me, personally, involves the distinguished gentleman who presides over what we usually refer to as "the other body." I refer to that great and beloved American, Speaker Sam Rayburn, who today celebrates his 44th anniversary in Congress.

"Mr. Speaker" is one of the few men in history who occupies at the same time the position of a legend and the position of a living force. His personality is stamped on this Nation and on its laws. But at the same time he is still helping to make those laws, and millions of Americans are grateful that he is at the helm. . . .

People will come, and people will go, but Speaker Rayburn will always remain as the promise of the eternal youth and the eternal vigor of the institutions of this Nation.

Mr. Mike Mansfield, Senator from Montana. Mr. President, I wish to join the distinguished majority leader [Mr. Johnson], as well as my other colleagues, in extending congratulations and best wishes to "Mr. Democrat," the Speaker of the House of Representatives, the Honorable Sam Rayburn, of Texas.

As one who learned much at the feet of this great American, while serving in the House, I wish to say that his advice was always sound, his counsel always good, and his understanding as broad and as deep as could be.

I wonder if it is known, Mr. President, that approximately one-third of the Senate membership are graduates of Mr. Sam's school of experience. In this group is our majority leader, the senior Senator from Texas [Mr. Johnson], as well as many other Members on both sides of the aisle. This group is a living example of the training achieved under Speaker Rayburn. Personally, Mr. President, and collectively, we wish to "Mr. Sam" the best of everything in the years ahead. He has represented his district, his State, our Nation, and the free world well.

Mr. Albert Gore, Senator from Tennessee. Mr. President, few men have imprinted themselves so indelibly upon the history of the 20th century as has Speaker Sam Rayburn. His life and public service have been exemplary in many respects. The confidence he has enjoyed from his colleagues in the House of Representatives is in all

[15] *Congressional Record* (Daily Edition), vol. 103, no. 37 (March 4, 1957), pp. 2623-2625.

respects unexcelled in the history of our Nation. His power of persuasion, his wisdom, his kindness, his patience, are renowned.

Perhaps it might be well at this moment to give recognition to the service he has rendered to the United States Senate. The training he has given in parliamentary practice and procedure, to many Members of this body when they were Members of the House, has contributed to their usefulness, and parliamentary skill, as well as to the debate and the procedures of the Senate of the United States Congress. Mr. Rayburn's service has been outstanding in so many ways that in a brief moment of tribute it is impossible to set forth its many facets. He is a truly great Texan, a truly great American, a truly great world leader of our time, who has enjoyed the confidence of the great and the small, the many and the few, the respect of all.

Mr. Everett Dirksen, Senator from Illinois. Mr. President, anniversary occasions are high ground where one can stand and look back and see whence he came, survey the contemporary scene, and then look forward to see where the course goes.

This is an anniversary occasion with which I can associate myself, because I think it is the 23d anniversary of the day I became a Member of the House of Representatives, and there I for the first time made the acquaintance of the very distinguished Member from Texas [Mr. Rayburn] the present Speaker of the House. . . .

In those early days, Mr. Rayburn was a member of the Committee on Interstate and Foreign Commerce, and he left his impact on durable legislation which has had a profound effect upon the country. He was one of a great many Texans who served in the Congress. . . .

We can salute the great State of Texas, first because it sends such competent and able persons, and, secondly, because it keeps them here. They grow in the job. They become able legislators. They develop a great perspective.

So I salute at once not only Sam Rayburn, the great, impartial Speaker that he is, but the great State of Texas as well, whence comes our great majority leader. I am happy to immerse myself in this anniversary for the Speaker of the House, which also happens to be an anniversary for myself.

QUESTIONS FOR STUDY

1. In your opinion which of these speeches seems best to achieve its purpose? In less than 500 words explain your answer.
2. Willard Hayes Yeager says, "Skill in making of speeches of praise and blame is dependent upon a knowledge of human virtues. . . ."[16] What virtues do the speakers suggest that Rayburn possesses?
3. Some of the speakers gave specific facts about Rayburn. What are the purposes in citing these facts?
4. Make a careful comparison of the statements of Senators Gore and Dirksen. How do their methods of development vary? Also compare their choice of language and sentence structure. Which is the more effective?
5. Write a 500-word theme in which you carefully analyze one of these speeches.
6. After carefully reading these speeches, write a 500-word speech of your own in honor of Speaker Rayburn. For additional biographical facts, consult *Who's Who* and *Current Biography.*
7. Prepare in less than 200 words a speech of commendation about an outstanding man in your community.

[16] Willard Hayes Yeager, *Effective Speaking for Every Occasion,* Prentice-Hall, Inc., 2nd ed., 1951, p. 84.

Readings on the Stimulating Speech

Brigance, William Norwood, *Speech: Its Techniques and Disciplines in a Free Society,* Appleton-Century-Crofts, Inc., 1952, chap. 23, "Speeches on Special Occasions."

Crocker, Lionel, *Public Speaking for College Students,* American Book Company, 3rd ed., 1956, chap. 16, "How to Be Interesting."

Gilman, Wilbur E., Aly, Bower, and Reid, Loren, *The Fundamentals of Speaking,* The Macmillan Company, 1951, chap. 14, "Impressing."

Gray, Giles W., and Braden, Waldo W., *Public Speaking: Principles and Practice,* Harper & Brothers, 1951, chap. 10, "The Occasional Speech."

McBurney, James H., and Wrage, Ernest J., *The Art of Good Speech,* Prentice-Hall, Inc., 1953, chap. 16, "The Methods of Evocation."

Monroe, Alan H., *Principles and Types of Speech,* Scott, Foresman and Company, 4th ed., 1955, chap. 21, "The Speech to Stimulate"; chap. 27, "Speeches of Tribute."

Oliver, Robert T., and Cortright, Rupert L., *New Training for Effective Speech,* The Dryden Press, 1951, chap. 21, "The Speech for A Special Occasion."

White, Eugene E., and Henderlider, Clair R., *Practical Public Speaking: A Guide to Effective Communication,* The Macmillan Company, 1954, chap. 15, "Speeches of Special Types."

Persuasive Speeches

Convincing and actuating speeches are sometimes referred to under the title of persuasive speeches. The two types are alike in that they both seek changes in the listeners; they differ in the degree of change demanded. The first asks only for a change of belief, an opinion or a conviction; while the second seeks an overt response—action.

THE CONVINCING SPEECH

In the convincing speech the speaker may say, "Don't you agree that the proposal is an excellent one?" or "Won't you concede that my analysis is sound?" or "Is it not evident that the proposal has merit?" Abraham Lincoln gave this type of speech at Cooper Union, February 27, 1860. Well aware that his New York listeners had to be won subtly, the tall Illinois politician argued that nothing in the proper division of local from federal authority or in the Constitution forbade the Federal government from controlling slavery in the Federal territories. General Douglas MacArthur (see p. 61) gave a convincing talk before the joint session of Congress, April 19, 1951, placing foremost as his purpose the defense of his strategy and character. In a speech quoted below, Lester Markel argued that the printed word has a future. In these three examples cited, the speakers have sought from the listeners only mental agreement. In each case the speaker moved the listener toward action, but he stopped short of asking for an overt response.

Other examples of convincing talks are the following:

George Washington's "Farewell Address."

Wendell Phillips' "Toussaint L'Ouverture."

George W. Curtis' "The Puritan Principle Under the Law."

Henry W. Grady's "The New South."

Characteristics of the convincing talk are the following:

1. Prior to the speech, the speaker and listeners disagree over the proposition.

2. The speaker's goal is a covert response, a change of opinion or belief.

3. The proposition is one of fact or value. It asserts the existence of a truth, a value or a relationship.

4. The supporting materials include facts, and reasons for acceptance of the proposition.

5. The speech usually demands an intellectual rather than an emotional commitment.

THE ACTUATING SPEECH

The actuating talk seeks to move the listeners to act on the proposition. In contrast to the convincing talk which asked the listeners to agree or to concede, this talk asks the listeners to vote, to contribute, to donate, to support, to write, to join. The speaker says: "You ought to buy. . . ." or "You should give. . . ." or "You should join the organization. . . ."

This type of talk is given at the revival meeting, at the bond drive and the political rally. Before the legislature votes, both supporters and opponents are likely to give powerful speeches designed to win converts.

The actuating speech is more difficult than the convincing talk, for many times, although the listeners are in accord with a proposition, they hesitate to reveal their position through action. They prefer the satisfaction of remaining inconspicuous.

The characteristics of this type of talk are the following:

1. The speaker and listeners are in disagreement as to the desirability of acting on the proposition.

2. The speaker seeks to move the listener to pursue a course of action.

3. The proposition is one of policy. For example, it may be worded as follows: "You should buy. . . ." or "You should refuse to pay. . . ."

4. The speaker often does not announce his real goal until the end of the speech.

5. The speaker frequently uses a kind of psychological rather than logical organization. He may order his points on the basis of: (1) importance, (2)

interestingness, (3) complexity or (4) acceptability.

6. The speaker seeks to use impressive language which is highly suggestive and carries strong emotional overtones.

7. The speaker hopes to enhance his persuasiveness by demonstrating his vital concern for his cause, for cherished institutions, and for the personal welfare of his listeners.

8. The delivery is vigorous, direct and enthusiastic.

Persuasion takes many forms. The four excerpts quoted in the following pages well illustrate this point.

THE VANISHING FAMILY FARM[17]
by Eric Sevareid

1. The showdown on farm policy seems to be developing faster than expected. A strong Congressional push for restoring high, rigid supports is under way, Administration conferences are going on in an atmosphere of crisis, and Secretary Benson is reported to be weakening under the intramural pressures of his party's election strategists. Obviously, some sort of financial rescue operation is coming.

2. Beneath the surface of these policy quarrels over stopgap measures, a profound change is coming over agricultural life in the country. It may be progress, it may just be inevitable, but it does have its tragic aspects, and it is happening with remarkable rapidity. An American way of life as old as our deepest traditions is passing away. The source spring of much of our moral outlook, our conceptions of individualism, our politics, our folklore is drying up. The small family-size farm and farm-family life are vanishing, as fast as the Indian villages vanished a century ago. And America is never going to be quite the same.

3. Almost everywhere one sees this unstoppable tide of change. Three family farms adjoin the small weekend property this reporter maintains in the foothills of the Virginia Blue Ridge. One, of some three hundred acres, has just been inherited by an ex-G.I. farmer with a large family. He will try to sell, and then rent a much larger farm in order to make ends meet. The next farm, about a hundred acres, is still run by the seventy-five-year-old man who has lived there all his life. He still works dawn to dark, owns nothing approaching a luxury; sons in the city support him.

4. The third farm, about a hundred and thirty acres, is also operated by an intensely hard-working dirt farmer and his efficient wife; they have no phone, no car, and all expenses are pared to a spartan minimum. His gross cash income last year was four hundred dollars.

5. Generations of children grew up on these three farms, but the end has come. No small farmers will buy these places when their owners die out, for no profit is possible. They will all end up, eventually, as part of great properties owned by corporations or by city businessmen who can make farming pay on a very large scale or who will run them for tax-deduction purposes.

6. Now this is not the best farming land in the country, but the same thing is happening in the best soil regions. You get an idea from a year-long study just published by the Farmers Union Grain Terminal Association in Saint Paul. They studied forty-three hundred family-run farms in good farming country—Wisconsin, Minnesota, the Dakotas, and Montana.

[17] From a radio broadcast over CBS, reprinted in *The Reporter*, February 9, 1956, p. 6.

7. Here are some of their findings: Net income before taxes in 1954 was twenty-five hundred dollars—that means fifty dollars a week. To net this much required, from the family, about five thousand working hours in the year, more than twice the standard for most city workers. If you figured a five per cent return on investment, then it would come to four hundred and fifty dollars for the whole year, earned by the labor alone. While home construction booms around every great city, very few new farm homes have been built in thirty-five years.

8. In these five farm states, in a five-year period, thirty-eight thousand farm homes have disappeared. That means one family in thirteen gave up the life they had tried to live. This rate of failure seems to be on the increase.

9. In that region, as in back-country Virginia, the story is the same: The independent farmer and his family are leaving the land; the home is vanishing and the business office is taking over.

QUESTIONS FOR STUDY

1. "Good speaking to television and radio audiences is based upon the same general principles as good speaking to other audiences."[18] Do you agree? Can a radio news commentary be compared to a speech delivered in a face-to-face situation? In the present case what elements are the same and what ones are different?

2. In a news commentary, what is the broadcaster's goal? Is it to inform, to stimulate, or to persuade? To support your opinion, give examples from the broadcasts of commentators you have heard. In this speech, what is Sevareid's goal?

3. In considering this speech, two critics could not agree upon the speaker's goal. One said it was to explain the nature of the farm problem, and thus it was an informative speech. The other maintained that the speaker's goal was to prove a proposition, and thus it was an argumentative speech. What evidence can you find to support each point of view? Base your answer upon a careful study of Sevareid's use of supporting materials.

4. After carefully outlining this talk answer the following questions:
   a. What is the central thought or proposition? How many times is it stated?
   b. What are the supporting points of the talk?
   c. What is the plan of organization?
   d. How many kinds of supporting material are used? Why?

5. In Par. 2 notice that Sevareid restated the same ideas several times. What is his purpose? In what way does he give emphasis to the topic sentence of the paragraph? What emotional appeals do you find in this one paragraph?

6. Does the speaker prove his point? From his evidence, is he justified to make the following generalization: "The independent farmer and his family are leaving the land. . . ."? What additional evidence would strengthen his case?

7. Generally, a proposition of fact is part of a proposition of policy.[19] What is the speaker's larger unstated proposition of policy?

8. Should a commentator "interpret" the news or just report the news?[20] Perhaps you would like to write an essay on this subject.

9. This speech is a good illustration on the one-point speech.[21] After studying the

---

[18] Gilman, Aly, and Reid, *op. cit.*, p. 413.

[19] See Gray and Braden, *op. cit.*, pp. 208-220.

[20] See Elmer Davis, "News and the Whole Truth," *The Atlantic Monthly*, August, 1952, p. 32.

[21] Monroe, *op. cit.*, pp. 238-247.

speech carefully, decide what are the basic requirements of this type of speech.

10. Prepare a one-point speech on a controversial local, state, or national problem.

THIS TIME THEY DON'T HAVE TO DIE[22]

A Newspaper Advertisement

1. You're hearing it—the word you hoped you wouldn't hear again—"Refugees!"

2. The news headlines are back too—telling again how people must run for their lives—because they're Jews.

3. The Hitler days are supposed to be gone. But are they?

4. In Egypt, 50,000 people are being driven out—because they are Jews.

5. Egypt's new nationality law prohibits citizenship to almost all Jewish men and women. Remember the Nuremberg Laws?

6. Most Jewish-owned firms of importance have been confiscated. Remember Nazi Germany?

7. Police visit homes at midnight to make arrests or order expulsions. Remember Hitler's Gestapo?

8. More than 11,000 Jewish refugees, terrorized and stripped penniless, have been forced from Egypt in a few short months.

9. But Egypt isn't all. There are 17,000 new Jewish refugees who recently fled Hungary and Communist terror. Thousands are in Austria still, sitting on their suitcases, waiting for the chance to begin life again.

10. Have you been reading about still other refugees running from countries where anti-semitism has flared up anew? Well, those reports are true, too.

11. Yes, 1957 will be a refugee year—with more than 100,000 Jewish men, women and children facing disaster and death, taking to the roads, crowding into camps, searching for safety and freedom.

12. The same old, terrible business?—No! There's this difference: This time we can save them.

13. We can save them if we act quickly enough and give enough.

14. We can get them to free lands—including Israel. For this time, there is an Israel, a place where Jewish refugees are wanted and welcome.

15. So give today. Give your increased gift to the regular United Jewish Appeal. Then, to save more lives, to rescue the new refugees, give a great "Over and Above" gift to the $100,000,000 UJA Emergency Rescue Fund.

QUESTIONS FOR STUDY

1. In what ways is this magazine advertisement like a persuasive speech?

2. These paragraphs are packed full of emotional appeals. Make a list of them.

3. What type of inference is used in the first eight paragraphs?

4. The advertisement falls into four steps: (1) the attention step, (2) the problem step, (3) the solution step and (4) the action step. Indicate the paragraphs which fall under each division. After familiarizing yourself with Monroe's motivated sequence, divide the advertisement on the basis of that scheme of organization.[23]

5. "Much persuasion occurs in the form of figurative language which relies for its

[22] The advertisement was placed in the New York Times, February 28, 1957, by United Jewish Appeal.

[23] See Monroe, op. cit., chap. 16.

persuasive power upon colorful images."[24] What figurative language do you find in these paragraphs?

6. "Slanting consists of selecting descriptive methods to encourage acceptance or rejection."[25] What evidence do you find of slanting in these paragraphs?

7. Brembeck and Howell (p. 161) explain *signal* response and symbol response as follows: "The signal response occurs in the form of automatic and relatively uncritical reaction. Symbol response takes a little more time, is critical, and involves consideration not only of the stimulus but also of the context." Is the advertiser seeking a signal or symbol response? Point out specific words and phrases to support your answer.

8. Make a list of the *facts* which are included in these paragraphs. Now write a paragraph using these facts, but use report language only.[26] In class compare your paragraph with that of other members of the class.

9. Many words and phrases suggest positive or desirable qualities, while other words suggest negative or undesirable qualities. The words *free lands* or *gift* would have a positive quality for most persons, while *refugees* and *run for their lives* are negative in their implications. Make a list of positive words and phrases and another list of negative words and phrases. Compare your list with those of your classmates. How do you explain variations in interpretation?

10. After a careful investigation of the problems in the Middle East, prepare a defense or refutation of an idea found in this speech.

EXCERPT FROM "THE FUTURE OF THE PRINTED WORD"[27]
by Lester Markel

1. My assignment is a large one. The Future of the Printed Word is a subject that requires almost as much crystal-gazing as The Outlook for Krushchev, Life on a Flying Satellite, or How Will Grace Kelly Do When She Plays the Palace.

2. But I shall go at it logically, even though, as some one has said, logic is a systematic way of going wrong with confidence. I shall try to define the printed word, to describe its past and its present and to peer into its future.

3. I do not wonder, what with television, with color to come (hues presumably will be added to cries), with Cineramic-telescopic-three-D-and-four-F movies, with pictures beckoning and bemusing us from all sides and in all shapes, I do not wonder that the question is raised: has the printed word a future?

4. I firmly believe that it has.

5. Let us start with an examination of what is, to me, a basic fallacy. It is said, repeatedly, that "one picture is worth ten thousand words"—and this is surely a Kodak age. But I ask: what pictures and what words? There are pictures that do speak eloquently—pictures like Michelangelo's or El Greco's or, at times, photographs, like Brady's of Lincoln. But they are rare indeed; most pictures are only snapshots; as momentary as a flicker of the eye or of the lens.

6. And then I ask: what words? What pictures can speak as eloquently as certain phrases, well-known but still echoing—phrases such as these:

24 Winston Lamont Brembeck and William Smiley Howell, *Persuasion, A Means of Social Control*, Prentice-Hall, Inc., 1952, p. 147.

25 *Ibid*, p. 152.

26 See *Ibid*, pp. 159-160.

27 Delivered at the Third National Editor-Educator Conference, New York City, February 23, 1956. Found in *Vital Speeches of the Day*, April 1, 1956, pp. 381-384.

7. Churchill, addressing the House of Commons in 1940: "I have nothing to offer but blood, toil, tears, and sweat."

8. Or Benjamin Franklin: "They that can give up essential liberty to obtain a little temporary safety deserve neither liberty nor safety."

9. Or Franklin Roosevelt: "The only thing we have to fear is fear itself."

10. Or Socrates: "I am a citizen not of Athens or Greece, but of the world."

11. Or Lincoln: "That this nation, under God, shall have a new birth of freedom. . ."

12. Or finally, Voltaire: "I disapprove of what you say, but I will defend to the death your right to say it."

13. As you read or hear passages such as these, you become certain that the word has more impact, much more impact, than the picture. But there then arises the question as to whether the spoken word makes a deeper impress than the printed one. I do not deny that, on state occasions, at great moments in history, the spoken word can be an atomic force. And it can doubtless weave a hypnotic spell, especially in presidential election years. But, in the long run, the printed word has an authority that the spoken word can never have; because it reaches beyond the limited audience for the spoken word—an audience limited if not in size then surely in time and in depth—and because it is set down definitively in black and white. . . .

14. As a case history, let us consider the newspaper and television. I select this because I happen to know something about it (logic again!) and because what applies to the newspaper applies, also, in important respects, to all printed matter.

15. Many newspapers are having what might be called a case of DT's. I do not think this acute ague is warranted. This is why:

16. There are two areas in which the mass media compete for attention—the entertainment field and the information field.

17. As for the entertainment field, printed words can supply a good deal else, but they cannot furnish pictured motion and action drama. Therefore, TV now has the edge in the entertainment category and will increasingly add to that edge, especially with color on the horizon.

18. Television is also making an effort in the non-entertainment, the information area. You meet the press on television, you meet your Congress there, your authors meet their critics there. The commentators and the columnists appear not infrequently on the not-so-silver screen. And there is no doubt that television has done an important job in covering some spot news, such as the McCarthy hearings, the coronation of the Queen and the World Series.

19. Yet, on the whole, TV has not done a good news job. Moreover, even if it were doing that job well, I do not believe it can take the place of the newspaper, for these, among other, reasons:

20. First, the newspaper (and the book and the magazine) is there when you want it, for reading at a time and at a speed at which you want to read it. You are not required to tune in at a certain hour when there may be other becks or calls. You are not required to proceed at the pace set by the broadcaster, who may be either too breath-taking or too snore-inducing for you.

21. Second, the newspaper (again, like the book and the magazine) supplies perspective—which TV cannot supply. On television every page is the front page. Each item gets the same emphasis from the commentator whether it be the report of an H-Bomb explosion or a communique on the latest zyrations of Zsa Zsa, or especially a commercial.

22. News on TV is basically a bulletin business supplemented by newsreel film.

23. The programs are often determined by the nature and quality of the pictures. Thus, if the newscaster happens to have some fine shots of the Abominable Snowman of the Himalayas, these will be allotted ten minutes, whereas the Secretary of State may have only 60 seconds. The other night, for example, one station led off its nightly news period with shots of a mentally unbalanced man climbing around the upper girders of the Queensboro Bridge. The second item on the broadcast was a State Department announcement that our Far Eastern foreign policy was being radically revised. Thus is perspective lost.

24. In contrast with this kind of treatment, there is the first page of the newspaper, which gives the reader—or should give him—a birds-eye view and evaluation of the news.

25. Third, the newspaper—and books and magazines—can supply the kind of background which television can never supply both because of TV's time limitations and its demand for "hot copy." In these complicated days explanation is needed—and that requires research and space.

26. Fourth, the news in the newspaper is complete—or should be. On television it is limited. For example, I am a great admirer of the "Meet the Press" program, yet, often I find that the time limit has expired before some of the vital questions are answered.

27. Finally, the newspaper, like the other printed media, supplies the written word—in contrast with the spoken word. And the written word still carries more potential authority because it is set down with deliberation and it is there to be seen and pondered upon rather than snatched from the air waves.

28. All this explains why TV, which is basically an entertainment medium, cannot take the place of the newspaper, which is—or should be—an information medium. It indicates that the newspaper must stick to its last, which is to provide the news comprehensively and comprehensibly. . . .

QUESTIONS FOR STUDY

1. How did the speaker attempt to win a favorable hearing? What attention and interest devices does he include?
2. The present speech asked for mental agreement. To what question of policy does the proposition of this speech point? In other words, is there an implied action suggested by the speech?
3. Prepare a sentence outline of the portion of the speech quoted. After careful study, determine whether the argument is sound.
4. This speech was delivered to an audience of editors and educators. Would these same arguments have been appropriate for an audience of television executives? What changes would you recommend for the latter type of audience?
5. On what bases could you argue that the goal of this speech was to stimulate and not to convince?
6. After carefully reviewing the characteristics of the convincing speech on p. 139, list the ways this talk is a typical convincing talk. In what ways is it not typical?
7. Select an idea from these paragraphs and prepare a defense or a refutation of it. Use the following plan of organization.
   a. State the idea from the speech in one sentence. You may use a direct quotation or paraphrase an idea.
   b. State your point of view in one sentence.

c. Give your supporting material to prove your point.

d. Summarize what you have said.

"WAR MESSAGE TO CONGRESS"[28]

by Franklin D. Roosevelt

1. Yesterday, December 7, 1941—a date which will live in infamy—the United States of America was suddenly and deliberately attacked by naval and air forces of the Empire of Japan.

2. The United States was at peace with that nation and, at the solicitation of Japan, was still in conversation with its government and its Emperor looking toward the maintenance of peace in the Pacific. Indeed, one hour after Japanese air squadrons had commenced bombing in Oahu, the Japanese ambassador to the United States and his colleague delivered to the Secretary of State a formal reply to a recent American message. While this reply stated that it seemed useless to continue the existing diplomatic negotiations, it contained no threat or hint of war or armed attack.

3. It will be recorded that the distance of Hawaii from Japan makes it obvious that the attack was deliberately planned many days or even weeks ago. During the intervening time the Japanese Government has deliberately sought to deceive the United States by false statements and expressions of hope for continued peace.

4. The attack yesterday on the Hawaiian Islands has caused severe damage to American naval and military forces. Very many American lives have been lost. In addition American ships have been reported torpedoed on the high seas between San Francisco and Honolulu.

5. Yesterday the Japanese government also launched an attack against Malaya.

6. Last night Japanese forces attacked Hong Kong.

7. Last night Japanese forces attacked Guam.

8. Last night Japanese forces attacked the Philippine Islands.

9. Last night the Japanese attacked Wake Island.

10. This morning the Japanese attacked Midway Island.

11. Japan has, therefore, undertaken a surprise offensive extending throughout the Pacific area. The facts of yesterday speak for themselves. The people of the United States have already formed their opinions and well understand the implications to the very life and safety of our nation.

12. As Commander-in-Chief of the Army and Navy, I have directed that all measures be taken for our defense.

13. Always will we remember the character of the onslaught against us.

14. No matter how long it may take us to overcome this premeditated invasion, the American people in their righteous might will win through to absolute victory.

15. I believe I interpret the will of the Congress and of the people when I assert that we will not only defend ourselves to the uttermost but will make very certain that this form of treachery shall never endanger us again.

16. Hostilities exist. There is no blinking at the fact that our people, our territory and our interests are in grave danger.

17. With confidence in our armed forces—with the unbounding determination of our people—we will gain the inevitable triumph—so help us God.

[28] Delivered to Congress, December 8, 1941. Found in Samuel I. Rosenman (ed.), *The Public Papers and Addresses of Franklin D. Roosevelt, 1941 Volume,* Harper & Brothers, 1950, pp. 514-515.

18. I ask that the Congress declare that since the unprovoked and dastardly attack by Japan on Sunday, December 7th, a state of war has existed between the United States and the Japanese Empire.

QUESTIONS FOR STUDY

When he [Roosevelt] went before the Congress on the morning of December 8, he was taking his stand before the bar of history, and he knew it. . . . The brief speech that he then gave represented Roosevelt at his simplest and most direct. Every word of this was Roosevelt's own except for the next to last sentence, which was largely suggested by Hopkins, and which is the most platitudinous line in the speech. Roosevelt's only literary flourish was his phrase, "a date which will live in infamy." . . .

There was none of Churchill's eloquent defiance in this speech. There was certainly no trace of Hitler's hysterical bombast. And there was no doubt in the minds of the American people of Roosevelt's confidence. I do not think there was another occasion in his life when he was so completely representative of the whole people. . . . They recognized Pearl Harbor as a tragedy and a disgrace—and that recognition provided a boost to national pride which expressed itself in tremendous accomplishment. . . .[29]

1. Carefully study the speech and the statement from Sherwood. In your opinion what was the general goal or end of the speech? Is it to stimulate, to convince, or to actuate. Defend your answer in a three-minute speech or a 300-word statement. In preparation you may wish to read other books on Roosevelt.
2. After analyzing the organization of the talk, answer the following questions:
    a. What is the proposition of the speech?
    b. How do you explain the placing of the proposition?
    c. Divide the speech into an introduction, discussion, and conclusion. In light of the occasion and the attitudes of the audience, how do you explain the amount of time devoted to each part?
    d. Divide the speech according to the following plan: attention step, problem step, solution step and action step. (Pay particular attention to the last two sentences.)
    e. If you planned the speech, would you have reversed the last two sentences? Why or why not?
3. Does the speech indicate that it was planned entirely for the immediate audience or does it show that it also adapted his greater audience?
4. What motive appeals does Roosevelt utilize in this speech? Look for indirect appeals as well as direct appeals.
5. Robert Sherwood describes the next to the last sentence as "the most platitudinous line of the speech." Do you agree? What is the purpose of the sentence?
6. Samuel I. Rosenman says that Cordell Hull, Secretary of State, "urged the President to deliver a full-dress speech to Congress, setting forth the long history of Japanese-American relations, our efforts to attain a peaceful solution, and the final perfidy of the Japanese."[30] In your opinion why did Roosevelt choose a short speech for Congress?

[29] Robert E. Sherwood, *Roosevelt and Hopkins, An Intimate History*, Harper & Brothers, 1948, pp. 436-437.
[30] Samuel I. Rosenman, *Working with Roosevelt*, Harper & Brothers, 1952, p. 307.

7. Roosevelt is reported to have delivered this speech in six and a half minutes.[31] What was his word rate per minute? How does this rate compare with the speaking rate for other speeches? Explain his slowness of delivery in terms of audience and the occasion.
8. If possible listen to a recording of this speech. With a pencil, mark off how Roosevelt phrased the speech.
9. Study carefully the language of the speech. Note the number of "loaded words" used. Compare the number with some of the other speeches in the section.

Readings on Convincing and Actuating Talks

Baird, A. Craig, and Knower, Franklin H., *General Speech: An Introduction,* McGraw-Hill Book Company, 2nd ed., 1957, chap. 16, "Argumentative Speaking"; chap. 17, "Persuasive Speaking."

Brigance, William Norwood, *Speech: Its Techniques and Disciplines in a Free Society,* Appleton-Century-Crofts, Inc., 1952, chap. 7, "Persuasion and Public Opinion"; chap. 8, "The Seven Lamps of Planning a Speech to Persuade."

Bryant, Donald C., and Wallace, Karl R., *Fundamentals of Public Speaking,* Appleton-Century-Crofts, Inc., 1953, chap. 18, "Persuasive Speaking"; chap. 19, "Motives and Basic Lines of Thought"; chap. 20, "Partisans, Neutrals and Opponents."

Crocker, Lionel, *Public Speaking for College Students,* American Book Company, 3rd ed., 1956, chap. 23, "Persuasion"; chap. 24, "Techniques of Persuasion."

Gilman, Wilbur E., Aly, Bower, and Reid, Loren, *The Fundamentals of Speaking,* The Macmillan Company, 1951, chap. 16, "Persuading."

Gray, Giles W., and Braden, Waldo W., *Public Speaking: Principles and Practice,* Harper & Brothers, 1951, chap. 9, "Argumentative Speeches"; chap. 11, "Forms of Support."

McBurney, James H., and Wrage, Ernest J., *The Art of Good Speech,* Prentice-Hall, Inc., 1953, chap. 15, "The Methods of Advocacy."

Monroe, Alan H., *Principles and Types of Speech,* Scott, Foresman and Company, 4th ed., 1955, chap. 22, "The Speech to Convince."

Oliver, Robert T., and Cortright, Rupert L., *New Training for Effective Speech,* The Dryden Press, 1951, chap. 17, "The Speech to Convince"; chap. 18, "The Speech to Persuade."

White, Eugene E., and Henderlider, Clair R., *Practical Public Speaking: A Guide to Effective Communication,* The Macmillan Company, 1954, chap. 14, "The Speech to Persuade."

[31] *Ibid,* p. 307.

Chapter VIII

SPEECH CRITICISM

Edmund Burke—the eighteenth-century author, statesman, and speaker—once declared:

> In a free country, every man thinks he has a concern in all public matters; that he has a right to form and a right to deliver an opinion upon them. They sift, examine, and discuss them. They are curious, eager, attentive, and jealous; and by making such matters the daily subjects of their thoughts and discoveries, vast numbers contract a very tolerable knowledge of them, and some a very considerable one. And this it is that fills free countries with men of ability in all stations.[1]

In other words, Burke was saying that the exercise of critical abilities contributes to the development of greatness. What is true of criticism generally is also true of speech criticism, considered specifically.

What is speech criticism? It is a judicious evaluation of one or more of the interacting elements of the speech situation: the speaker, the speech, the occasion, and the audience. A broad outline of the speech critic's lines of investigation is presented in Chapter I, "What to Study." This entire book has, in reality, been an elaboration of the ideas suggested in that section. The "Questions for Study" were devised to develop the appreciations, insights, and standards necessary for judicious evaluation. Many of the exercises provided opportunities for speech criticism.

The purpose of this chapter is twofold: (1) to provide definitions of the critical function, and (2) to supply examples of speech criticism.

With Freedom of Speech Goes Responsibility

A. Craig Baird, for many years Professor of Speech at the State University of Iowa and author of several significant speech texts, believes strongly in the speaker's obligation to be morally responsible for what he says and in the listener's duty to evaluate carefully what he hears. In a commencement address at his own University, Dr. Baird gave a significant overview of public address

[1] Quoted by Harold F. Harding, "The College Student as a Critic," *Vital Speeches of the Day*, September 15, 1952, p. 736. From letter dated October 31, 1777.

in our society. In his analysis he presented the bases for sound criticism. Notice the elements that this renowned teacher stressed in his presentation.

EXCERPT FROM SPEECH ENTITLED
"RESPONSIBILITIES OF FREE COMMUNICATION"[2]
by A. Craig Baird

1. Obviously the times call for . . . worthwhile talk and reply. As thousands of orators have told us, ours is a government of talk. For our political system to work without constant breakdowns, we must have open and unimpeded channels of speech, public assembly, press, radio, motion pictures, and television. Only thus can we have mature opinion and action.

2. To keep these channels open and to use them wisely is the job of all. We are not suggesting that university graduates abandon their pursuit of law, engineering, or other interests. We do not expect them to become soap box orators, columnists, or meet-the-press televisors. But we do expect all who have the university stamp to be socially minded, well informed on what is going on in Washington and Berlin. We do expect them to be articulate in talking and writing and to have insight into these things. This we visualize as free and universal communication in political service.

3. The question is, are these channels of communication unduly blocked today? In many respects, yes! But if we assume that these freedoms of speech and press are to continue, are the privileges of such free communication wisely used? Who, for example, does most of the talking and writing? In our talks and scripts have we kept pace with the loud speakers and other gadgets? Has the technology of communication far outstripped our art here just as our atomic and hydrogen bombs may have outstripped our skill in knowing what to do with *them?* Have other people, less responsible, cornered the air or the newsprint? If given the floor, are we capable of defending ourselves and exposing the loose talk of others?

4. Do we really understand the human beings with whom we think we are communicating? Finally, do we have the mental and moral maturity to know and direct wisely the great truths we would expound and even fight for? These are the questions that concern the public. They also concern the universities that have accepted the responsibility for training in free communication.

5. How shall we make our political talk effective? First, we must understand what we are to communicate and why. . . .

6. A second mark of worthwhile communication is that of efficient thinking. He who speaks and writes should do so with fact and reason. Here again university education gives us support. The university furnishes technique for ferreting out facts and a methodology for evaluating evidence and inference. This is what we mean by efficient thinking. The most distinguishing characteristic of a university is at this point. It has a ceaseless quest for facts and a discriminating evaluation of principles, premises, and conclusions.

7. If communication is to be more than so many words, speakers and writers must have this skepticism of mere assertion. We must at least reject communication as the primitive art of arousing the emotions. Our purpose in the group is at least to put reason rather than emotionalism on top. Too many discussions of military training, steel strikes and candidates for presidential nominations are developed in storm

[2] Complete text in *Vital Speeches of the Day*, September 1, 1952, pp. 699-701.

clouds of passion. College graduates as well as reporters and congressional investigators must join in the search for intelligent answers to intelligent questions. Truly the race continues to be between public information and public confusion. . . .

8. A third test of effective free communication lies in the communicator's good will. He must have an awareness of his audience. He must be sensitive to their attitudes, traditions, superstitions. When Russians and Americans debate in the Security Council on procedural matters or in the endless Big Four Conference in Paris, they have done so along parallel lines. The bogging down has been due not simply to the military and ideological differences. The words just don't transfer the meanings.

9. But the problem of conversing with an audience where grave issues are at stake is more than a vocabulary difficulty. If we would communicate not only with hostile peoples, but with more friendly ones next door, we must enter into their modes of thinking and living. The communicator, to bridge the gap between himself and his auditors or readers, must be at the bottom a person of good will.

10. Good will, we think, is not simply a sentimental slogan of our culture. It is a deeply ingrained trait of western civilization. Aristotle, that ancient expounder and teacher of sound communication, and still recommended reading for all political speakers and writers, held that good will was one of the three essentials for anyone whose personality would count with an audience. . . .

11. The practical end of political speaking and writing is to give effective support to truth—or whatever we regard as truth. As John Milton in his stormy protest to the British Parliament in 1644, in his defense of a free press, proclaimed:

> Who knows not that truth is strong
> Next to the Almighty?
> Truth needs no policies, no strategems, no
> Licensing, to make her victorious.

We have no right to cry fire in a crowd where there is no fire, no right to stir up chaos by demagoguery, no right to use communication for Hitlerian ends. This reunion of communication with ethics is the underlying principle and major concern of all worthwhile discourse.

12. What is our conclusion? We are sojourners in a political world that seems forever topsy-turvy. Constantly to restore its equilibrium is our job. We must continually make decisions about our Koreas. And these decisions cannot wait. As Ralph Perry, of Harvard, says, "For each problem comes a moment of decision. The choice must be made before it is too late. Otherwise all is meaningless."

What the Critic Does

Another Professor of Speech, Harold F. Harding of The Ohio State University, spoke to a University of Michigan audience on the role of the college student as a critic of public address. His speech carefully defines what a critic does and why his work is significant.

EXCERPT FROM A SPEECH ENTITLED
"THE COLLEGE STUDENT AS A CRITIC"[3]
by Harold F. Harding

1. The critic I believe is the true complimenter to the creative artist. His abiding interest is in standards and in preserving and improving them. He often holds out alone, takes abuse and scorn, is misunderstood, reviled, and is only seldom praised for the contribution he makes.

2. But the critic is a stimulator. He helps mature our appreciation. And he does this by showing the defects of the inferior and by forcing our attention to the superior. . . .

3. It is the main business of the critic . . .
    to discover the facts,
    to compare, for example,
       promise with performance
       theory with practice
       good with bad
       past with present
       present with probabilities,
    to evaluate effects and
       give an appraisal,
    to recommend,
       and finally,
    to act and to lead others—
       not to accept blindly or follow meekly.

4. "A wise scepticism is the first attribute of a good critic," James Russell Lowell tells us. And if we are to cultivate this habit we must constantly seek more knowledge, better knowledge, and wiser interpretations of knowledge. "Erudition and Knowledge build the background of criticism, prepare and open the way for it, and last but not least, are a test and a trial for its conclusions; but they play a subordinate part in the critical act itself."

5. The critic has high responsibilities. These are some of his commandments:
    Thou shall not misrepresent.
    Thou shall not knowingly color or slant.
    Thou shall not omit what should be told.
    Thou shall not misuse the office by seeking private gain. . . .

6. Let us get back to the matter of the methods and the means of the rhetorical critic. He arrives at his judgments independently. He sets his own standards. He constantly seeks the evidence—the intent, the man himself, what he said, how it was received. He respects the tradition—and in rhetorical criticism this means, of course, the monumental works of Aristotle, Cicero, Longinus, and Quintilian. But he adapts to the needs of today. He estimates and re-estimates. Above all, he must ultimately take a position—for or against. He cannot earn his pay sitting on a fence. . . .

7. The criticism of the work of speakers and orators is not concerned with beauty nor permanence, but with effect. Rhetorical criticism is concerned with the ideas of masses of people as influenced by their leaders rather than with the ideas of solitary

[3] Harding, *op. cit.*, pp. 733-736.

thinkers or poets. It examines the wielder of public opinion as one handling a technique of power.

Comments on Contemporary Speaking by a Political Scientist

Speech teachers are not the only academic critics of public speaking. William G. Carleton, Professor of Political Science at the University of Florida, considers "clear and effective speech in our American democracy . . . more necessary today than at any time in history." Speaking before the annual convention of the Southern Speech Association in 1951, he indicts the current level of public address.

EXCERPT FROM A SPEECH ENTITLED
"EFFECTIVE SPEECH IN A DEMOCRACY"[4]
by William G. Carleton

1. There has been a decline in the art of delivering a speech. There is the failure to convey a feeling of deep earnestness. (There is seriousness, yes, a simulated and stereotyped seriousness, the seriousness of dullness, of banality.) There is a lack of animation, of passion, of fire; a lack of rhythm and of music. The speaker today rarely communicates to his hearers the electric tension of a nervous system and a brain working at high gear—under control, of course, and always held in leash by reasonable and intellectual restraints—a nervous system and a brain working under immediate pressure, under the stimulation of having to think rapidly and out loud, and responding with flexibility, spontaneity, imagination, verve, vividness, and punch.

2. The truth is that too many speakers today are afraid to concede anything to the immediate occasion and to the moment. They perhaps come too well prepared. I do not mean, of course, the preparation of a well-stored mind, which is the preparation of a lifetime. Nor do I mean the preparation which thinks out ahead of time the reasoned organization of a speech, an analysis of the propositions and the alternatives, how one topic will flow logically from the preceding one, and even many of the striking and quotable phrases. There can never be too much of this kind of preparation. But I do mean that speakers nowadays often come too well prepared in meticulous detail; they leave nothing to chance, to the occasion; they ignore the possibilities of cutting here and expanding there while in action; they do not yield sufficiently to the delights of spontaneous asides and anecdotes, of vivid illustrations thought of on the spur of the moment. Too many speakers use too many notes; the notes are too copious; and worse still, more and more speakers read their speeches. Even when notes or even manuscripts are in order, often the speaker does not know when to interpolate new material, when to depart from the too well prepared sheaf of papers he holds in his hand. . . .

3. There has been a deterioration in the literary style of speeches. Politicians, lawyers, and ministers, the ranks from which most of our speakers are drawn, live in a busy and hurried age; they have less and less time for reading, reflection, and

[4] For complete text, see the *Southern Speech Journal,* September 1951, pp. 2-13.

the maturing of their own literary styles; they do not read the masters and the classics as they once did. They are readers of newspapers and periodicals in an age when newspapers and periodicals are less literary and more journalistic. Practitioners of the art of public speaking today are apt to piece together a speech from newspaper clippings and current editorials. Or worse still, the busy public man, engrossed with a thousand and one duties and increasingly dependent upon experts in technical fields for the intellectual materials covering his job, calls upon numerous ghost writers to prepare his speeches. Paragraphs from many sources are then assembled and fitted together into a speech.

4. What is the result of all this? The result is the loss of honesty in style, even the disappearance of style altogether. The result is that too often our contemporary speeches are pallid, synthetic hodgepodges that might well be produced by public relations firms or advertising agencies, hodgepodges devoid of unity, philosophy, perspective, integrity, personality, or craftsmanship. This results in productions without figures of speech and vivid illustrations, without cryptic phrases and terse aphorisms, without lights and shades, wit and humor, roll and rhythm. Even when speeches are not ghost-written, the ghost-written ones, representing as they do the speeches of our very highest politicians, are coming to set the pattern, and so today speeches that are not ghost-written are coming to sound ghost-written, synthetic, stereotyped. . . .

5. Most important of all, in our time there has been serious deterioration in the content of public addresses, but content cannot be separated from style, for style and content go hand in hand and it is difficult to distinguish cause and effect.

6. American speeches today, even those by leading statesmen, for the most part have ceased seriously to examine fundamental policy, to discuss first principles, to isolate and analyze all the possibilities and alternative courses with respect to a given basic policy. For the most part American speeches today assume a given policy; they proclaim it rather than debate it; they enumerate "points of a program" necessary to implement the assumed policy and to reach the assumed goal; they confirm the faith of their followers in the assumed policy and goal; they rally enthusiasm; they exhort to action. The result is that speeches today are rarely intellectually comprehensive or cogently analytical. The result of this tendency toward mere enumeration and exhortation is to render formal public address superficial and arid; speeches sound like advertising copy in which one takes pains not to mention competing products (that is competing ideas, competing alternatives of policy) for fear that the public might become acquainted with competing products (that is, competing ideas, competing alternatives of policy). One simply ignores competing ideas and alternative policies— or dismisses them with an epithet—and repeats the virtues of his own idea or his own policy. But things in this world are relative, and a given candidate, idea, or policy makes intellectual sense only in relation to other candidates, ideas and policies. The failure in a single speech to examine, analyze, discuss, and debate alternative points of view with respect to a given policy robs that speech of deep intellectual content and conviction, and is not even fair to the point of view held by the speaker. Intellectually, the speaker is selling short his own point of view when he fails to examine it fairly in relation to other points of view.

7. The development of mass democracy and the growing complexity of public problems seem to have combined to give American politicians and other public speakers the idea that issues must be flagrantly over-simplified to reach the intelligence of the average citizen. This is a mistaken attitude and in many cases a cynical and snobbish one. Where speakers fail, they usually fail because they "speak down" to audiences. Every great speech in history has aimed high; every great speech in

history has assumed a generous degree of virtue, intelligence, and maturity in those to whom it was addressed.

Several Views of a General's Speech to Congress

On April 19, 1951, General Douglas MacArthur, having been relieved of his command in the Far East, spoke to a Joint Session of Congress. (For further information, see pp. 60-63). The speech immediately became the subject of great controversy. Under the auspices of the Speech Association of America, a symposium of critics evaluated the speech. Included on the panel were members of Congress, journalists, and teachers. Three of the fourteen comments are presented here.[5]

ROBERT S. KERR: A CONGRESSIONAL CRITIC

1. I listened earnestly and carefully to General MacArthur's speech. I looked for unity. I didn't find it. I watched for an acknowledgment of the necessity to maintain the integrity of civilian control of the military power. It was not there. I searched for language that would give hope of a limited conflict and a purpose to prevent the spread into world-wide conflagration. He did not provide it.

2. I listened for words which would promote cooperation between this nation and our allies for collective security. Those words were not spoken. I expected him who had been in command of the United Nations forces to acknowledge and report on his stewardship and tell how to strengthen the common front. He did not even mention the United Nations or a single ally.

3. I hoped he would show the way to promote peace and prevent more or larger war. He was not looking in that direction.

4. Instead, if I understood him, he sounded a call for an expanded war, a second front for sure, and a third front, if it came. The General spoke sadly, but I was much sadder because I was convinced that his plan would not lead us upward to the goal of peace, but would hurl us downward to the awful road of total war.

RICHARD H. ROVERE: A JOURNALIST CRITIC

1. As a literary critic and political observer, I view the speech solely from the literary and political points of view. I am not qualified to criticize oratory or elocution.

2. As a piece of composition, the speech seemed to me a good deal but not a great deal better than the general run of public prose in the United States today. MacArthur has eloquence of a kind, but it strikes me as a rather coarse eloquence. He never shades his meanings, never introduces a note of humor, never gives the feeling that he is one man, only one, addressing himself to other men. His language is never flat and bloodless; neither is it flabby and loose-jointed, as so much writing

[5] For the complete symposium, see Frederick W. Haberman, "General MacArthur's Speech: A Symposium of Critical Comment," *Quarterly Journal of Speech,* October, 1951, pp. 321-331. Used by permission.

of this sort is. But to me there is rather a fetid air about it. It does not leave me with the impression that a cool and candid mind has been at work on difficult matters of universal concern. Instead, it leaves me with the impression that a closed and in a sense a rather frantic mind has been at work to the end of making an appeal to history—not neglecting to use any of the rule-book hints on how to do it. I think not of history but of second-rate historian as I read the speech.

3. Form and content are, if not inseparable, very closely related. Politically, Mac-Arthur's speech seemed extremely weak to me. This is not, I think, because I am opposed to his politics; I believe he could have made out a much stronger case for himself. But he never came to grips with the issues. For example, he wanted to have it that he was being persecuted for "entertaining" his particular views. This, of course, is rubbish. He got into trouble not for the political and military views he entertained (no doubt he was right in saying they were entertained by many of his colleagues) but for seeking to usurp the diplomatic function. He never sought to answer the objections to his position that rest on political and economic facts recognized by both sides: that if we followed him, we would be abandoned by several allies; that if Russia invaded Europe, which he has admitted might be an early consequence of his policy, the industrial balance would favor the Communist world; that, like it or not, American power does have its limitations. MacArthur's policy may be sounder than Truman's. But this contention cannot be sustained without facing these stubborn facts about the world today. MacArthur, in his speech, never faced them.

A. CRAIG BAIRD: AN ACADEMIC CRITIC

1. General Douglas MacArthur will be ranked as one of America's outstanding military orators. Partly because of disciplinary and strategic restraints, few modern soldiers have achieved reputations as outstanding speakers. Exceptions occur when military command and political leadership have merged, or when American public opinion of the present decade has invited nation-wide, untrammeled reports from such five-star heroes as George Marshall, Dwight Eisenhower, and Douglas MacArthur.

2. General of the Army MacArthur, before the Joint Session of Congress, on April 19, 1951, was deeply eloquent in his Apologia. His defense was in the tradition of Robert Emmet, before the Dublin court that had condemned him.

3. The General adequately fulfilled the speaking demands of the situation, with its expectancy of powerful eloquence that should exist "in the man, in the subject, and in the occasion." He is an orator by temperament, by habit, and by long exercise. Before Congress he realized Webster's criterion of the orator as one who possesses boldness, manliness, and energy.

4. The mode of his discourse, in spite of its logical texture, was primarily personal and ethical—a vindication of his intellectual integrity, wisdom, and good will. The historical-philosophical overview, the delineation of the new strategic frontier in the Pacific, the speech structure and movement, the language at times somewhat Churchillian—all these exalted the mature judgment and common sense of the speaker. The general's understanding of the vast Eastern populations, his sympathy for them, his implications of his own destiny strongly enforced his assumptions about his own character.

5. MacArthur in this dramatic setting was heroic in his bearing, movements, and gestures. His voice was by turns self-confident, convincing, stern, scornful, righteous.

6. What were his limitations? His sonorous delivery, occasional volatile phrasing, and calculated peroration were defects due to Asian rather than to Attic style. Pericles would presumably have composed and delivered this oration with more artistic subtlety, sense of order, freedom from extravagance, with more intellectual severity and emotional balance.

7. If MacArthur had not been a soldier for the past fifty-two years, he could have become a statesman of stature. For he has much of the parliamentary grand manner and an eloquence that the age has not outgrown.

A Student Criticism of a Famous Speech

The previous examples in this chapter have been broad in their treatment, considering the whole of contemporary American public address or evaluating an entire speech. In contrast, Dorothy Ann Cresap Bishop limits her criticism of Bryan's "Cross of Gold" address to an analysis of ethical appeal, a single aspect of the speech.

BRYAN'S USE OF ETHICAL PROOF IN THE "CROSS OF GOLD" SPEECH[6]
by Dorothy Ann Cresap Bishop

1. At the Democratic Convention of 1896, William Jennings Bryan delivered his now famous "Cross of Gold" speech in the debate over the adoption of the platform. In an atmosphere highly charged with emotion, Bryan gave the final speech in behalf of the majority or bimetallists. The outcome of the speech would determine whether Bryan would be selected as the presidential candidate of the party. His immediate speech purpose, therefore, was to move the convention to action, that is, to gain the adoption of the bimetallism platform, while his ultimate goal was to win the nomination. In the light of these two purposes, and of the temper of the convention, Bryan wisely chose non-logical instead of logical appeals.

2. Bryan recognized that his youth and his comparatively brief political experience were handicaps when contrasted with the experience of his opponents who were long-established, well-known party members. Recognizing that some considered him a presumptuous upstart, Bryan opened as follows:

I would be presumptuous, indeed, to present myself against the distinguished gentlemen to whom you have listened if this were a mere measuring of abilities; but this is not a contest between persons.

However Bryan followed this direct tribute to the opposition with an indirect tribute to himself:

The humblest citizen in all the land [Bryan], when clad in the armor of a righteous cause is stronger than all the hosts of error [the gold Democrats]. I [not the opposition] come to speak to you in defense of a cause as holy as the cause of liberty—the cause of humanity.

[6] Completed in Speech 217 at Louisiana State University.

Again he reminded his audience that:

> We object to bringing this question down to the level of persons. The individual is but an atom; he is born, he acts, he dies; but principles are eternal; and this is a contest over a principle.

3. Bryan continued to use indirection and implication to establish his ethical appeal. He discussed the split in the party and the advent of the silver Democrats. He said:

> . . . our silver Democrats . . . are now assembled . . . to enter up the judgment already rendered by the plain people of this country. . . . New leaders [among them the speaker] have sprung up to give direction to this cause of truth.

The implication was clear; the silver Democrats and Bryan were the true representatives of the people, consequently they were in the better position to elect a president.

4. Bryan again minimized the contest between himself and the old-party members such as Hill of New York and Russell of Massachusetts by saying, "We do not come as individuals." Bryan, as an individual, could pay tribute to Hill, but he suggested that "the people" would never be willing to put Hill "in a position where he could thwart the will of the Democratic party." Bryan emphasized his devotion to his cause by repeating his regret of the necessity to oppose his distinguished opponents.

5. Bryan expressed no ill-will toward the people of the Atlantic states, but he announced his determination to see that his constituents were treated as equals. He said that only a matter of necessity to uphold principle over special interests of the individual drove him to "defy them."

6. By condemnation of the principles of the gold Democrats, Bryan of course elevated his own status. In support of the income tax he explained:

> It simply intends to put the burdens of government justly upon the backs of the people. I am in favor of an income tax. When I find a man who is not willing to bear his share of the burdens of government which protects him, I find a man who is unworthy to enjoy the blessings of a government like ours.

By implication Bryan represented himself as worthy, his opposition as "unworthy."

7. On the question of national bank currency Bryan aligned himself with Benton, Jackson and Jefferson. "I stand with Jefferson rather than with them [the gold Democrats]. . . ." The gold Democrats supported an alternative in the event of failure of free coinage. Bryan expressed his position as follows:

> When we advocate a policy which we believe will be successful, we are not compelled to raise a doubt as to our own sincerity by suggesting what we shall do if we fail.

Bryan suggested that he was confident but that his opposition lacked confidence.

8. Bryan further established his ethical appeal by pointing out the enhanced possibilities of gaining an election with a silver platform:

> Three months ago, when it was confidently asserted that those who believe in the gold standard would frame our platform and nominate our candidates, even the advocates of the gold standard did not think that we could elect a president.

The reason? Here Bryan skillfully cast an unfavorable reflection on the gold Democrats. ". . . there is scarcely a State here today asking for the gold standard which is not in the absolute control of the Republican party." But Bryan did not wish to stir up unnecessary party discord; consequently he turned from the Democrats to attack the Republican platform "which declared for the maintenance of the gold standard until it can be changed into bimetallism by international agreement." Bryan aligned himself with the nationalistic spirit, the anti-Great Britain sentiment, as he declared that no "man who will declare that he is in favor of fastening the gold standard upon the country [the gold Democrats], or who is willing to surrender the right of self-government and place the legislative control of our affairs in the hands of foreign potentates and powers [the Republicans]" can win an election. He outlined the advantage of position a silver platform would have over a gold platform in the contest with the Republicans. The implication—Bryan not only supported the "struggling masses, who produce the wealth and pay the taxes of the country" as opposed to the "idle holders of idle capital," but also he supported the true interests of the party as an organization. He again developed his position, as pro-American rather than pro-foreign interests, with the highly emotional ". . . instead of having a gold standard because England has. . . . let England have bimetallism because the United States has it."

9. Bryan's emotional conclusion is fraught with implied ethical appeal. By the close of the speech he had assumed complete accord with his audience; therefore, he assumed that what he first outlined as true of a wing of the party was true of the whole. He reminded his audience that he had behind him and the silver Democrats the "producing masses of this nation and the world" supported by the commercial and laboring interests. In his final sentence he aligned himself, as he did in his opening paragraph, with the cause of humanity by announcing (this time to the Republicans, not to the gold Democrats), "You shall not press down upon the brow of labor this crown of thorns, you shall not crucify mankind upon a cross of gold."

10. Bryan's use of ethical appeal in the "Cross of Gold" speech is a masterpiece of subtlety. His choice of non-logical appeals was apt for the occasion and purpose.

11. Bryan focused attention upon the probity of his character by several means. He associated himself completely with his message and his message with what is virtuous and elevated—with the cause of humanity. He tempered praise of himself by keeping it entirely indirect. He gave high praise of his clients and cause, but not to the direct derogation of those who opposed his clients. He linked his opponents and their cause with that which is not virtuous—self-interest, special privilege to the few, destruction of the possibility of Democratic success, foreign domination, and, finally, the crucifixion of mankind. He sought to minimize the charges leveled against himself—that is, of being a destroyer of business interests, of the nation's economy, of party harmony. He referred to experience—his own experience with and support from the masses as well as to the experience of distinguished Americans and Democrats of the past. His humility and devotion to a principle above the interest of the individual established his sincerity.

12. Bryan proved his sagacity by the use of common sense—what was best not only for the people as a whole but for the Democratic party. He gave evidence of tact and moderation; he pointed out that his outright defiance of the gold interests came only after all other methods of gaining a hearing had failed. He displayed good taste in his criticism—by declaring not a note of bitterness and retaliation but his determination to see right prevail. He displayed broad familiarity with the issues of the day and proceeded to justify his concentration on the currency issue. He created the impression that, if time allowed and the occasion demanded, he could give an exhaustive treatment of the subject. He knew that his audience was familiar enough with his decisions on the tariff and money question in the House of Representatives

to accept his conclusions without complete proofs.

13. Finally, Bryan established his good will toward his audience. He demonstrated that he held no personal rancor. He chastised the gold advocates; yet he was principally concerned with the success of the party as a whole. He identified himself thoroughly not only with the masses—the rank and file of the party—but with the party as an organization. He was straightforward in his criticism and in the advocacy of his cause. He knew that the expression of humility and the almost complete elimination of personal reference would offset personal reasons for giving the speech. He displayed his personal qualities as a messenger of the truth of the cause of the bimetallism platform.

14. The immediate success of Bryan's speech is seen in the results of the voting which followed. The proposal to adopt the minority gold report, the subject of the debate, was defeated by more than two to one. The Hill amendment to commend the then incumbent Democratic National Administration was defeated by a vote of 564 to 357. Two qualifying amendments to the free coinage of silver platform were defeated without roll call. Not only did Bryan establish his cause as worthy, but he so well established himself as the man to carry that cause to victory that the convention, on the first ballot, elected him as the standard bearer.

EXERCISES

1. Listed below are the names of contemporary speakers honored by Tau Kappa Alpha, national forensic organization, as "Speaker-Of-The-Year" in the indicated category.[7] The criteria for selection are effective, responsible, and intelligent speaking.

National Affairs	*Religion*	*Labor*
Harry S. Truman	Ralph W. Sockman	James B. Carey
Paul H. Douglas	Fulton J. Sheen	Walter P. Reuther
Dean Acheson	Louis H. Evans	John L. Lewis
Adlai Stevenson	G. Bromley Oxnam	George Meany
Dwight D. Eisenhower	Norman Vincent Peale	James P. Mitchell
Clifford P. Case	George Buttrick	
John F. Kennedy	James A. Pike	

Educational, Scientific and Cultural Activities	*Business and Commerce*
Robert M. Hutchins	Eric Johnston
Ralph Bunche	Paul G. Hoffman
W. Norwood Brigance	Michael V. DiSalle
James B. Conant	Clarence B. Randall
Edward R. Murrow	Henry Ford, II
Frank C. Baxter	Merle Thorpe
Eleanor Roosevelt	Harlow H. Curtice
Eric Sevareid	Erwin D. Canham

[7] For future lists consult the spring issue of the *Speaker,* official publication of Tau Kappa Alpha.

Life magazine prepared the following list of twelve American preachers, "selected solely for effectiveness in the pulpit, as determined by a polling of ministers, priests and theological schools of all faiths."[8]

Dr. Louis Hadley Evans

Dr. Theodore P. Ferris

Dr. Ralph Washington Sockman

Dr. Howard Thurman

Rabbi Abba Hillel Silver

Dr. Norman Vincent Peale

Dr. George Arthur Buttrick

Dr. Robert James McCracken

The Rev. William (Billy) Graham

Dr. Joseph R. Sizoo

Very Rev. Robert Ignatius Gannon

Most Reverend Fulton J. Sheen

Prepare a report evaluating a speaker from any of the above groups. You may wish to limit yourself to a consideration of a single speech aspect such as:

background and speech training

occasion

speech goal or speaker's purpose

methods of preparation

sources of material

audience adaptation

ethical proof

organization

forms of support

style

Check *Current Biography, Who's Who in America,* and current periodicals for information on the speakers. Their speeches can probably be located in *Vital Speeches of the Day* or *Representative American Speeches.*

2. The following articles are examples of speech criticism. Review one of them for your class.

Arnold, Carroll C., "Invention in the Parliamentary Speaking of Benjamin Disraeli, 1842-1852," *Speech Monographs,* 1947, pp. 66-80.

Arnold, Carroll C., "The Speech Style of Benjamin Disraeli," *Quarterly Journal of Speech,* December, 1947, pp. 427-436.

Auer, J. Jeffrey, "Tom Corwin: 'Men Will Remember Me as a Joker,'" *Quarterly Journal of Speech,* February, 1947, pp. 9-14.

Behl, William A., "Theodore Roosevelt's Principles of Invention," *Speech Monographs,* 1947, pp. 93-110.

Behl, William A., "Theodore Roosevelt's Principles of Speech Preparation and Delivery," *Speech Monographs,* 1945, pp. 112-122.

Braden, Waldo W., "William E. Borah's Senate Speeches on the League of Nations, 1918-1920," *Speech Monographs,* 1943, pp. 56-67.

Brandenburg, Earnest, "Franklin D. Roosevelt's International Speeches: 1939-1941," *Speech Monographs,* 1949, pp. 21-40.

Brembeck, Cole S., "Harry Truman at the Whistle Stops," *Quarterly Journal of Speech,* February, 1952, pp. 42-50.

Bryant, Donald C., "Colonel Isaac Barré—Cossack of the Opposition: The Opening of His Career," *Quarterly Journal of Speech,* February, 1944, pp. 55-64.

Chester, Giraud, "Contemporary Senate Debate," *Quarterly Journal of Speech,* December, 1945, pp. 407-411.

Clark, Robert D., "The Oratorical Career of Bishop Matthew Simpson," *Speech Monographs,* 1949, pp. 1-20.

Crowell, Laura, "Franklin D. Roosevelt's Audience Persuasion in the 1936 Campaign," *Speech Monographs,* March, 1950, pp. 48-64.

[8] "Great Preachers," *Life,* April 6, 1953, pp. 126-133.

Gehring, Mary Louise, "Russell H. Conwell: American Orator," *Southern Speech Journal*, Winter, 1954, pp. 117-124.

Huber, Robert, "Dwight L. Moody: Master of Audience Psychology," *Southern Speech Journal*, May, 1952, pp. 265-271.

McCall, Roy C., "Harry Emerson Fosdick: Paragon and Paradox," *Quarterly Journal of Speech*, October, 1953, pp. 283-290.

Mills, Glen E., "Daniel Webster's Principles of Rhetoric," *Speech Monographs*, 1942, pp. 124-140.

Perkins, Lindsey S., "The Oratory of Benjamin Ryan Tillman," *Speech Monographs*, 1948, pp. 1-18.

Reid, Loren D., "Speaking in the Eighteenth Century House of Commons," *Speech Monographs*, 1949, pp. 135-143.

Runion, Howard L., "An Objective Study of the Speech Style of Woodrow Wilson," *Speech Monographs*, 1936, pp. 75-94.

Thompson, Wayne N., "A Case Study of Dewey's Minneapolis Speech," *Quarterly Journal of Speech*, December, 1945, pp. 419-423.

Windes, Russel, Jr., and Robinson, James A., "Public Address in the Career of Adlai E. Stevenson," *Quarterly Journal of Speech*, October, 1956, pp. 225-233.

SELECTED REFERENCES

Readings on Rhetoric and Speech Criticism for Advanced Students
(See list on pp. 10-11)

The Nature and Scope of Rhetoric

Bryant, Donald C., "Aspects of the Rhetorical Tradition: The Intellectual Foundation," *Quarterly Journal of Speech*, April, 1950, pp. 169-176.

Bryant, Donald C., "Aspects of the Rhetorical Tradition—Emotion, Style and Literary Association," *Quarterly Journal of Speech*, October, 1950, pp. 326-332.

Bryant, Donald C., "Rhetoric: Its Function and Its Scope," *Quarterly Journal of Speech*, December, 1953, pp. 401-425.

Clark, Donald Lemen, "The Place of Rhetoric in a Liberal Education," *Quarterly Journal of Speech*, October, 1950, pp. 291-295.

Hunt, Everett Lee, "Rhetoric and Literary Criticism," *Quarterly Journal of Speech*, November, 1935, pp. 564-568.

Hunt, Everett Lee, "Rhetoric as a Humane Study," *Quarterly Journal of Speech*, February, 1955, pp. 114-117.

Parrish, W. M., "The Tradition of Rhetoric," *Quarterly Journal of Speech*, December, 1947, pp. 464-467.

Approaches to Rhetorical Criticism

Crandell, S. Judson, "The Beginnings of a Methodology for Social Control Studies in Public Address," *Quarterly Journal of Speech*, February, 1947, pp. 36-39.

Ewbank, Henry Lee, Sr., "Four Approaches to the Study of Speech Style," *Quarterly Journal of Speech*, November, 1931, pp. 458-465.

Griffin, Leland M., "The Rhetoric of Historical Movements," *Quarterly Journal of Speech*, April, 1952, pp. 184-188.

Hochmuth, Marie, "The Criticism of Rhetoric," A History and Criticism of American Public Address, Longmans, Green and Co., vol. III, 1955, pp. 1-23.

Holland, Virginia, "Rhetorical Criticism: A Burkeian Method," Quarterly Journal of Speech, December, 1953, pp. 444-450.

Lee, Irving J., "Four Ways of Looking at a Speech," Quarterly Journal of Speech, April, 1942, pp. 148-155.

Wrage, Ernest J., "Public Address: A Study in Social and Intellectual History," Quarterly Journal of Speech, December, 1947, pp. 451-457.

Wrage, Ernest J., and others, "Symposium: Criticism and Public Address," Western Speech, Spring, 1957, pp. 69-118.

Opportunities for Research

Aly, Bower, "The History of American Public Address as a Research Field," Quarterly Journal of Speech, October, 1943, pp. 308-314.

Baird, A. Craig, "Opportunities for Research in State and Sectional Public Speaking," Quarterly Journal of Speech, October, 1943, pp. 304-308.

Brigance, William Norwood, "Whither Research," Quarterly Journal of Speech, November, 1933, pp. 552-561.

Dickey, Dallas C., "Southern Oratory: A Field for Research," Quarterly Journal of Speech, December, 1947, pp. 458-463.

Lang, William C., "Public Address as a Force in History," Quarterly Journal of Speech, February, 1951, pp. 31-34.

O'Brien, Joseph F., "A Re-Examination of State and Local Oratory as a Field for Study," Quarterly Journal of Speech, February, 1951, pp. 71-76.

Park, Joseph H., "The Oratory of British Nineteenth-Century Statesmen," Quarterly Journal of Speech, December, 1951, pp. 441-447.

Thompson, Wayne N., "Contemporary Public Address as a Research Area," Quarterly Journal of Speech, October, 1947, pp. 274-283.

Wiley, Earl W., "State History and Rhetorical Research," Quarterly Journal of Speech, December, 1950, pp. 514-519.

An Overview of Rhetorical Criticism

Thonssen and Baird, Speech Criticism, The Development of Standards for Rhetorical Appraisal, the Ronald Press Co., 1948. This book is considered the standard reference in the field of rhetorical criticism. It not only summarizes the principles of criticism but also traces their historical development from the Greek world. The student would do well to read the entire work. However, of particular interest will be: chap. 8, "Determining the Areas of Investigation," chap. 9, "Establishing the Authenticity of Texts," chap. 10, "Reconstructing the Social Settings," chap. 17, "The Measures of Effectiveness," chap. 18, "Toward a Philosophy of Rhetoric."

Index